Rob,
It is the Government
it is the Patriot that
from the government!

UNALIENABLE RIGHTS

And the Denial of the U.S. Constitution

MICHAEL E. LEMIEUX

PublishAmerica
Baltimore

First printing

PublishAmerica has allowed this work to remain exactly as the author intended, verbatim, without editorial input.

ISBN: 1-60441-785-4 (softcover)
ISBN: 978-1-4489-2899-6 (hardcover)
PUBLISHED BY PUBLISHAMERICA, LLLP
www.publishamerica.com
Baltimore

Printed in the United States of America

UNALIENABLE RIGHTS

And the Denial of the U.S. Constitution

MICHAEL E. LEMIEUX

Table of Contents

About the Author

Michael LeMieux was the first son born to Raymond Lemieux and Lana Robie in a small town called Midwest City, Oklahoma. His family hails from Newmarket New Hampshire along the shores of the Lamprey River just outside Portsmouth. Michael was one of seven children raised in a military family that moved around the world, and lived as a child in New Hampshire, Puerto Rico, Delaware, and Spain.

At 17 he enlisted in the U.S. Army and served a tour in South Korea, rising quickly through the enlisted ranks and even served as an enlisted aide to then Major General Hank "the Gunfighter" Emerson who instilled the spark of patriotism. As the enlisted aide for General Emerson he had the opportunity to drive President Gerald Ford during his visit there in 1974.

In 1980, having not yet seen enough of the world, he changed services to the U.S. Navy. As a sailor he traveled to many nations of the world participating in humanitarian missions that included the Philippines, Australia, Mauritius, Mogadishu Somalia in Africa, Karachi Pakistan, Diego Garcia in the Indian Ocean, and Scotland.

His military travels have allowed him to live in places in Europe such as Spain, Scotland, Germany, and Italy. He also served combat tours in Kuwait and Afghanistan.

Mr. Lemieux was medically retired from the National Guard due to injuries received in Afghanistan for which he was awarded the Purple Heart.

The last eight years of his National Guard career was as a paratrooper; working tactical military intelligence for the 19TH Special Forces group. He has written numerous intelligence reports and briefings and has presented his findings at all levels of the DOD from General Officers to Special Operations mission briefs.

He currently lives in Bellevue, Nebraska, with his wife, Robin, eldest son, Spencer, their daughter, Latricia, and granddaughter, Madison. His youngest son now resides in Utah.

He currently works as an intelligence defense contractor to the U.S. Government which gives him unique insight into the operations of the government.

He has a Bachelors degree in Computer Science from Weber State University and is an avid researcher of constitutional law and history.

Acknowledgments

As no man goes through life on his own, I would like to graciously thank my parents, Raymond and Lana LeMieux, for instilling in me correct principles and a love for God and country. To my wife, Robin, for her generous support, and dedication. I would also like to acknowledge Major Curtis Mathiasen for his guidance, knowledge, and honesty in reviewing this work. You were a great help.

INTRODUCTION

President Andrew Jackson, at his farewell address on March 4, 1837, stated:

> *"It is well known that there have always been those among us who wish to enlarge the powers of the general government, and experience would seem to indicate that there is a tendency on the part of this government to overstep the boundaries marked out for it by the Constitution. Its legitimate authority is abundantly sufficient for all the purposes for which it was created, and its powers being expressly enumerated, there can be no justification for claiming anything beyond them. Every attempt to exercise power beyond these limits should be promptly and firmly opposed, for one evil example will lead to other measures still more mischievous; and if the principle of constructive powers or supposed advantages or temporary circumstances shall ever be permitted to justify the assumption of a power not given by the Constitution, the general government will before long absorb all the powers of legislation, and you will have in effect but one consolidated government. From the extent of our country, its diversified interests, different pursuits and different habits, it is too obvious for argument that a single consolidated government would be wholly inadequate to watch over and protect its interests; and every friend of our free institutions should be always prepared to maintain unimpaired and in full vigor the rights and sovereignty of the states and to confine the action of the general government strictly to the sphere of its appropriate duties."*

The America of our forefathers, the ideals of liberty established in a republic protected by a constitution and government, does not exist today.

Our freedom was taken over at our nation's weakest moment (during the civil war) and has continually and gradually had powers, rights, and privilege, usurped; by those sworn to protect and defend our freedom. The greatest danger we face to American freedom today is not terrorism, it is not Russia's or China's long-range nuclear missiles, or even the flood of illegal aliens across our borders; it is our own civic apathy and cowardice toward government domination. According to Merriam-Webster's dictionary, apathy is defined as a "lack of feeling or emotion, or lack of interest or concern." They define civic as: "of or relating to a citizen, a city, citizenship, or community affairs." Thus civic apathy would be defined as a lack of interest or concern with one's citizenship or community. Much of this apathy has been brought about by conditioning in our youth due to the lack of proper instruction by parents, schools and community leaders. But the cost of this apathy, as I will show throughout this book, is possibly the future existence of this nation, our freedom and way of life, and possibly the enslavement of the entire planet.

America was founded on the ideal that no man or government should stand above all others, that indeed, as our Declaration of Independence espouses, "all men are created equal." Our government was established by the people, and for the people, and the government draws it's power from the people it governs. It is the natural inclination of any group or governing body to expand what power they may have, for the greater good of course. We all know the adage that "power corrupts and absolute power corrupts absolutely." By its very nature power will wear on ALL men regardless of how noble or righteous they profess or seem to be. We have seen great ministers fall to temptation and greed. There are senators and congressmen who feel they are above the law, and governmental agencies who have spoken outright that they do not need to answer the questions of citizens, and that their response will be shown by enforcement (read force). There is a line from the movie "V for Vendetta" that provides a prospective rarely seen in today's media, "*the people should not fear their government, the government should fear the people*." This follows the founding fathers' vision that the government is subservient to the people, and that the power of the government is derived from the people and not from their position.

From the inception of our government the nation has been in a constant state of change. We have progressed in nearly every area of our human existence; except we seem to have forgotten or lost the true meaning of our countries freedom. In an effort to help spark a renewed understanding of what we have lost we will discuss the following concepts:

- The federal government has passed, and enforces laws outside the scope of federal jurisdiction.
- The federal schemes of socialistic public welfare are an affront to the Constitution and the personal liberties of all Americans.
- The government has usurped the states' authority over its citizens by creating a second class 'Federal' citizen that most every American has been forced into.
- The presidents have passed laws outside of their Constitutional powers, and have usurped powers never intended for the executive branch.
- The Supreme Court has illegally acted as legislature by passing judgments that created law and mandated legislature to Congress.
- The financial power structure in the United States today is illegal and against the Constitution. The Congress has unconstitutionally given away its responsibilities and powers to non-governmental organizations and are held sway by them.
- The tax scheme as enforced today is unconstitutional, illegally enforced, and according to our founding fathers, immoral.
- Americans have lived in a constant state of emergency since the civil war, giving dictatorial powers to the executive branch usurping rightful powers from congress.
- The demonization of America's militia.
- The usurping of the people's right to keep and bear arms.
- Why the government won't stop illegal immigration.
- Property rights stolen from all Americans.
- Excessive limitations on free speech.
- The curtailment and loss of many of your Fourth Amendment rights.
- The misapplication of emergency powers by the federal government.
- The missing common law.
- The missing rights of the citizens.
- The fraud of the Sixteenth Amendment by all branches of government.

Did you read the preceding and think "conspiracy theory"? I agree that some people take these things a little too far; however, if only 25% of what I discuss here is as I present it we are still in bad shape as citizens of this country. Everything I present is based on the statements of the founding fathers, federal statutes and code, statements from congress and congressional research papers, and Supreme Court rulings. I am merely presenting them to you to help you make your own determinations.

When our country was first formed, it was a union of individual states. Each state had representation in all aspects of the government; the state was a buffer between the people and the federal government. Thomas Jefferson said in 1821, "*When all government, in little as in great things, shall be drawn to Washington as the Center of all power, it will render powerless the checks provided of one government on another and* ***will become as venal and oppressive*** *as the government from which we separated.*" How well he understood the true nature of government. He realized what a government was capable of and if not held in check, it would tend to usurp more and more power until it had taken all there was.

The federal government was not designed to be a bureaucracy that had, for the most part, any effect on the populace of the country. In fact, the only power granted by the Constitution to the federal government lay in ensuring that government did not trespass against the citizens. It was the responsibility of the individual states to deal with the needs of the people. Federal legislative control was designed only to have jurisdiction only within the District of Columbia and the areas ceded by the states to the federal government for forts, (and other federal sites as needed) or to make laws dealing with interstate commerce or dealing with foreign nations. Since the federal government was created, it has slowly and methodically grown in size and scope until it has permeated every aspect of our lives. Another quote from Thomas Jefferson, "*Government big enough to supply everything you need is big enough to take everything you have .... The course of history shows that* ***as a government grows, liberty decreases.***" I believe the current federal position towards its citizens has proven this axiom to be all too true.

There seems to be a misunderstanding in America today about what rolls the constitution and "Bill of rights" play in regard to the American Citizens. Many believe that this venerable document grants, or is a guarantor, of our individual freedoms. We often hear people talking about their "Constitutional Rights" or "rights guaranteed by the Constitution"; however, they are mistaken. The Constitution has very little to do with the American citizen. It was written to establish a Federal Government and to place the boundaries by which that government would operate. The constitution was never designed to provide or enumerate the rights of the citizens but to restrain the federal government from meddling in state and ultimately citizen affairs.

Much has been written about the history and evolution of events and societies leading up to the formation of our constitution. Though I may touch on aspects of constitutional origins, that is not the focus of this writing. Instead, I will attempt to show what we have lost due to our collective apathy and fear of our government, which no longer follows constitutional doctrine.

My research over the past few years has been a journey of awareness and awakening. Much of what I thought to be common knowledge turned out to be common misunderstanding. What I once believed it took to be a good citizen was an understanding founded in ignorance. Over the next few chapters I will attempt to show that the vision of freedom which our founders once had has been all but lost, and we are on the verge of losing all that our soldiers and heroes of the past have died for. If we do not take back the republics upon which this nation was founded, we may be doomed to repeat the failures of all the mighty republics that have come before us.

Preface

Declaration of Independence

Many of us in high school civic classes or college political science classes have had to read the Declaration of Independence. Entire volumes have been written on the importance and meanings contained within the Declaration of Independence and I would encourage all of you to read not only the founding documents but the writings of those who lived during that time. As a refresher, I have included the first couple paragraphs for you here: (The text in its entirety is found in the appendix.)

IN CONGRESS, JULY 4, 1776

The unanimous Declaration of the thirteen united States of America

When in the Course of human events it becomes necessary for one people to dissolve the political bands which have connected them with another and to assume among the powers of the earth, the separate and equal station to which the Laws of Nature and of Nature's God entitle them, a decent respect to the opinions of mankind requires that they should declare the causes which impel them to the separation.

We hold these truths to be self-evident, that ***all men are created equal****, that they are* ***endowed by their Creator with certain unalienable Rights,*** *that among these are Life, Liberty and the pursuit of Happiness. — That to secure these rights, Governments are instituted among Men,* ***deriving their just powers from the consent of the governed, — That whenever any Form of Government becomes destructive of these ends,***

> ***it is the Right of the People to alter or to abolish it, and to institute new Government****, laying its foundation on such principles and organizing its powers in such form, as to them shall seem most likely to effect their Safety and Happiness. Prudence, indeed, will dictate that Governments long established should not be changed for light and transient causes; and accordingly all experience hath shewn that mankind are more disposed to suffer, while evils are sufferable than to right themselves by abolishing the forms to which they are accustomed. But when a long train of abuses and usurpations, pursuing invariably the same Object evinces a design to reduce them under absolute Despotism, it is their right, it is their duty, to throw off such Government, and to provide new Guards for their future security. — Such has been the patient sufferance of these Colonies; and such is now the necessity which constrains them to alter their former Systems of Government. The history of the present King of Great Britain is a history of repeated injuries and usurpations, all having in direct object the establishment of an absolute Tyranny over these States. To prove this, let Facts be submitted to a candid world.*

The preceding statement was made to the King of England at a point when the colonists believed they could no longer suffer the oppression of their government. In this statement they established a rule or hierarchy of sovereignty unique to America. Prior to this time most, but not all, governments were established by a King, dictator, or ruling class which laid edicts upon its subjects and promised them protection for which taxes and other homage was paid, and all law came from that source. Whatever laws were created was done so at the pleasure of the ruler and without concern for their subjects. In some societies it was quite common for the ruler to claim he had divine guidance or to say that he spoke for God. In some cases rulers claimed to be God in the flesh. The bottom line is they had the ability to lord over all aspects of the people's lives for good or bad. Freedom was only granted to nobility either through birth or through the grace of the ruler.

However, here in this great land, the people said no more. We have suffered oppression, taxation, and the taking of our land and our property; and it is wrong. Here we established that God, our creator, by the very act of our creation, instilled upon us our rights; and those rights were not granted by any government. Our new government was to be created by the people, drawing its power from the people solely for the purpose of protecting those rights. As soon as the government turns to make unjust demands upon the people, or usurp power where it is not entitled, it is the right of the people to correct or abolish that government and start anew.

It is not enough just to declare that men are free, there must be a means by which to control a government once it is created. That mechanism is the Constitution for the United States. It takes more than mere words on parchment to change the nation and to change history. It takes brave men and women who are willing to take responsibility for their actions and to act as truly free people.

Sovereignty

Now would be a good time to bring up a point of sovereignty. Sovereignty is defined as

1. supreme power; especially over a body politic or
2. freedom from external control: autonomy, or
3. controlling influence, or
4. One that is sovereign; especially: an autonomous state".

According to the earliest Supreme Court decision, Chisholm V. Georgia (US) 2 Dall 419, 454, 1 L Ed 440, 455 @DALL 1793 pp471-472 "*...at the Revolution, the sovereignty devolved on the people; and they are truly the sovereigns of the country, but they are sovereigns without subjects...**with none to govern but themselves**; the citizens of America are equal as fellow citizens, and as joint tenants in the sovereignty.*"

In most nations the government is sovereign and the people are it's subjects. Our forefathers, after years of subjugation to the Kings of England, believed that the people should be sovereign and that the government should only be in existence to ensure the continuance of freedom for the people. Governmental power was to be derived from the consent of the people; but the people were to be the supreme sovereign, though sovereign without subjects other than themselves.

"*None to govern but themselves*", is a statement of profound meaning. Not only does it substantiate that we are a populace of equals, but it says that we have the right to self govern. By inference that means unless ones' actions harm another, one is free to go and to do as they please, as any true sovereign does. Each man is a king unto himself; and with the knowledge that all those around him were equals, people treated each other accordingly, as was the custom of the day. This sounds wonderful, doesn't it? How have we strayed from such a free society; to where we are totally regulated, watched, and licensed as we are today?

The federal government has said that they are sovereign and thus immune from suit by the people unless they (the government) give permission to be sued. This is not an arbitrary stance, but one founded in history, foreign law, and as the Supreme Court has said, it is Constitutional.

The primary reasoning for sovereign immunity is to ensure that a government cannot be controlled by another group, whether they are another sovereign nation, member states, or even the people. This protects the government from undo influence or from those trying to stall or hinder the government through frivolous lawsuits. This has another unintended consequence; it distances itself from those it serves.

What does the Constitution say about government immunity? Article 1, Section 6, Clause 1 states: *"They shall in all Cases, except Treason, Felony and Breach of the Peace, be privileged from Arrest during their Attendance at the Session of their respective Houses, and in going to and returning from the same; and for any Speech or Debate in either House, they shall not be questioned in any other Place."* I do not see where the government derives it's broad immunity position. According to this the only place immunity is granted is in either house during session and traveling to and from session. Nor can they be tried for what they say during any speech or debate within either house. There is a maxim in law, "where none is expressed, non can be implied". This goes to not making inferences or to expand the meaning of a thing when it is not specifically expressed.

Each and every representative and government official has sworn an oath to protect and defend the Constitution of the United States. If they pass laws contrary to the Constitution, if they support actions by their superiors contrary to the Constitution, if they enforce laws shown to be in conflict with the Constitution, if they ignore their responsibilities as assigned within the constitution they are in violation of their oaths of office and should be removed.

Which raises another question, what are these "public servants" afraid of? Why do they hide behind an illegal claim of immunity, if there is nothing to hide? By definition, immunity is not required by those who have done nothing wrong. We have heard the government tell us, many times, "You do not have to fear the government, if you are doing nothing wrong." The same could be said by the citizens to the government, you don't need to hide behind immunity, if you've done nothing wrong.

One may ask, with the governments "claim" to sovereign immunity in place, if they cannot sue, what recourse is available to the American Citizen when they have grievance with a government that places itself above the people and the law?

There are three recourses available to us when our government does not respond to it's people; however, there are only two peaceful means by which to achieve a satisfactory conclusion. The first is a petition for redress of grievances. This allows citizens to petition the Government in writing to present narrative of a grievance or a wrong committed and to ask for correction or enlightenment. It should, at least, provide a means for the government to respond to why it believes a wrong has, or has not, been committed and to provide a remedy to its citizens. The "We the People Foundation" had submitted a petition to various government agencies to answer various questions that the foundation thought were unconstitutional but have yet to receive a reply. They then sued in the District Court of D.C. to have their petitions answered. The D.C. Court, in "We the People V United States Civil Action No. 04-1211 31 August 2005, ruled that"

> *"The Supreme Court, however, has held that "the First Amendment* ***does not impose any affirmative obligation on the government to listen, to respond*** *or, in this context, to recognize the association and bargain with it."* (Bold added)

The government has no obligation to listen or respond. Does this sound like a government of, for, and by the people? Not to me! One of the primary reasons we went to war with England, among others, was the lack of response by the English government to the petitions of the American colonies. What good would it be to have a right of petition if the government could unilaterally ignore any petition it wished to ignore? When the people lose their voice in government and the government turns its back on its people, the people have no recourse but to remove that government and return it to its rightful state.

The D.C. ruling was appealed to the Appellate Court who ruled, not surprisingly, with the government upholding the right of the people to petition but that the government had no requirement to respond stating:

> *"We need not resolve this debate, however, because we must follow the binding Supreme Court precedent. See Tenet v. Doe, 544 U.S. 1, 10-11 (2005). And under that precedent, Executive and Legislative responses to and consideration of petitions are entrusted to the discretion of those Branches."*

In other words the Court has placed itself above the Constitution and its decisions are final. Others have argued that the previous decisions were based upon petitions against state official's not federal government, which was the basis of the prior decisions. This court, however, ruled that the meaning would apply regardless, based on the 14th Amendment guarantee of the First Amendment upon the states. The appellate Court stated:

> *"...the Supreme Court flatly stated that the First Amendment,* ***which has been incorporated against the States by the Fourteenth Amendment, does not provide a right to a response to or official consideration of a petition.*** *"* (Bold added)

The importance of the 14th Amendment cannot be overstated as it sets the framework for every encroachment of our individual rights (which I will discuss in detail in chapter 3).

Regardless of the reasons for the founding fathers to include the right of petition, the Appellate Court ruled the Fourteenth Amendment does not specify the requirement of a response, and therefore there is no requirement to do so. In effect the Fourteenth Amendment rewrote the Constitution for the benefit of the federal government and not for the protection of the people by establishing a predominate "Federal Citizen" above that of a state citizen. We now find ourselves in the same, if not worse, position than our country was in the year 1775.

At present the "We the People Foundation" has submitted an appeal of the case to be heard by the entire panel of appellate judges. The outcome of which, I am sure, will make it's way to the Supreme Court. President John F. Kennedy once said: *"Those who make peaceful change impossible will make violent revolution inevitable."* History and the future await our courts decision.

The second peaceful means is to tuck our tail between our legs and cower to the omnipotent government that has allowed us to most humbly serve the federal corporate machine. However, most hard working, honest patriotic Citizens would not find this an attractive course of action, and far too many of the ignorant are already willing to do just this.

The third option, when dealing with an oppressive government, is referenced in the Declaration of Independence. It is simply to replace that government and install a constitutional one. Many may jump to the conclusion that this automatically means a revolution, it does not. The choices are an awakening of the American people to vote out of office the corrupt and replace them with constitutional fundamentalist that will peacefully return freedom to our country. The alternative is a revolt by the enlightened patriots who know well where the bondage our current course takes us.

Republic Vs Democracy

"I pledge allegiance to the Flag of the United States of America, and to the Republic for which it stands: one Nation under God, indivisible, with Liberty and Justice for all."

So much is spoken today about the spread of democracy and how truly democratic countries are the saving grace in this new age of political enlightenment. After the close of the Constitutional Convention in Philadelphia on September 18, 1787, a woman by the name of Mrs. Powel asked Dr. Benjamin Franklin what kind of government we would have. His response to her was, "*a Republic, if you can keep it*". Our founders knew that only by vigilant watch of the citizenry could a Republic be maintained. If left alone and democracy were to gain a foothold, it would take a rebellion to restore the rightful government. There is a distinct difference between a democracy and a democratic process. A democracy is nothing more than majority, or mob rule; and is a form of government our founders did not accept. The democratic process is the means by which our forefathers chose for the selection of our representatives, nothing more.

Let's first take a look at the meanings of Democracy and Republic:

- Democracy literally means "rule by the people" or rule of the majority. Blacks Law Dictionary, Seventh Edition, describes democracy as: *"Government by the people, either directly or through representatives."* This is what our government has devolved to today, and it is not a new thing. Democracies have been around since before the Roman era and were a part of the Greek and Athenian governments. There are many countries that have claimed to be democracies solely because they have democratic elections. Iraq was identified as a democracy, in that they elected their dictator. In their most basic form, democracies are mob rule.
- The definition of Republic from Blacks Law Dictionary, Seventh Edition: *"A system of government in which the people hold sovereign power and elect representative who exercise that power."* Here we have the people as sovereign and the representative (government) as the servant, which more accurately conveys the meanings of the writers of the Constitution.

In fact, and in operation, republics and democracies are antithetic to each other. Republics operate under the rule of law, democracies rule under the operation of law (mob rule). James Madison said "*Democracies have ever been spectacles of turbulence and contention; have ever been found incompatible with personal security or the rights of property; and have in general been as short in their lives as they have been violent in their death.*"

From the creation of our republic, the only democratic mechanism was how we chose our leaders. Over time we have slowly slipped into legislation by polling where those who have gained political power care only to get elected or reelected and to maintain the status quo. We are now more a social democracy than we are a republic. The social democracy rules by what the majority want and can be swayed by fad and political manipulation. Regardless of how you look at democracy it is a collectivist view (what is best for the whole) even at the peril of the minority.

A pure democracy is one in which the majority rules. Everyone in town votes to build a new park. That sounds good, and everyone can benefit from it. But wait! What if they want to take your house and land to build the new park? Now it's the whole town voting for the new park and just you voting against it. In a democracy you lose, end of story.

In a republic, we operate under the rule of law that protects the minority from the majority. For most things, under our democratically elected representatives, the majority vote for laws. The main difference is there are certain things that cannot be done away with, period. In our system those things are enclosed within the Constitution and more specifically the bill of rights, which tells the government you may go this far and no further. This is the line in the sand that you cannot cross. In this way, regardless of what the majority wants, the rights of ALL are equally protected. The function of the Bill of Rights is to enumerate a minimum set of rights against which the government cannot trespass.

You will notice that nowhere in the Constitution is the word *democracy* used; however Article 4, Section 4 states, "*The United States shall guarantee to every State in this Union a Republican Form of Government...*" The writers wanted to ensure that the destructive and factious Democracy would not get a foothold in our government.

Throughout the Constitution there is a balance between the collectivist and the individualist position. The Collectivist view, simply stated, is that the government can have a free reign in what it does as long as it can be shown that it is for the greater good of the country. The individualist view, by contrast, defends the minority from the whim of the majority.

Another major difference between the collectivist and individualist is that of personal responsibility. The collectivist believes that the needs of the many outweigh the needs of the one. They believe there is some responsibility to provide to those who have not, what I call the Robin Hood syndrome. The individualist, on the other hand, believes a man is responsible for his or her own choices, and should be held responsible for those choices. The problem comes with enactment. I may personally give thousands of dollars each year to charity; but however, I reserve the right to not give should my personal circumstances change. Who is best to determine these circumstances other than myself? However, if I am not given a choice as to who I will support by my labor and earnings then I am being forced into mandated welfare, and back to a collectivist view of government.

Mandated welfare from the state is legalized thievery, nothing less. The individualist will argue, "What right do you have to take what I have worked so hard to obtain to give to someone who does not work for it?" The collectivist will argue that we are all a part of the whole and by strengthening the weakest part, the whole is made better. I would argue that this is debatable. Any system that rewards failure, idleness, or poor choices in life, will have little incentive to correct it. To have a government provide health care, food, housing, education etc. to a sector of the population other than those who have worked to earn it, builds resentment by both parties. Those who have worked for what they have will look down on others who have received the benefit without working for it. The recipient of the government handout will not value what he has been given because he did not earn it. The public housing schemes in our major cities are proof of this. Individually owned houses, built during the same timeframe as welfare housing, are still in great shape and have increased in value, while the welfare housing is scheduled for demolition. Why is that? Could it possibly be that the tenants of the welfare housing do not care for the property, because it is not theirs? They did not pay for it, and they are not going to spend their money on something they do not own or pay for. It is common human nature, and no amount of welfare is going to change that.

Ronald Reagan once said, *"...man is not free unless government is limited. There's a clear cause and effect here that is as neat and predictable as a law of physics: As government expands, liberty contracts."* The more government expands its powers into our daily lives the less real freedom we will have.

The Establishment of Government

The preamble to the Constitution reads: "***We the People of the United States***, *in Order to form a more perfect Union, establish Justice, insure domestic Tranquility, provide for the common defence, promote the general Welfare, and secure the Blessings of Liberty to ourselves and our Posterity, do ordain and establish this Constitution for the United States of America."*

[Emphasis added.]

Unique to the United States is that we are a nation established by it's people, and not mandated by the government. When America was first colonized, the populations grouped together for reasons of religious affiliation, security, commerce, and for the amenities that towns and cities provide to their inhabitants. We could thank the King of England for his harshness in dealing with the colonies, as this is what brought them together; and as the Declaration of Independence relates, it was not a whimsical decision. The founders stated in the Declaration of Independence that breaking with the government they had known "*...should not be changed for light and transient causes; and accordingly all experience hath shewn that mankind are more disposed to suffer, while evils are sufferable than to right themselves by abolishing the forms to which they are accustomed*"

The colonists needed to decide how to govern themselves without having the burdens and corruption they had experienced under the King of England. They decided on a government that did not gain power by virtue of position, or birth right. They created a government that would derive its powers from the very same people they were to lead. **The people** would be the masters of their own destiny as Sovereigns; and the government would be created by them, answerable to them, and bound by the power of their creation, as enumerated by the Constitution **for** the United States of America.

The very opening of the Constitution establishes who is represented by this document, "we the People" **of** the United States. **We the people** have banded together from a group of independent states, to unite together for the purpose of creating a new government. You may have noticed the wording of the final phrase above; it is not the Constitution '**of**' the United States but '**for**' the United States. We, the people, establish the federal government and assign the government its scope and limits; it is not the federal government assigning the limits to us, the people.

The government was formed for the following reasons:

- ***to form a more perfect Union***—This was not the first governing document that guided us, as most states had constitutions and the Articles of Confederation, etc. this document was to expound on those to create a more perfect union.

- ***establish Justice, insure domestic Tranquility***—This phrase is to ensure that we would be a nation of laws and not be ruled by the whims of her rulers. Justice was to provide the people equality before the law, and to provide a means of resolution without resorting to violence. I will expound more on this during the discussion on the amendments.
- ***provide for the common defence***—One of the shortcomings identified during the years of the Articles of Confederation was the inability to fund or raise forces for the defense of the union as a whole. Part of forming a more perfect union was to allow for a federal government which had the ability to protect the nation as a whole.
- ***promote the general Welfare***—Much has been said and done on this topic; and as this subject also comes up again under Article 1, Section 8 of the Constitution, we will not address it here (see chapter 2). However, I would like to pose one question for you to ponder, "Does the government have a right to use your money for charity?"
- ***and secure the Blessings of Liberty to ourselves and our Posterity***— The Constitution was to provide freedom for all the generations that would follow. Our forefathers were looking to protect future generations, as well as themselves. When we look at what we have done in our government and see the burdens we have placed on our children, it appears we have forgotten this role of the Constitution. More on this topic later.

I want to impress upon you that these five reasons were the sole purpose for the governments' existence, nothing more. The governments' responsibility is as a protector of the union, not a dominator of the union.

When reading the constitution, we must first look at the plain text, or meaning of what is said. If we are still uncertain of its meaning then we should consult the writings of the authors and other periodicals written around that time. Next, as the framers of the Constitution were educated men who were well versed in English Common Law and who spoke with a common understanding of the language in use. We can reasonably assume that much of what was written was done so in the common law manner. The Supreme Court in SMITH v. STATE OF ALABAMA, 124 U.S. 465 (1888), was a case of state versus federal authority. Mr. Smith had been operating a train that hauled passengers within Alabama. However, a few months earlier the federal government had mandated that all train operators must be tested and licensed, under their authority to regulate commerce. Smiths claim was that the federal position was only in "interstate" commerce and had no authority for "intrastate" commerce. Much of the courts discussion was based upon the states use of common law and that there was no national common law. However, the court interjected, with exception, the Constitution when they stated: "*There is, however, one clear exception to the statement that there is no national common law. The* ***interpretation of the constitution*** *of the United States is necessarily influenced by the fact that its provisions are* ***framed in the language of the English common law, and are to be read in the light of its history****. The code of constitutional and statutory construction which, therefore, is gradually formed by the judgments of this court, in the application of the constitution and the laws and treaties made in pursuance thereof, has for its basis so much of the common law as may be implied in the subject,* ***and constitutes a common law*** *resting on national authority.*" (Bold added)

From the writings of the founding fathers, we also know that the powers that were defined by the constitution were to be limited and general and were not to be used against the citizens. James Madison, in Federalist 45 said, "*The powers delegated by the proposed Constitution to the federal government are few and defined . . . to be exercised principally on external objects, as war, peace, negotiation, and foreign commerce.*" Notice that all of these items deal with generalities of government and with national and foreign issues, not individual issues.

One premise I want to point out is that no **authority/power** is granted to any office of the federal government that cannot be directly tied to the U.S. Constitution. Any law, power, or authority that cannot be tied directly to the Constitution is automatically reserved to the states or to the people, and the federal government is prohibited to exercise outside of this restriction. Secondly, it is the **responsibility** of the people to keep watch and to correct the government if it steps outside of its authority.

Article 1, of the Constitution describes the legislative body of the government, which shall consist of a Senate and House of Representatives. Sections one through seven deal with the numbers of senators and representatives, how they are elected, the terms of office, compensation, responsibilities, and the process for raising revenue. Section eight speaks of Congress' powers and **enumerates** the areas in which they may enact that power. Section nine places limitations on the powers of Congress, and section ten deals with how the states interact with Congress.

Let us start by enumerating the 18 areas to which congress may act, based on section 8 of Article 1:

1. The Congress shall have Power To lay and collect Taxes, Duties, Imposts and Excises, but all Duties, Imposts and Excises shall be uniform throughout the United States; [**One of the problems with the Articles of Confederation was that there was no mention of how to fund the Federal government. This was part of the "build a more perfect union", as mentioned in the preamble**.]
2. To pay the Debts and
3. Provide for the common Defense and general Welfare of the United States [**See General Welfare, Chapter 2**].
4. To borrow Money on the credit of the United States;
5. To regulate Commerce with foreign Nations, and among the several States, and with the Indian Tribes; [**It says "regulate among the states" not within the states**]
6. To establish a uniform Rule of Naturalization, and
7. Uniform Laws on the subject of Bankruptcies throughout the United States;
8. To coin Money, regulate the Value thereof, and of foreign Coin, and [**Congress is the only one that can coin money, not the Federal Reserve**]
9. Fix the Standard of Weights and Measures;
10. To provide for the Punishment of counterfeiting the Securities and current Coin of the United States;
11. To establish Post Offices and post Roads;
12. To promote the Progress of Science and useful Arts, by securing for limited Times to Authors and Inventors the exclusive Right to their respective Writings and Discoveries; [**this allows for patents, copyrights, and other creative property laws**]
13. To constitute Tribunals inferior to the supreme Court;
14. To define and punish Piracies and Felonies committed on the high Seas, and Offenses against the Law of Nations;
15. To declare War, grant Letters of Marque and Reprisal, and make Rules concerning Captures on Land and Water; [**What constitutional authority is granted to anyone else to engage in war if congress does not declare war? See War Powers, Chapter 8**]

16. To raise and support Armies, but no Appropriation of Money to that Use shall be for a longer Term than two Years; To provide and maintain a Navy; To make Rules for the Government and Regulation of the land and naval Forces; To provide for calling forth the Militia to execute the Laws of the Union, suppress Insurrections and repel Invasions; To provide for organizing, arming, and disciplining, the Militia, and for governing such Part of them as may be employed in the Service of the United States, reserving to the States respectively, the Appointment of the Officers, and the Authority of training the Militia according to the discipline prescribed by Congress;
17. To exercise exclusive Legislation in all Cases whatsoever, over such District (not exceeding ten Miles square) as may, by Cession of particular States, and the Acceptance of Congress, become the Seat of the Government of the United States, and to exercise like Authority over all Places purchased by the Consent of the Legislature of the State in which the Same shall be, for the Erection of Forts, Magazines, Arsenals, dock-Yards and other needful Buildings;—And [**Exclusive legislation over DC and federal enclaves *only*. No jurisdiction outside of those limited areas. See Federal Jurisdiction Chapter 1.**]
18. To make all Laws which shall be necessary and proper for carrying into Execution the foregoing Powers, and all other Powers vested by this Constitution in the Government of the United States, or in any Department or Office thereof.

Speaking specifically of congressional authority, as stated in Article 1, there are numerous examples where the congress has either given up its constitutional responsibilities or has passed laws that stepped outside the bounds of its authority. In some cases, amendments to bills have been tacked on to unrelated legislation or have simply been unread by the body of the legislature. In either case they were either complicit in their actions or negligent in their duties by voting for laws they have not read. We have heard many times how ignorance of the law is no excuse, or more correctly, is no defense. Why is it that those that create the law are not required to know the laws they vote upon?

The next 18 chapters will outline just some of the areas that the government, both federal and local, have strayed from the Constitution, and have stolen unalienable rights of the American people. But just as importantly, I will show how we, the American people, have failed our government and our posterity. How we have failed by ignorance of our civil duties, complacency of trusting government and not keeping watch (not my job), fear of retribution, moral cowardice to stand for the principles that have made this country great, **FREEDOM**.

CHAPTER 1
FEDERAL JURISDICTION

Webster's New Collegiate Dictionary, 1977, defines the following words:

De Facto: Exercising power **as if** legally constituted (emphasis added)

De Jure: By right: of right

"Color" of law:

2a: An outward often deceptive show:

2b: A legal claim to or appearance of a right, authority, or office

2c: A pretense offered as justification

2d: An appearance of authenticity

Colorable:

1: Seemingly valid or genuine

2: Intended to deceive

Jurisdiction:

1: the power, right, or authority to interpret and apply the law

2: the authority of a sovereign power to govern or legislate

3: the limits or territory within which authority may be exercised: Control

Black's Law Dictionary 7th Edition defines these same words:

De facto: Latin meaning "In point of fact"

1. Actual; existing in fact; having effect even though not formally or legally recognized <a de facto contract>
2. Illegitimate but in effect <a de facto government>

   De facto government:

   1. A government that has taken over the regular government and exercises sovereignty over a nation.

2. An independent government established and exercised by a group of a country's inhabitants who have separated themselves from the parent state.

De jure: Latin meaning "as a matter of law." Existing by right or according to law. In this sense, it is contrary of de facto.

"Color" of law: "The appearance or semblance without the substance, of a legal right. The term usually implies a misuse of power made possible because the wrongdoer is clothed with the authority of the state. *State action* is synonymous with *color of law* in the context of federal civil-rights statutes or criminal law.

Jurisdiction:

1. A government's general power to exercise authority over all persons and things within its territory.
2. A court's power to decide a case or issue a decree.
3. A geographic area within which political or judicial authority may be exercised.
4. A political or judicial subdivision within such an area

As previously noted, when dealing with federal jurisdiction or any part of government, you need to understand the difference between De Facto and De Jure. According to Blacks Law Dictionary, seventh edition, De Facto means: *"[Latin "In point of fact"1. Actual; existing in fact; having effect even though not formally or legally recognized. 2. Illegitimate but in effect.*" Blacks goes on to define De jure as: *"[Latin "as a matter of law"] Existing by right or according to law."* De Jure jurisdiction is the legal right to do so; De Facto jurisdiction is the ability in fact to do so. If the government passes a law or establishes dominion over an area of society, not granted by the Constitution it looses De Jure standing, but may still operate as law because it has De Facto capability by use of the police or military.

Another way of looking at this is that a government may have the power to do something (De Facto) though not have the legal right to do so (De Jure). For instance, if Congress passes a law which is in conflict with the Constitution, or the President passes an executive order which is in conflict with the Constitution, the act creates law but does not make it right or constitutionally lawful. However, under statute law, it may well be enforced by police action and be totally unconstitutional, yet it carries the color and weight of law. This is our current situation.

This change from De Jure to De Facto government did not happen over night, but by a long string of events starting as far back as Abraham Lincoln and the War Between the States. There is not one action or event, but a long series of actions and events, as well as the passage of time. When something happens that affects the nation as a whole, or in large part, the government naturally reacts.

Often that reaction creates laws or, occasionally, amendments to the Constitution. As time progresses we look at the words of the law or amendment, but have lost the meaning or the reason for it's existence, and we start applying the law against those it was not meant to affect. For example, the 14th Amendment was enacted to ensure that the freed slaves received protection, under the Constitution. This amendment did not affect the population of the Union who were already citizens or their posterity; you can not give to someone what they already have.

Today, however, much of what the government does is based on the assumption that ALL Americans today are 14th Amendment citizens. On your voter application form, and many other federal documents, they ask for you to affirm that you are a United States Citizen, and as you will learn in the Chapter on Citizenship, there are 3 definitions of citizen within our government. When I enquired as to which definition they were using, I was told the 14th Amendment. We will get into this in greater detail throughout the book, but for now it is important to have an understanding of De Facto and De Jure jurisdictions.

The Constitution recognizes three levels of jurisdiction.

1. **The People;** the people have jurisdiction over their own lives to the extent they do not infringe upon others, and from which all other levels derive their power.
2. **The State;** the state or more correctly "the individual states of the union."
3. **The Federal;** the federal government was created by the people. It was enacted by the Constitution and it sets firm limits upon which the government may operate. However, when I speak here of jurisdiction I am speaking of State and Federal jurisdiction. The line differentiating between the two has become blurred or nearly indistinguishable in the last 100 years.

Since the time of the Declaration of Independence, the thirteen original colonies had grown and divested to statehood with operating constitutions of their own. Each had agreed and signed the Declaration if Independence to formally unite against England and proclaim their freedom to the world. Indeed, they were in fact sovereign state nations, independent and unique from each of the other confederated states.

In 1777, one year after declaring their freedom from England, the Articles of Confederation (see appendix) was adopted. Article II states: *"Each state retains its sovereignty, freedom, and independence, and every Power, Jurisdiction and right, which is not by this confederation expressly delegated to the United States, in Congress assembled."* A definite separation of state and federal jurisdiction existed by law. What is not expressly delegated to the Federal was to remain in the state. At this point in history it did matter what state you lived in, as each state had the ability to define the law of the land within their respective states.

Notice also the use of the word Confederation. A confederation is an agreement between two or more states or nations. Each state/nation was independent and had its own constitution, legislative and judicial bodies, as well as independent leaders, with virtually no ties to any federal system. Seeing the need to deal with foreign nations, and to ensure all states were represented, they created a compact in the form of the Articles of Confederation as to how they would work together.

This idea of state power and sovereignty continued even at the constitutional convention in 1787, where Article 1, Section 8, Clause 17 was drafted, to ensure the federal government was limited in scope and jurisdiction:

> "*To exercise exclusive Legislation in all Cases whatsoever, over such District (not exceeding ten Miles square) as may, by Cession of particular States, and the Acceptance of Congress, become the Seat of the Government of the United States, and to exercise like Authority over all Places purchased by the Consent of the Legislature of the State in which the Same shall be, for the Erection of Forts, Magazines, Arsenals, dock-Yards, and other needful Buildings.*"

Under the Articles of Confederation the states were the supreme governing body, and the federal government had very little power or funding. During the Constitutional Convention the states wanted to guarantee a strong state and a limited federal government. This sentiment was expounded on in the Federalist papers #43 stating:

> "*The indispensable necessity of complete authority at the seat of government carries its own evidence with it. It is a power exercised by every legislature of the Union, I might say of the world, by virtue of its general supremacy. Without it not only the public authority might be insulted and its proceedings*

interrupted with impunity, but a dependence of the members of the general government on the State comprehending the seat of the government for protection in the exercise of their duty might bring on the national councils an imputation of awe or influence equally dishonorable to the government and dissatisfactory to the other members of the Confederacy. This consideration has the more weight as the gradual accumulation of public improvements at the stationary residence of the government would be both too great a public pledge to be left in the hands of a single State, and would create so many obstacles to a removal of the government, as still further to abridge its necessary independence. The extent of this federal district is sufficiently circumscribed to satisfy every jealousy of an opposite nature. And as it is to be appropriated to this use with the consent of the State ceding it; as the State will no doubt provide in the compact for the rights and the consent of the citizens inhabiting it; as the inhabitants will find sufficient inducements of interest to become willing parties to the cession; as they will have had their voice in the election of the government which is to exercise authority over them; as a municipal legislature for local purposes, derived from their own suffrages, will of course be allowed them; and as the authority of the legislature of the State, and of the inhabitants of the ceded part of it, to concur in the cession will be derived from the whole people of the State in their adoption of the Constitution, every imaginable objection seems to be obviated."

"The necessity of a like authority over forts, magazines, etc., established by the general government, is not less evident. The public money expended on such places, and the public property deposited in them, require that they should be exempt from the authority of the particular State. Nor would it be proper for the places on which the security of the entire Union may depend to be in any degree dependent on a particular member of it. All objections and scruples are here also obviated by requiring the concurrence of the States concerned in every such establishment."

As is laid out here, Madison explains the need of separation of jurisdiction so as not to impede the necessary functions of the federal government, especially in times "on which the security of the entire Union may depend". The flip side is that the federal government is thus limited to jurisdiction only in those areas ceded to it. How has so much federal law found its way to work directly on the people when it has no jurisdiction outside of federal enclaves?

The matter of federal versus state jurisdiction has been before the Supreme Court many times, and their rulings have reinforced the idea of separate and distinct jurisdictions. One of the earliest court cases was United States v. Bevans, 16 U.S. (3 Wheat.) 336 (1818), a murder case being brought by the federal government. The crime took place onboard the USS Independence while at port in Boston Harbor, Massachusetts. The Federal government stated they were trying the case under the admiralty jurisdiction; however, the State argued it had jurisdiction to all areas within the state that had not been ceded to the Federal government. The court wrote the following:

> *"What, then, is the extent of jurisdiction which a state possesses?*
>
> *"We answer, without hesitation, the jurisdiction of a state is co-extensive with its territory; co-extensive with its legislative power," 3 Wheat., at 386, 387.*
>
> *"The article which describes the judicial power of the United States is not intended for the cession of territory or of general jurisdiction. ... Congress has power to exercise exclusive jurisdiction over this district, and over all places purchased by the consent of the legislature of the state in which the same shall be, for the erection of forts, magazines, arsenals, dock-yards, and other needful buildings."*
>
> *"It is observable that the power of exclusive legislation (which is jurisdiction) is united with cession of territory, which is to be the free act of the states. It is difficult to compare the two sections together, without feeling a conviction, not to be strengthened by any commentary on them, that, in describing the judicial power, the framers of our constitution had not in view any cession of territory; or, which is essentially the same, of general jurisdiction," 3 Wheat., at 388*

The Supreme Court has given us the extent of federal jurisdiction. It is over "this district", meaning Washington D.C., lands purchased by "consent of the legislature of the state"; which is defined only for "... forts, magazines, arsenals, dock-yards, and other needful buildings." That's it! The federal government can only have jurisdiction where the state has ceded that territory to the federal government. If it has not, then the federal government has no jurisdiction.

There have been numerous cases dealing with the jurisdiction between state and federal governments, overwhelmingly siding with Bevens. The problem is not one of law or jurisdiction, but one of an over-reaching or extension of power it does not legally have. As we discussed in the last chapter, this amounts to De Facto government. A government acting as if legal, but it is not, it is forced upon the inhabitants, **as if** it were legal. For instance, the federal government has graciously stated they will help the states in combating the evils of drugs. Under the Department of Justice is the Drug Enforcement Agency (DEA), which is a part of the Executive Branch of government. The mission of the DEA is to "enforce the Controlled Substances laws and regulations of the United States and to bring to justice those organizations involved in the growing, manufacturing or distribution of controlled substances". I am not an advocate for the legalization of controlled substances; however, I am an advocate who believes that where the federal government does not have a clear Constitutional mandate, they are exceeding their authority. The states have the ultimate and final say for all laws within their jurisdiction—regardless of federal law. In today's world, the states are so bound to governmental dole that any confrontation with the federal government and the latter threatens the withholding of funds to the state, thus forcing capitulation by the state to the federal government. By law, this is called blackmail and extortion—a technique that if used by you or I, would land us in jail for a very long time.

The Tenth amendment to the Constitution states "*The powers not delegated to the United States by the Constitution, nor prohibited by it to the states, are reserved to the states respectively, or to the people.*" Here too, as in the Articles of Confederation, powers to the federal government are limited to only those delegated. All other powers or jurisdiction are reserved to the states or to the people.

To further illustrate the jurisdictional separation, this time in reverse. In the case of SRA v. Minnesota, 327 U.S. 558, 66 S.Ct. 749 (1946), the government was selling a post office building to a company called SRA. Under the sales contract, an "ad valorem" tax on the equitable interest was to be applied by the state. SRA refuted the state's claim stating the tax was really an unlawful tax on U.S. property as the property was federal, and claimed it could not be taxed by the state. The Court held:

> *"In the absence of some such provisions, a transfer of property held by the United States under state cessions pursuant to Article I, Section 8, Clause 17, of the Constitution would leave numerous isolated islands of federal jurisdiction, unless the unrestricted transfer of the property to private hands is thought without more to revest sovereignty in the states. As the purpose of Clause 17 was to give control over the sites of governmental operations to the United States, when such control was deemed essential for federal activities, it would seem that the sovereignty of the United States would end with the reason for its existence and the disposition of the property. We shall treat this case as though the Government's unrestricted transfer of property to non-federal hands is a relinquishment of the exclusive legislative power," 327 U.S., at 563, 564.*

It, therefore, becomes clear that once the federal government no longer has need for and transfers property into private hands, jurisdiction immediately reverts back to the states. Why then do we have so many "federal" laws operating within the states of the union, clearly outside of their jurisdiction?

One reason is the amount of federal land that has been taken by the federal government and is under federal jurisdiction. Nearly the entire western United States and 95% of Alaska is under federal jurisdiction due to declarations that those lands are "public lands" even though they are contained within the states of the union. In most cases the states have ceded land and jurisdiction over to the federal government, or as part of the states acceptance into the union, it was agreed to by the state when joining the union, a clear violation of the Constitution.

A recent case in point is Rapanos v. United States, in which the Federal Government tried three times to gain control over Rapanos' property using the Wetlands Act. The Wetlands Act authorizes the US Government to have jurisdiction in relation to *navigable* waterways and adjoining wetlands. However, Mr. Rapanos' property is 20 miles from the nearest navigable waterway. This battle has been ongoing for more than 12 years, costing thousands of dollars. What crime did Mr. Rapanos commit that would cause him to face the wrath of the Federal Government? He moved sand, which was on his own property, without a permit! The Federal Government argues that under the Wetlands Act they can regulate all the water in the nation. So far, the government has not found a sympathetic judge who will send Mr. Rapanos to prison. The past three attempts have been thrown out by the courts. On June 19th 2006, the Supreme Court ruled that:

> *"The average applicant for an individual permit spends 788 days and $271,596 in completing the process, and the average applicant for a nationwide permit spends 313 days and $28,915—not counting costs of mitigation or design changes. ...In this litigation, for example, for backfilling his own wet fields, Mr. Rapanos faced 63 months in prison and hundreds of thousands of dollars in criminal and civil fines. See United States v. Rapanos,235 F. 3d 256, 260 (CA6 2000). ...The Corps has also asserted jurisdiction over virtually any parcel of land containing a channel or conduit—whether man-made or natural, broad or narrow, permanent or ephemeral—through which rainwater or drainage may occasionally or intermittently flow. On this view, the federally regulated "waters of the United States" include storm drains, roadside ditches, ripples of sand in the desert that may contain water once a year, and lands that are covered by floodwaters once every 100 years. Because they include the land containing storm sewers and desert washes, the statutory "waters of the United States" engulf entire cities and immense arid wastelands. In fact, the entire land area of the United States lies in some drainage basin, and an endless network of visible channels furrows the entire surface, containing water ephemerally wherever the rain falls. Any plot of land containing such a channel may potentially be regulated as a "water of the United States." ...In sum, on its only plausible interpretation, the phrase "the waters of the United States" includes only those relatively permanent, standing or continuously flowing bodies of water "forming geographic features" that are described in ordinary parlance as "streams[,] ...oceans, rivers, [and] lakes." See Webster's Second 2882. The phrase does not include channels through which water flows intermittently or ephemerally, or channels that periodically provide drainage for rainfall. The Corps' expansive interpretation of the "the waters of the United States" is thus not "based on a permissible construction of the statute."*

*Chevron U. S. A. Inc. v. Natural Resources Defense Council, Inc., 467 U. S. 837, 843 (1984). ...Because the Sixth Circuit applied the wrong standard to determine if these wetlands are covered "waters of the United States," and because of the paucity of the record in both of these cases, the lower courts should determine, in the first instance, whether the ditches or drains near each wetland are "waters" in the ordinary sense of containing a relatively permanent flow; and (if they are) whether the wetlands in question are "adjacent" to these "waters" In the sense of possessing a continuous surface connection that creates the boundary-drawing problem we addressed in Riverside Bay view. * * * We vacate the judgments of the Sixth Circuit in both No. 04–1034 and No. 04–1384, and remand both cases for further proceedings."*

Though a little long, the preceding shows the depth to which the federal government has used De Facto law to expand the scope of their power and influence. To be able to stretch navigable waterways to drainage ditches on the side of the road and to encompass entire cities is absurd. The case is not over, but solely remanded back to the courts. Basically the Supreme Court stated that the government had not made their case against Rampos and can try again with a different argument.

James Madison once wrote: "*I believe there are more instances of the abridgment of freedom of the people by gradual and silent encroachment of those in power than by violent and sudden usurpations.*" This is as true today as it was when it was written; and we have seen from the Rampos case, it has gone much further than just mere encroachment but to the absurd.

Another example of usurped jurisdiction is that of parks and "public" lands which the Federal Government says falls under their jurisdiction. According to the Constitution, the Congress, (meaning the Federal Government), shall have power to *"exercise exclusive Legislation in all Cases whatsoever, over such District (not exceeding ten Miles square) as may, by Cession of particular States, and the Acceptance of Congress, become the Seat of the Government of the United States, and to exercise like Authority over all Places purchased by the Consent of the Legislature of the State in which the Same shall be, for the Erection of Forts, Magazines, Arsenals, dock-Yards and other needful Buildings."*

The first 13 states of the union have very few and small areas identified as federal lands. The states that have since joined the union have had huge tracks of land taken, in some cases by "eminent domain", or "purchases"; however, the Supreme Court has also ruled on this issue. In Pollard v. Hagan, 44 U.S. (3 How.) 212 (1845) and Fort Leavenworth R. Co. v. Lowe, 114 U.S. 525 (1885) it was ruled that the federal government may obtain by cessation from the state or purchase or even when acquired with ceding by the state their jurisdiction only pertains to "*Forts, Magazines, Arsenals, dock-Yards and other needful Buildings.*" All other lands are under the jurisdiction of the state equally with the property of private individuals.

Yet today, we still see the government grabbing up land all across the country for its control. A recent example is the acquisition of the Grand Staircase-Escalante National Monument in 1996 by President Clinton. In his speech announcing the taking he ensured Utah's school children that they would be taken care of from the riches contained within the land. This federal land grab encompasses approximately 1.9 million acres of Utah state territory. As a stunning coincidence, this is nearly the exact size of the geological society estimation of a rich coal bed discovered within the monument. In fact, according to a January, 1997 Utah Geological Survey document entitled "A Preliminary Assessment of Energy and Mineral Resources within the Grand Staircase—Escalante National Monument" Compiled by M. Lee Allison, State Geologist: *"Of the 62 billion tons of coal in the Kaiparowits coal field* ***(which lies almost entirely within the monument)*** *we calculate that at least 11.3 billion tons is recoverable. A one-percent increase in our coal recovery estimate amounts to more than 100 million tons of coal. At the current average price of $19.50 per ton of coal, the additional coal is worth nearly $2 billion, of which about $160 million in royalties would be paid."*

There is no authorization, within the Constitution, for the federal government to take lands from the states. As we have shown above, the federal government is restricted on what it can obtain lands from the states, and it does not include multi-million acre "monuments." A monument is what we have on the mall in Washington D.C., buildings and other needful structures, not the riches of the states.

In The Federalist Papers No. 78, Alexander Hamilton tells us:

> "*There is no position which depends on clearer principles than that every act of a delegated authority, contrary to the tenor of the commission under which it is exercised, is void.* ***No legislative act, therefore, contrary to the Constitution, can be valid.*** *To deny this would be to affirm that the deputy is greater*

than his principal; that the servant is above his master; that the representatives of the people are superior to the people themselves; that men acting by virtue of powers may do not only what their powers do not authorize, but what they forbid."

Again, this highlights the De Facto methods of our current government. It passes a "law" that allows the federal government to take land, although unconstitutional. Then the government sites that law as the government's right to perform an unconstitutional act. Because a law is passed, does not mean it is valid.

However, many a man who was right has been buried, jailed, or has had family members killed by overreaching government agencies. Just because you are right does not mean they will let you get away with it. Case in point, the Second Amendment states the right to keep and bear arms shall not be infringed; yet, in some states, if you walk down the street carrying a six-shooter on your hip, you will see how quickly your rights will be infringed. Even with the right to "carry openly", if someone else phones the police with a "man with a gun" complaint, you can be cited for disturbing the peace, even though you have done nothing wrong.

Another example of governmental overreaching is ***United States v. Lopez***, 514 U.S. 549 (1995) in which Lopez was walking near a school in San Antonio, Texas. Lopez had in his position a concealed .38 caliber handgun and 5 cartridges. He was charged with violating the federal Gun Free School Zone Act of 1990, 18 U.S.C. 922(q). He argued that the federal government had no legal authority to act, and no jurisdiction, within the boundaries of the state.

The governments' argument was that carrying a gun near schools leads to violent acts and has an adverse affect on the area, and it thereby negatively affects commerce. They also stated that having crimes in the vicinity of schools leads to poorer learning, due to fear of the guns, which leads to a weaker economy, and thereby, negatively affects commerce. With this kind of circular logic, any area in the United States could be placed under the jurisdiction of the Federal regime.

Correctly, the Supreme Court did not see it this way. The Court determined that the Commerce Clause did allow the Federal Government broad lawmaking powers, but they were not unlimited powers, and they did not apply to carrying handguns. They further specified that there was no evidence that carrying handguns affected the economy on a massive scale.

Chief Justice Rehnquist wrote the opinion of the court stating that

Congress had the power to regulate only the channels of commerce, the instrumentalities of commerce, or persons or things in interstate commerce, even if the threat comes from intrastate activities, and action that substantially affects interstate commerce. With the governments reasoning, Congress could be found to regulate anything. He further commented that since the Constitution created enumerated powers by which Congress was bound, they could not have such broad reaching powers.

He concluded that:

> "*To uphold the Government's contentions here, we would have to pile inference upon inference in a manner that would bid fair to convert congressional authority under the Commerce Clause to a* ***general police power*** *of the sort retained by the States. Admittedly, some of our prior cases have taken long steps down that road, giving great deference to congressional action. The broad language in these opinions has suggested the possibility of additional expansion,* ***but we decline here to proceed any further****. To do so would require us to conclude that the Constitution's enumeration of powers does not presuppose something not enumerated, and that there never will be a distinction between what is truly national and what is truly local. This we are unwilling to do.*

This is a great finding, which reiterates; that Congress must stay within the bounds set by the Constitution, and to do otherwise, would be to convert the Commerce Clause into a police power. The part I find troublesome is the courts unwillingness to make a distinction between what is national and local jurisdiction, as this will do nothing but embolden Congress to continue in its expansion of power and have only to worry about losing the occasional case.

Taken directly from the Department of Justice's own web-site we find: "*When instances are reported to the United States Attorney of offenses committed* ***on land or in buildings occupied by agencies of the Federal government****—unless the crime reported is a Federal offense regardless of where committed, such as assault on a Federal officer or possession of narcotics—****the United States has jurisdiction only if the land or building is within the special territorial jurisdiction of the United States.****"* [Bold added]

Where, then, does the DOJ/DEA/executive branch get its' constitutional authority to perform law enforcement within the states of the Union? Let us look at an excerpt from the Law: (Note: I do not condone the illegal use of controlled substances, and personally find the use of such substances a blight on our communities, and on life in general. However, I provide this example as an illustration of congressional thinking and not a supportive argument for the use of controlled substances.)

Title 21 United States Code (USC)
Controlled Substances Act

SUBCHAPTER I—CONTROL AND ENFORCEMENT
Part A—Introductory Provisions

Section 801. Congressional Findings and Declarations: Controlled Substances

The Congress makes the following findings and declarations:

(1) Many of the drugs included within this subchapter have a useful and legitimate medical purpose and are necessary to maintain the health and **general welfare of the American people.** [Emphasis added]

(2) The illegal importation, manufacture, distribution, and possession and improper use of controlled substances have a substantial and detrimental effect on the health and **general welfare of the American people.** [Emphasis added]

(3) A major portion of the traffic in controlled substances flows through **interstate and foreign commerce**. Incidents of the traffic which are not an integral part of the interstate or foreign flow, such as manufacture, local distribution, and possession, nonetheless have a substantial and direct effect upon interstate commerce because—[Emphasis added]

(A) after manufacture, many controlled substances are transported in **interstate commerce,** [Emphasis added]

(B) controlled substances distributed locally **usually have been transported in interstate commerce** immediately before their distribution, and [Emphasis added]

(C) controlled substances possessed **commonly flow through interstate commerce** immediately prior to such possession. [Emphasis added]

(4) Local distribution and possession of controlled substances **contribute to swelling the interstate traffic** in such substances. [Emphasis added]

(5) Controlled substances manufactured and distributed **intrastate cannot be differentiated from controlled substances manufactured and distributed interstate**. Thus, it is not feasible to distinguish, in

terms of controls, between controlled substances manufactured and distributed interstate and controlled substances manufactured and distributed intrastate. [Emphasis added]

(6) Federal **control of the intrastate** incidents of the traffic in controlled substances is essential to the effective **control of the interstate incidents** of such traffic. [Emphasis added]

(7) The United States is a **party to the Single Convention on Narcotic Drugs, 1961**, and other international conventions designed to establish effective control over international and domestic traffic in controlled substances.

(Pub.L. 91-513, Title II, Section 101, Oct. 27, 1970, 84 Stat. 1242.)

I find it interesting, from the section above, how so much is tied into General Welfare of Americans, however, the Federal Government does not have a constitutional mandate for the welfare of *American citizens,* only for the General Welfare of the United States, the country, as a whole. I will get into this more in the General Welfare section (Chapter 2).

I want to point out the logic used by the government, which is, because they cannot ascertain that a controlled substance is manufactured or distributed intrastate (within a state), they will **assume** it is interstate (between states), and, therefore, they have jurisdiction. Secondly, because so much of the controlled substances flow from foreign and interstate commerce, and the federal government has jurisdiction on foreign and interstate commerce, they **assume** all controlled substances are interstate commerce so they have jurisdiction. Talk about a self-licking ice cream cone! Using this sort of logic allows the government to pass any law about anything, because all things have the propensity to be used in interstate commerce. They would not be able to determine if an item was solely manufactured and sold intrastate, so the federal has jurisdiction over all things. This is ridiculous and totally against what the founding fathers wrote.

An example of this is the medical marijuana issue in California. In 1996 California passed proposition 215 which legalized the attainment of marijuana for certain medical treatments. The manufacturers and dispensers (usually the same person/business) were licensed with the state to perform this state legal function. The marijuana was known to be a local source, grown locally, and dispensed locally in accordance with the state law. The federal government, however, saw this as a direct affront to federal law and took steps to arrest those involved and confiscate their products with a clear knowledge of the **intrastate** position of the defendants.

Furthermore, the government's position is not based on fact, but only the assumption of such. They no longer have to find fact to enforce laws against Americans, they simply have to assume jurisdiction, and then they can act. Preposterous!

Look again at where congress has jurisdictional/legislative power: Article I, Section 8, Clause 17, states;

> *"To exercise exclusive legislation in all cases whatsoever, over such* ***district*** *(not exceeding ten miles square) as may by cession of particular states, and the acceptance of Congress, become the* ***seat of the government*** *of the United States, and to exercise like authority over* ***all places purchased by the consent of the legislature of the state*** *in which the same shall be, for the erection of forts, magazines, arsenals, dock-yards, and other needful buildings..".* [Emphasis added]

Unless specifically prohibited to the state, all other places not enumerated were to be under the jurisdiction of the state.

Look at the phrase *"interstate commerce"*, which much of today's legislation and jurisdiction **is purported to rely upon**. The governments' position is that if two or more states are involved, or if a foreign entity is involved, then the federal government has jurisdiction over all aspects of the venture regardless of what it is. Let's see if this position is constitutionally correct. The Constitution states in Article 1, Section 8: *"To regulate Commerce with foreign Nations, and among the several States, and with the Indian Tribes."* What did the founders mean by regulating commerce? Madison wrote in Federalist 42 that the primary reason to regulate commerce was to ensure equitable treatment between all the states. He states specifically:

> *"A very material object of this power was the* ***relief of the States which import and export through other States****, from the improper contributions levied on them by the latter. Were these at liberty to regulate the trade between State and State, it must be foreseen that ways would be found out to load the articles of import and export, during the passage through their jurisdiction, with duties which would fall on the makers of the latter and the consumers of the former.* ***We may be assured by past experience, that such a practice would be introduced by future contrivances****; and both by that and a common knowledge of human affairs, that it would nourish unceasing animosities, and*

not improbably terminate in serious interruptions of the public tranquility."

Southern states wanted to ensure that there would be a level playing field and that the only power the federal government would have was in ensuring no favoritism or benefit would be allowed "between the states." It is totally beyond the scope for the federal government to be involved in all areas of manufacture and sale of goods. In fact, the belief was that the federal government had jurisdiction between the states; but the jurisdiction stopped at the state line.

In the Supreme Court case U.S. v. Cruikshank, 92 U.S. 542 (1875), Chief Justice Waite's ruling included the following statement:

"In the formation of a government, the people may confer upon it such powers as they choose. The government, when so formed, may, and when called upon should, exercise all the powers it has for the protection of the rights of its citizens and the people within its jurisdiction; but it can exercise no other. The duty of a government to afford protection is limited always by the power it possesses for that purpose."

Justice Waite affirms the federal jurisdiction as a protection of citizen rights and the people, but it can exercise no other. Obviously this identifies that innate "limited" scope of government in America to be only what the people have given them, not what they can get away with. Because the government does a thing does not make that thing legal or valid.

Justice Waite continues stating:

*"**The government of the United States is one of delegated powers alone. Its authority is defined and limited by the Constitution.** All powers not granted to it by that instrument are reserved to the States or the people. No rights can be acquired under the constitution or laws of the United States, except such as the government of the United States has the authority to grant or secure. All that cannot be so granted or secured are left under the protection of the States."*(Bold added)

These powers are delegated, limited, and defined. They are not to be expansive or broadly defined, but limited in scope and authority to only the defined powers within the Constitution.

In speaking of the first amendment right of the people, Justice Waite stated:

"The particular amendment now under consideration assumes the existence of the right of the people to assemble for lawful

> *purposes,* ***and protects it against encroachment by Congress. The right was not created by the amendment; neither was its continuance guaranteed, except as against congressional interference****. For their protection in its enjoyment, therefore, the people must look to the States. The power for that purpose was originally placed there, and it has never been surrendered to the United States."* (Bold Added)

This, as with every other amendment, places the correct position and jurisdiction of the federal government in its correct perspective. The Constitution does not create rights, nor by the Constitution do the rights rely for continuance "***except as against congressional interference***". Now look at the thousands of laws that place interference with citizen's rights, and ask yourself if you really think Congress is abiding by this position? I think not! A prime example is flag burning; the Congress has said that the burning of the American flag is a personal expression protected by the First Amendment. However; the act of burning the cross is against federal law. I understand the reasoning behind this, and what a burning flag represents; however, the concept is exactly the same. Laws that protect one group should protect other groups who perform similar actions. The concept of burning an item as protected expression should be the same regardless of the item. By not applying the law consistently, we place one group above another giving them a "protected" status. Whether we like the message or not; the law must to be applied equally to a flag burner as it is to a cross burner.

Another example is a student charged with a hate crime because he threw a Koran in the toilet. However, there is no consequence for throwing a Bible in the toilet. How insane our laws have become! Laws are enacted to protect all citizens, not just a small section of society. Lastly, just because someone is offended does not give the government the right or jurisdiction to curtail the right of saying an offensive thing. Its called freedom, and the closer we stay to freedom, the further away we will stay from slavery.

Justice Waite also speaks on the jurisdiction and authority of the federal government in relation to the states, saying:

> *"The fourteenth amendment prohibits a State from denying to any person within its jurisdiction the equal protection of the laws; but this provision does not, any more than the one which precedes it, and which we have just considered, add any thing [92 U.S. 542, 555] to the rights which one citizen has under the Constitution against another. The equality of the rights of*

> *citizens is a principle of republicanism. Every republican government is in duty bound to protect all its citizens in the enjoyment of this principle, if within its power. That duty was originally assumed by the States; and it still remains there.* ***The only obligation resting upon the United States is to see that the States do not deny the right.*** *This the amendment guarantees, but no more.* ***The power of the national government is limited to the enforcement of this guaranty.*** *"* (Bold added)

The power of the United States is to insure that the states abide by the Constitution. It has no power against the people, other than through the states, to guaranty the rights of the citizens.

It is important to remember the concept of jurisdiction as we progress through the upcoming chapters. As with many aspects of our government, I do not believe that all laws, as they are written, are unconstitutional; but I do believe that how they are enforced often goes beyond the scope and jurisdiction of the law, and that makes them unconstitutional. As with the preceding example of the drug laws, the government then is free to use that logic to enforce a myriad of other laws in the same fashion.

Chapter 2
General Welfare

The term "General Welfare" has probably been used more to enslave man than any other term. This is akin to your father telling you "It's for you own good." Other terms used, synonymous with General Welfare, are "what is best for all," "for their best interest," "for the public good," etc., etc. That is not what the founders meant by General Welfare. There have been many articles written on this term—some in favor of expanding governmental power, others on limiting governmental power. It is my position that the latter is correct. If the founders wished congress to have such broad, sweeping power, they would not have gone through the trouble of enumerating what powers they did have.

On March 3, 1817, President James Madison, one of our founding fathers, vetoed a bill for the appropriation of funds on a federal public works initiative, which deals with the general welfare clause. His letter is as follows: (Bold added.)

> *To the House of Representatives of the United States:*
>
> *Having considered the bill this day presented to me entitled "An act to set apart and pledge certain funds for internal improvements," and which sets apart and pledges funds "for constructing roads and canals, and improving the navigation of water courses, in order to facilitate, promote, and give security to internal commerce among the several States, and to render more easy and less expensive the means and provisions for the common defense,"* ***I am constrained by the insuperable difficulty I feel in reconciling the bill with the Constitution of the United States*** *to return it with that objection to the House of Representatives, in which it originated.*

The ***legislative powers vested in Congress are specified and enumerated*** *in the eighth section of the first article of the Constitution, and it does not appear that the power proposed to be exercised by the bill is among the enumerated powers, or that it falls by any just interpretation with the power to make laws necessary and proper for carrying into execution those or other powers vested by the Constitution in the Government of the United States.*

"The power to regulate commerce among the several States" can not include a power to construct roads and canals, and to improve the navigation of water courses in order to facilitate, promote, and secure such commerce with a latitude of construction departing from the ordinary import of the terms strengthened by the known inconveniences which doubtless led to the grant of this remedial power to Congress.

To refer the power in question to the clause ***"to provide for common defense and general welfare" would be contrary to the established and consistent rules of interpretation****, as rendering the special and careful enumeration of powers which follow the clause nugatory and improper.* ***Such a view of the Constitution would have the effect of giving to Congress a general power of legislation instead of the defined and limited one hitherto understood to belong to them****, the terms "common defense and general welfare" embracing every object and act within the purview of a legislative trust. It would have the effect of subjecting both the Constitution and laws of the several States in all cases not specifically exempted to be superseded by laws of Congress, it being expressly declared "that the Constitution of the United States and laws made in pursuance thereof shall be the supreme law of the land, and the judges of every state shall be bound thereby, anything in the constitution or laws of any State to the contrary notwithstanding." Such a view of the Constitution, finally, would have the effect of excluding the judicial authority of the United States from its participation in guarding the boundary between the legislative powers of the General and the State Governments, inasmuch as questions relating to the general welfare, being questions of policy and expediency, are unsusceptible of judicial cognizance and decision.*

A restriction of the power "to provide for the common defense and general welfare" to cases which are to be provided for by the expenditure of money would still leave within the legislative power of Congress all the great and most important measures of Government, money being the ordinary and necessary means of carrying them into execution.

If a general power to construct roads and canals, and to improve the navigation of water courses, with the train of powers incident thereto, be not possessed by Congress, the assent of the States in the mode provided in the bill can not confer the power. ***The only cases in which the consent and cession of particular States can extend the power of Congress are those specified and provided for in the Constitution.***

I am not unaware of the great importance of roads and canals and the improved navigation of water courses, and that a power in the National Legislature to provide for them might be exercised with signal advantage to the general prosperity. ***But seeing that such a power is not expressly given by the Constitution, and believing that it can not be deduced from any part of it without an inadmissible latitude of construction and reliance on insufficient precedents; believing also that the permanent success of the Constitution depends on a definite partition of powers between the General and the State Governments, and that no adequate landmarks would be left by the constructive extension of the powers of Congress as proposed in the bill, I have no option but to withhold my signature from it,*** *and to cherishing the hope that its beneficial objects may be attained by a resort for the necessary powers to the same wisdom and virtue in the nation which established the Constitution in its actual form and providently marked out in the instrument itself a safe and practicable mode of improving it as experience might suggest.*

James Madison,
President of the United States"

President Madison, throughout this admonition to the House, refers to specified and enumerated powers of Congress. He went on to state that this was the established and consistent rule of interpretation for the powers of congress, and to give a broad interpretation would give Congress a general power of legislation, **which it did not have**. Within the context of "general welfare" the congress **must** stay within the enumerated boundaries set by the Constitution. He concluded by stating that if the Congress did not have these defined and limited powers they would be able to legislate anything using the common defense and general welfare clauses, and this was wrong. If it was wrong then, then it is wrong now.

The meaning of words has a tendency to change, over time, so we must determine what the founders meant. In order to establish a proper context for this discussion I will refer to Webster's Dictionary from 1828 which gives the definition of Welfare as:

1. *"Exemption from misfortune, sickness, calamity or evil; the enjoyment of health and the common blessings of life; prosperity; happiness;* ***applied to persons.****"*
2. *"Exemption from any unusual evil or calamity; the enjoyment of peace and prosperity, or the ordinary blessings of society and civil government;* ***applied to states****."*

The founders knew, very specifically, the meaning of general welfare when they wrote it into the Constitution. Notice the distinction between the definitions as applied to persons and to states. Clearly, when speaking of "general welfare", they knew a government could not provide for the specific "welfare" of every citizen to include sickness, health, prosperity, and happiness. No government in the world could provide such a thing. The government could only provide general welfare, an opportunity to enjoy peace, prosperity, and the "ordinary blessing of society."

The 1977 Webster's New Collegiate Dictionary defines welfare as:

1. *"The state of doing well esp. in respect to good fortune, happiness, well-being, or prosperity."*
2. *"Of, relating to, or concerned with welfare and esp. with improvement of the welfare and disadvantaged social groups."*

Notice the not so subtle change in identification of "social welfare" in the more recent definition. The 1828 version speaks of state welfare more in what could be deemed "well being" whereas the newer definition focuses on "improvement of welfare and **disadvantaged groups**." This follows more in line with Russia than it does with the founding fathers.

From a legalistic point of view, Blacks Law Dictionary, Seventh Edition defines welfare as:

1. "Well-being in any respect; prosperity.

a. Corporate welfare. Governmental financial assistance given to a large company, usu. In the form of a subsidy.
b. General welfare. The public's health, peace, morals, and safety.
c. Public welfare. A society's well-being in matters of health, safety, order, morality, economics, and politics.

2. A system of social insurance providing assistance to those who are financially in need, as by providing food stamps and family allowances.

Notice how much more expansive the definition of welfare becomes as we get closer to the "law". What James Madison admonished the House of Representatives for, and the bill he would not sign into law, has become the mantra of the present government, Democrat or Republican, "General Welfare."

So what does the word **General** mean? The 1977 Webster's New Collegiate Dictionary defines general as:

1. Involving or applicable to the **whole**.
2. Involving, relating to, or applicable to **every member** of a class, kind, or group.
3. applicable to or **characteristic of the majority** of individuals involved
4. Relating to, determined by, or concerned with **main elements** rather than limited details.
5. **Not confined by specialization** or careful limitation
6. Belonging to the **common nature** of a group of like individuals.
7. Holding superior rank or taking precedence over others similarly titled.

The common thread that runs throughout is that general means of the whole or for everyone. Not some small sector of the whole or a privileged group. The percentage of welfare of the whole is but a small amount, yet we take from the whole for the benefit of the few. This is wrong. Congress was given specific enumerated powers on what it could and could not legislate. To expand beyond that scope, no matter how well intentioned, goes against the Constitution and against the American citizen. "General Welfare" are those things which allows the whole of society to flourish, it does not encompass special interest groups.

Thomas Jefferson wrote:

> "*I consider the foundation of the Constitution as laid on this ground: That 'all powers not delegated to the United States, by*

> *the Constitution, nor prohibited by it to the States, are reserved to the States or to the people.' **To take a single step beyond the boundaries thus specially drawn around the powers of Congress is to take possession of a boundless field of power, no longer susceptible of any definition.**"* [Bold added]

Thomas Jefferson agreed with James Madison that Congress must be held within the bounds outlined. To allow the General Welfare clause to be used in a broad sense would allow Congress to assume a "**boundless field of power**." The founders knew that the government was to be of limited scope, power, and means. By design, it was not to be used to benefit any special interest groups, privileged class of persons, or groups in society. Rather, the Constitution was to be the guarantor of equality, where all people had a free society that allowed for the unrestrained pursuit of happiness.

In 1792, in a letter from James Madison to Henry Lee, responding to Lee's question, if the "general Welfare" clause was a grant of power, Madison replied, "*If not only the means but the objects are unlimited, the parchment [the Constitution] should be thrown into the fire at once*. (Brant, Irving the fourth President—a life of James Madison (Eyre & Spottis Woods (Publishers) Ltd. London 1920.

Quite plainly, James Madison believed the Constitution would be come worthless and fit only for firewood, should the "general welfare" clause be a grant of power. Yet if Madison were to come back to Washington today, I think he would have a fine fire of ancient parchment.

The Constitution was created by the people to establish a government that was limited. A government which could only perform what was enumerated for it to do. James Madison cautioned on interpreting the general welfare clause too liberally, "*If Congress can do whatever in their discretion can be done by money, and will promote the general welfare, the government is no longer a limited one....*" Thus, as with the 10th Amendment, the Federal was to be constrained and should only promote "general" welfare, not welfare for specific recipients.

The founding fathers knew, from their own experiences in England, of the division that was created as soon as an "entitled" class of citizen was created. They remembered the class warfare between the haves and have not's and the division that was created within that citizenry. Where one would be a recipient of welfare from the state, the state would have to find funds by taking them from another hard working Citizen. It is quite appropriate that the modern fairy tale of Robin Hood, which was set in England, in which the hero

steals from the rich, to give to the poor. Think of welfare, how it takes from us all to give to the "poor", but as with Robin Hood, theft is theft.

But our country was not founded upon a fairy tale told by Hollywood, but upon the hard work of honest citizens. Even in the colonies, before the Constitution, there were no "free rides". We all remember the stories of Captain John Smith, who became the leader of Jamestown in September 1608. Captain Smith established a "no work, no food" policy. The Citizens of Jamestown knew that the value that placed on something cannot be given but must be earned. We should not forget this lesson from our past. Today there is a sense of entitlement which comes into existence upon birth. Life is not fair. Some people will be born into riches, having never worked a day in their life. Others will have to struggle for every penny they earn. The constitution does not promise happiness, but only the pursuit thereof. Since the Constitution does promise Life, liberty and the pursuit of happiness, we ask the government only to protect us while we go about seeking it.

So where does Congress get it's power to spend "our money" on welfare programs? Congress's spending power comes from Article I, Section 8 of the Constitution, which states: *"The Congress shall have Power To lay and collect Taxes, Duties, Imposts and Excises, to pay the Debts and provide for the common Defence and general Welfare of the United States; but all Duties, Imposts and Excises shall be uniform throughout the United States."*

At first glance, it would appear that Congress may **collect** taxes and spend on:

1. "Paying the debts of the United States," and
2. "Provide for the common defence and general Welfare of the United States.

According to the Constitution these two lines describe what Congress can spend our tax money on, nothing else. But for the first 150 years of our Constitutional history there was no federal welfare. So how is it that we new spend billions upon billons each year for "welfare" programs?

As we have already read above, many of the founders of our nation did not want an all powerful, controlling government. They did not feel it was the governments place to provide the sustenance of life to every citizen. So from 1787 until 1937, virtually no legislation was passed that veered outside of the enumerated powers identified in Article 1, Section 8 of the Constitution. And the few that were, as we have shown above, were rejected.

However, in 1933 with the strain of the great depression, the new president, Franklin D. Roosevelt, our Constitutional world was about to be turned upside down in something called "The New Deal." For the next four years President Roosevelt saw the nation sinking deeper and deeper into despair and financial ruin. Seeing no other alternative he asked for and was granted executive powers "***similar to those necessary in time of war.***" During the 73rd session of Congress; legislation after legislation was expedited through the halls of Congress. Some bills were even voted upon, and passed, without ever being read.

By 1935 the first of the "New Deal" legislations were being reviewed by the Supreme Court. Eight out of ten of these statutes were found to be unconstitutional. FDR was furious and he declared war upon the Judiciary. He threatened to pass legislation to "stack" the courts by enacting legislation that would allow the president to appoint another Supreme Court Justice for every justice that was 70 years old or older if they did not retire. This would have added six new justices to the ranks of the Supreme Court and would ensure his bills were approved by the court. In one of his legendary fireside "chats", he stated: ***"we have therefore, reached the point as a nation where we must take action to save the Constitution from the Court and the Court from itself."***

Shortly thereafter two justices decided to change their vote in support of the "New Deal" statutes and thereby averted what would have amounted to the overthrow of the Supreme Court. By the end of his administration, President Roosevelt replaced five of the nine Supreme Court justices: Hugo Black, William O. Douglas, Felix Frankfurter, Robert Jackson and Frank Murphy.

It's effects however were felt far and wide, and across generations and opened the doors to any spending which avowed the "General Welfare" mantra. It continues to this day with ever increasing national debt in the trillions of dollars. All done in just 70 years! We lasted for 150 years without a welfare state and with no national debt. We now stand as the greatest debtor nation in history, all to support the "General Welfare"

One of the justices which changed their vote to support President Roosevelt in his welfare spending was Justice Roberts. In the 1936 case United States v. Butler, 297 U.S. 1, 65, 66, Justice Roberts, speaking of the "General Welfare" phrase, wrote:

> *"Since the foundation of the Nation sharp differences of opinion have persisted as to the true interpretation of the phrase. Madison asserted it amounted to no more than a reference to the other powers enumerated in the subsequent clauses of the*

> *same section; that, as the* ***United States is a government of limited and enumerated powers, the grant of power to tax and spend for the general national welfare must be confined to the numerated legislative fields committed to the Congress.*** *In this view the phrase is mere tautology, for taxation and appropriation are or may be necessary incidents of the exercise of any of the enumerated legislative powers. Hamilton, on the other hand, maintained* ***the clause confers a power separate and distinct from those later enumerated, is not restricted in meaning by the grant of them, and Congress consequently has a substantive power to tax and to appropriate, limited only by the requirement that it shall be exercised to provide for the general welfare of the United States.*** *Each contention has had the support of those whose views are entitled to weight. This court had noticed the question, but has never found it necessary to decide which is the true construction. Justice Story, in his Commentaries, espouses the Hamiltonian position. We shall not review the writings of public men and commentators or discuss the legislative practice. Study of all these leads us to conclude that the reading advocated by Justice Story is the correct one. While, therefore, the power to tax is not unlimited, its confines are set in the clause which confers it, and not in those of § 8 which bestow and define the legislative powers of the Congress.* ***It results that the power of Congress to authorize expenditure of public moneys for public purposes is not limited by the direct grants of legislative power found in the Constitution."***

The amazing thing is that Justice Roberts and others, for years, have found the bills expanding the "general welfare" clause of Congress to be unconstitutional. Note: One precept of the Judicial Branch is that of precedent. That once a position has been taken by the court, future courts are not to change that position for transient means. Here we have Justice Roberts, who admits that the Supreme Court has been divided on the meaning and latitude that should be given to the term "General Welfare." Yet, in 1936, with the pressure to preserve the Supreme Court and to appease President Roosevelt, the court changes it's position and gives Congress the power to tax and spend for anything they can attach, by any stretch of the imagination, to defense and welfare. Remember, the courts had shortly before ruled that 8 of 10 welfare bills originally passed by Roosevelt's Congress were found to be unconstitutional. Now 2 years later rules have changed and President Roosevelt and Congress get a free pass.

The most far reaching legislation of the Roosevelt era would, arguably be, the Social Security Act. To support the welfare mentality a more socialistic process had to be devised. A means by which the vast majority would be able to support the less fortunate, and to establish a mechanism that allowed for the dignified retirement for the many that lost their life savings during the depression. The sentiment was noble, though not constitutional. But just 10 years before President Harding stated: ***"Just government is merely the guarantee to the people of the right and opportunity to support themselves. The one outstanding danger of today is the tendency to turn to Washington for the things which are the tasks or the duties of the forty-eight commonwealths."*** Seventy five years ago none of our citizens turned to Washington, today none dare turn away.

I have heard from supporters of government welfare that "Congress may spend money to promote the general welfare, and what the general welfare is, changes with the times." It is natural for the meaning of words to change over time by common use and custom, this is true. The meaning of Constitutional terms, however, cannot be changed; it cannot change, because the meaning remains exactly what those that penned them meant it to say. This meaning cannot be changed by time or the Supreme Court. The Supreme Court based their decision to support the "New Deal" welfare reform, in part, on what General Welfare meant to President Roosevelt in the 20th century, they did not base it on what the founders of the Constitution meant it to mean. In this instance the Supreme Court was wrong.

It is important to point out that even with the agreed upon power congress has to tax, it cannot tax for things outside of the federal jurisdiction, or the purposes of the federal government. Secondly, the tax and purpose of the **tax cannot subvert or infringe on any other constitutional purpose or right**. To do so is paramount to destroying that right. The belief that if someone is given money, increases the general welfare of that person, and thus benefits the nation as a whole, is flawed. In order to provide a benefit to someone denotes that you would have to penalize others to obtain it. By that same logic, you would lower the general welfare of those you took from and thus have a gross negative effect on the total. This is a version of socialism, and socialism does not work.

One of the setbacks to Roosevelt's New Deal was decided in ***United States v. Butler,*** 297 U.S. 1 (1936), known as the Agricultural Adjustment

Act of 1933. The Act provided payments to farmers if they agreed to reduce production acreage. The Supreme Court decided while the tax itself was justified under the "General Welfare" clause, its intended use was "coercive" and thus unconstitutional based on the Tenth Amendment. It was reasoned that Congress had attempted to use the taxing power of congress to regulate agricultural production, which was deemed the sole jurisdiction of the States. Since the 1930's, as we have already discussed, the "General Welfare" mantra has been used to support more and more expansive spending by the federal government at the expense of the taxpayer.

To be balanced on this subject we must also look at what Alexander Hamilton had to say concerning General Welfare, the government has found his position to be the most supportive. Alexander Hamilton, as a Federalist, wanted a strong government and believed that the checks and balances inherent in the system would keep the government safe from tyranny. In the federalist papers, Hamilton maintained the clause confers a power separate and distinct from those enumerated. Congress, consequently, has a substantive power to tax and appropriate for government, limited only by the requirement that it can be shown to provide for the general welfare of the United States.

In the hands of unscrupulous men, the idea of separation of state and federal governments, checks and balances built into government, and enumeration of powers, would all be undermined; and in such hands would enable them to enslave the entire nation. If the government could have the power to pass any law, tax anyone for anything, at any degree, the citizenry would be powerless to resist. Our forefathers, having rebelled over a Tea tax of 3%, would not give the federal government the power to freely tax anything it wished? If those who wrote the Constitution wished that congress would have an open hand in determining what it could do, there would be no reason to enumerate the individual powers congress would have.

As recently as 1995, in United States vs. Lopez, (93-1260), 514 U.S. 549, the Supreme Court affirmed that the Constitution establishes a federal government with enumerated, and thus, limited powers. I refer the reader to the previous chapter on jurisdiction. The congress may pass any laws it sees fit to pass, under its jurisdiction; however, they are still constrained to only the enumerated powers, otherwise the power reverts back to the state or to the people. An accurate reading of the Constitution, therefore, brings much of Congress' authority into question.

Thomas Jefferson wrote concerning the General Welfare clause:

> *"...that Congress had not unlimited powers to provide for the general welfare, but were restrained to those specifically enumerated, and that, as it was never meant that they should provide for that welfare but by the exercise of the enumerated powers, so it could not have been meant they should raise money for purposes which the enumeration did not place under their action;* ***consequently, that the specification of powers is a limitation of the purposes for which they may raise money."***
> [Bold added.]

Let's take a look again at the pertinent part of Article 1, Section 8: *"to pay the Debts and* ***provide for the common Defence*** *and general Welfare of the United States".* Now look at the second phrase in bold, provide for the common defence. Some may say this was a phrase that enhanced or expanded the powers of Congress. To what extent did it expand their powers? Surely, both the defense and welfare clauses are general in nature. If you take the same logic with defense as Congress has with welfare, we could place soldiers in every town, on the borders, at airports, bus stations;—anywhere there is the possibility of attack against us. After all, if it aids in the common defense, it must be constitutional. What would happen if the government could detain anyone, at any time for questioning, but only for the common defense? What if they could open all mail, monitor electronic communications, monitor bank records, listen in on telephone calls, and bug our homes, churches, and meeting places, but only for the common defense? What if you could not question the manner in which this was done, as that *would* be unconstitutional? Many of you would be saying, that can't happen, we have rights, and those things are unconstitutional. Many of these things are being done, at varying degrees, right now!

Much of the abuse of this power has happened since the 1930's, as referenced above. What about evidence of enumerated powers closer to the time of the founders? President Buchanan on 24 February 1859, in an address to the House of Representatives, stated:

> *"It would require clear and strong evidence to induce the belief that the framers of the Constitution, after having limited the powers of Congress to certain precise and specific objects, intended by employing the words "dispose of" to give that body unlimited power over the vast public domain. It would be a strange anomaly indeed to have created two funds--the one by taxation, confined to the execution of the enumerated powers*

> *delegated to Congress, and the other from the public lands, applicable to all subjects, foreign and domestic, which Congress might designate; that this fund should be "disposed of," not to pay the debts of the United States, nor "to raise and support armies," nor "to provide and maintain a navy," nor to accomplish any one of the other great objects enumerated in the Constitution, but be diverted from them to pay the debts of the States, to educate their people, and to carry into effect any other measure of their domestic policy.* ***This would be to confer upon Congress a vast and irresponsible authority utterly at war with the well-known jealousy of Federal power which prevailed at the formation of the Constitution. The natural intendment would be that as the Constitution confined Congress to well-defined specific powers, the funds placed at their command, whether in land or money, should be appropriated to the performance of the duties corresponding with these powers.*** *If not, a Government has been created with all its other powers carefully limited, but without any limitation in respect to the public lands."*

How is it that here we find the limitation of Congress so plain, and yet the further we remove ourselves from the founding truths of the Constitution, the further from the truth and the more corrupt we become? It seems that where once the Congress asked "Where in the Constitution do we have the power to act?" Now it seems Congress is saying "We can do anything unless prohibited by the Constitution."

Now as government expands beyond its role of "general welfare," it strips the right from the states, or the people, to whom this responsibility would fall. During the first century of this nation there were no "welfare" programs like we have today. A man would turn to family and friends when he fell on hard times. If they were unable to help, there was the church and the community. After that they were on their own.

It is quite apparent that the government, although perhaps well meaning, has stepped beyond its power and jurisdiction into the roll of a parent over children. By steadily increasing the governments' charity role, it places the entire nation deeper and deeper into debt and slavery. Slavery, not only for ourselves, but for our children. At the current rate of debt accumulation, our children could possibly see tax rates as high as 65% or more in order to keep our country going.

And in my opinion, this is immoral, unconstitutional, and illegal. Unfortunately, as long as our country continues to give free handouts, there will always be those who will take advantage. Millions of illegal aliens flock across the borders each year, which inflates the welfare roles and the burden on our society. Socialism was never a viable option in any other country in the world. Why we think it will work here is beyond understanding.

In the next chapters I will discuss the powers and restrictions which were enumerated in the Constitution and discern if today's government is operating within the bounds set forth therein.

CHAPTER 3
14TH AMENDMENT

Have you ever looked at a picture with hidden images drawn inside of a larger image? There is one optical illusion of a young lady in a gown, but when you look at it a little differently, you can see a picture of an old woman. The fourteenth Amendment is a bit like that. When you first read it, it sounds straight forward, especially when viewed in historical perspective of President Lincoln after the civil war. However, I will present you a glimpse of the other picture, the ugly truth about the 14th Amendment, and how it relates to all of us today.

To build the complete picture of the 14th Amendment, we need to take into consideration the things that led up to the drafting of the amendment. We have been taught that the civil war was fought over slavery; which is partially correct, more accurately; however, it was fought over discriminatory trade laws against the south, and in the end, over money. (I do not agree with slavery of any kind, especially as was common during the time of the framers, however, I make the following observations of the nature of slavery during the early years to contrast the law during that time and where we are today.) When the six southern states joined the union, laws were established which allowed the slave states to continue slave ownership. From their writings we can see that slave owners believed they were as much protector as they were bondsmen.

In their declaration to cede from the union, the Confederates explained that because of Lincoln's election, and his stance to absolve slavery, the south felt betrayed. The congressional representatives from the northern states bound together to pass laws on the southern states which moved them toward the abolition of slavery. The south believed that the actions of the northern states to overrule the laws within the southern states was unconstitutional, and Texas felt betrayed because the federal government would not provide aid against the "ruthless savages" in it's fight with Mexico. This was also the era of the underground slave railroad which helped transport runaway slaves from the south—a time when skirmishes broke out and many southerners were killed. The South felt betrayed when those accused were not tried for their actions. This created a further divide between the north and south.

After the 1860 Election of President Lincoln, seven states formally ceded from the United States to form the Confederate States of America on February 4, 1861. They elected Jefferson Davis as their first president. The first seven states united were South Carolina, Mississippi, Florida, Alabama, Georgia, Louisiana, and Texas. After President Lincoln called up troops on 15 April, 1861, four more states joined the confederacy: Virginia, Arkansas, Tennessee, and North Carolina, bringing the total to 11 states.

The call up of troops was done by proclamation and was the forerunner to an executive order. The reason for such a measure was not just the announcement by the states that they were ceding from the union, but also a refusal by the southern states to sit and convene congress. By proclamation Lincoln called up 75,000 militia troops, and he ordered both houses of congress to convene. He summoned all representatives to meet on July 4th, 1861.

In both the Senate and house Journals of the 37th Congress, 1st Session, Pages 123 & 91, respectively, it is stated that the Civil War was not waged for the purpose of conquest or to overthrow the rights and established institutions of those States; it was waged to defend and maintain the supremacy of the Constitution and to preserve the Union with all equality and rights of the several States unimpaired and that as soon as these objects are accomplished; the war ought to cease.

At the conclusion of the war, congress proposed the 13th, 14th, and 15th Amendments—abolishing slavery, and creating and granting federal citizenship, and suffrage (voting) for **its** new citizens. The 13th Amendment was ratified December 6th, 1865. It is interesting to note that the last state to ratify this amendment was Mississippi on March 5th, 1995, a full 130 years after the initial ratification, for a total of 36 out of our current 50 states.

The 13th Amendment states:

> **Section 1.** *"Neither slavery nor involuntary servitude, except as a punishment for crime whereof the party shall have been duly convicted, shall exist within the United States, or any place subject to their jurisdiction".*

Section 2. *"Congress shall have the power to enforce this article by appropriate legislation."*

This was the first amendment which included an enforcement clause.

Why did congress feel it necessary to include the 2nd section which gave them power to enforce this legislation? It was because they did not have the power to do so by Article 1 of the Constitution. They were expanding their power. Remember earlier we spoke of Congressional Power? Congress had only the powers that were enumerated under Article 1, Section 8. They did not have any authority to enforce the 13th Amendment, as this power was not enumerated. Now we have what I call the initial marriage of the legislative and judicial branches of government. Congress needed to have power to enforce this amendment, to pass laws, (legislate), and to give the Supreme Court, (the judicial branch), the ability to side with congress via this amendment.

Up until this time, many of the states did not recognize blacks as *persons* who could become citizens. Even with the passing of the 13th Amendment, the Federal Government had no power within the states to effect the necessary changes to force the issue. In the case of Blair v. Ridgely, 97 D. 218,249, S.P. the Supreme Court held *"Prior to the adoption of the federal Constitution, states possessed unlimited and unrestricted sovereignty and retained the same ever afterward. Upon entering the Union, they retained all their original power and sovereignty..."* The Federal Government, therefore, could not force the states to do all that was required on the issue without granting this additional power.

One very important case of the time was Dred Scott v. Sandford, 60 U.S. 393 (1856), which required the 14th Amendment to overturn the Supreme Courts decision. The Dred Scott case was specifically about the rights of slaves, property owners, and the separation between federal and state jurisdiction. The case was brought by Dred Scott, a black man, who by Missouri law, could not be a citizen of that state and, therefore, could not bring suit. The court found in favor of Sandford, the defendant, due to the lack of jurisdiction. I would recommend everyone to read the Dred Scott case for a truly insightful look at a piece of American History.

The 14th Amendment was proposed by a rump Congress which did not include representatives and senators from most of the southern states. Had those southern congressmen been present, the Amendment would never have passed. *(A rump congress is defined as a legislature having only part of its original membership and therefore being unrepresentative or lacking in authority.) What is more astounding are the official history journals from the Senate Library entitled "Amendments to the Constitution, A Brief Legislative History," (dated 1985). Within this official history, the government acknowledges the maneuvering of the Senate to preclude the southern states from seating and voting on the 14th Amendment. They also show that at the time of the ratification of the 14th Amendment they did not have the requisite 28 states confirming the Amendment.

The 14th Amendment was passed by Congress on 13 June, 1866, and supposedly, it was ratified 9 July, 1868. There are those that believe that the Fourteenth Amendment was not properly ratified and that senators were excluded from the hearings and the vote in order to secure the necessary vote percentage. As our courts have said, once an amendment is on record as being ratified it becomes a political question which will only be resolved by political means. The political system has nothing to gain by admission of this ratification error, and is not likely to be reversed. I will write more on this later.

Prior to the signing of the 14th Amendment, on April 2, 1866, President Andrew Johnson issued the following proclamation:

> "*The insurrection which heretofore existed in the States of Georgia, South Carolina, Virginia, North Carolina, Tennessee, Alabama, Louisiana, Arkansas, Mississippi and Florida is at an end, and is henceforth to be so regarded.*"

As the southern states in question were allowed to vote on the 13th Amendment, why then were they barred from seating in the house and senate to vote on the 14th Amendment? Another interesting event was that many of the southern states had replacement representatives assigned by the northern congress to facilitate the necessary majority to pass the 14th Amendment, a clear violation of the Constitution.

Now that the separatist confederacy was stopped; the government still did not have power to change the individual state constitutions. In order to do this the federal government had to change the playing field. This was accomplished by the enactment of the 13th Amendment, freeing the blacks in the southern states. The problem with this was that while the 13th Amendment freed the slaves, it did nothing to change the laws of southern states. In fact, after the 13th Amendment was ratified, some states enacted what became to be known as "Jim Crow" laws, which disallowed blacks from owning property, guns, and certain jobs. Blacks also could not vote or hold public office, and there were many other restrictions which were in direct opposition to the new amendments and reconstruction acts.

In 1865 The Freedman's Bureau Act was established which aided the war department in dealing with refugees from the south. It assisted with relocation, feeding, clothing, and transportation of blacks fleeing the south.

In 1866 the Civil Rights Act was passed by Congress. It was vetoed by President Andrew Johnson, but the veto was overridden by Congress. This act was the forerunner to the 14th Amendment. This act made all persons born in the United States, citizens of the United States without regard to their previous condition, and it made those who denied blacks these rights guilty of a misdemeanor. Problems began when organizations such as the Ku Klux Klan (and others) ignored the act and defied the federal government. During this time, separatist and Klan groups did everything in their power to defeat attempts to integrate the blacks into the citizenry. These acts include murder, burning of homes, beatings and many other atrocious acts.

In 1870 to 1871, the Enforcement acts were put into place by congress to give further weight to the previous acts and to give criminal codes to violations of federal intent of the reconstruction amendments (13, 14, and 15). They also allow for federal prosecution under those codes.

Prior to the 14th Amendment the federal government had little or no jurisdiction over the citizens of the many states of the union. After the 14th Amendment the federal government became directly involved with the citizens, to the detriment of our entire society and the constitutional republican form of government. At this point, we lost the Constitution of our heritage and we entered a Constitutional dictatorship. Because we elect a new person every four to eight years does not change the dictatorial powers the office holds. If you have any doubt, review the thousands of executive orders/ proclamations that create law and executive organizations—all without congressional approval.

When dealing with the Constitution one must be able to interpret between what the founders meant by the words written. The authors of the Constitution were learned men who were educated in the English language and in proper legal construction. There are two primary rules I try to follow when reading the Constitution; first, what does the plain text say? Is it straight forward and easily understood? Second, what did the authors have to say about what was written? If you compare the earlier amendments ("Bill of Rights") with the later amendments, you will notice that, for the most part, the earlier amendments were fairly easy to understand.

We will start with Section 1 of the 14th Amendment, which reads:

> *"All persons born or naturalized in the United States, and subject to the jurisdiction thereof, are citizens of the United States and of the State wherein they reside. No State shall make or enforce any law which shall abridge the privileges or immunities of citizens of the United States; nor shall any State deprive any person of life, liberty, or property, without due process of law; nor deny to any person within its jurisdiction the equal protection of the laws."*

Most people believe that the United States, (the federal government that was enacted in the Constitution), consolidated the states and the people into a single nation; it did not. Remember the words in the opening of the Constitution, (See Appendix), *"in Order to form a more perfect Union"*? The Constitution modified the Articles of Confederation under which the federal government was created. As mentioned earlier, the Articles of Confederation had some shortcomings dealing with funding the government, taxing authorities etc.; but the government was already created. The creation of the federal government was not to be a ruler, but to be a guarantor of these (agreed upon) roles and responsibilities. It was secondary to the jurisdiction of the states; especially for anything that happened within that state. Each state was a separate government. The federal was created as a referee between the states, to deal with foreign governments, and to be protector.

The 14th Amendment attempts to change the very nature of our government and our Constitution. The very first sentence states, *"All persons born or naturalized in the United States, and subject to the jurisdiction thereof, are citizens of the United States and of the State wherein they reside."* For the first time, people outside the territories and federal enclaves of the government were granted (forced) into federal citizenship, which is separate and distinct from state citizenship. More importantly, it created a change in the order of government—now the federal citizen was placed ahead of the state citizen.

Note how the first section uses the distinction between person and citizen. "*...nor shall any State deprive any person of life, liberty, or property, without due process of law; nor deny to any person within its jurisdiction the equal protection of the laws."* As both words are used within the section, it must be assumed that there is a difference between them. It is also important to point out that once the identified "persons" were given citizenship, the mandate to the states reverted back to identifying them as persons. So who were the "persons" identified? Clearly they were not those who were born here and who were already citizens. The writers must have been referring to those "persons" who did not have the right to citizenship, or those of color.

The 14th Amendment was not written for those who were already citizens, it only affected non-citizens. This is an important point to remember; obviously you would not be granting citizenship to someone who was already a citizen. The government created a **federal** citizen who had all the protections and privileges due such a citizen. This was a means of overcoming the Jim Crow laws of the south and to give protection to the blacks throughout the country. The federal government already had citizens. Remember, people who lived in Washington D.C., the territories, and all federal enclaves were part of the Federal government; but they did not have state citizenship. They could not vote, and they had no constitutional rights as guaranteed by the states of the union.

It is important to point out that no member of Congress or the Supreme Court has ever equated a "citizen of the United States", as used in the 14th Amendment, with a native born Citizen of a state of the Union. It is also interesting to point out that there were people who fell into a grey area of citizenship, such as those that were born and or lived in Washington D.C. Because Washington D.C. is an enclave, not a state, they were not considered citizens and could not vote. It wasn't until the 14th Amendment that these people became federal citizens—separate and distinct from a state citizen.

If the 14th Amendment did not apply to everyone, then whom does this amendment apply? Are there any citizens alive today who can claim direct citizenship from pre 14th Amendment time? Remember from the preamble, which guaranteed this citizenship "to us and our posterity". Since that time the citizenry and standards of citizenry changed. Everyone could hold citizenship. Citizens were no longer only white land owners, but now citizens were women, blacks, Chinese, and Latinos, everyone may hold citizenship. Is there a difference between pre-14th Amendment citizens and post-Amendment citizens? Do they exist today?

We have already shown that there were Citizens identified prior to the 14th Amendment. The 14th Amendment could not change the original writers meaning of the term "Citizen" when the Constitution was drafted. Therefore, there were now two classes of citizens,—pre 14th Amendment white, male Citizens, and post 14th Amendment black, male citizens. This cannot change. The meaning of the Constitution remains the same as it did at the time it was written, period. All persons not falling into the pre-14th Amendment description are identified as 14th Amendment citizens. This is what the federal government presumes as well.

Obviously the definition of "Citizen of the U.S." used in the opening of the Constitution, refers to one class of citizen while the "citizen" of the United States as written in the 14th Amendment, refers to a different class of citizen. As the Supreme Court ruled in the Dred Scott decision, the term "Citizen of the United States" could never be used to mean people of African decent (or their posterity) brought here for the purpose of slavery.

We now have two distinct and separate classes of citizens: the first "**C**itizen of the United States," as defined in the opening of the Constitution, and "citizen of the United States," as defined in the 14th Amendment. Notice the subtle distinction in their presentation. In law, context is everything. Remember that the Federal government had very little interaction with the people in the states of the union. Now this had changed. For the first time, the federal government was in a position to dictate to the states how to deal with the federal citizens residing within each state. For the states' own Citizens, nothing really changed. For the federal citizens, however, the federal government could dictate to the states how they would be treated and also dictated what rights those citizens would have. The **C**itizen, pre-14th, had unalienable rights from their creator, now found themselves living among **c**itizens, post-14th Amendment, who had rights, and privileges granted by **their** creator—the federal government. This sheds a whole different light on the subject.

Suddenly the lines between Federal and State jurisdiction were blurred beyond recognition. What was designed to protect the rights of freed black slaves opened the door to federal encroachment, something the Founding Fathers had never intended. In order to protect all its citizens, the federal government began to make wide, sweeping generalities about all citizens. How could they know for certain who was and was not one of **their** citizens? They decided, therefore, to presume that **all** citizens were 14th Amendment citizens, unless they declared otherwise. This provided the easiest and most equitable approach to dealing with everyone, and it evenly offered protection to all its' citizens.

An interesting case in the late 1960's relied heavily upon the 14th Amendment and what that amendment means to the states and its citizens—the case was Dyett v. Turner (Utah 1968) 439 P.2d 266, 20 Utah 2d 403. This case illustrates the historical and political mindsets, as well as problems with the ratification of the 14th Amendment. This information comes from a Utah Supreme Court Justice as well as other pertinent documents.

I have included sections of the case dealing with the 14th Amendment.

Even though this is only a partial transcript, it is still quite lengthy, but worth the read:

439 P.2d 266, 20 Utah 2d 403 Dyett v. Turner (Utah 1968)
Gerald J. DYETT, Plaintiff, vs. John W. TURNER, Warden, Utah State Prison, Defendant No. 11089
SUPREME COURT OF UTAH
439 P.2d 266, 20 Utah 2d 403
March 22, 1968
ELLETT, Justice, wrote the opinion.
CALLISTER, J., concurs in the result.
HENRIOD, J., concurs in the result and reasoning.
CROCKETT, Chief Justice (concurring in the result):
TUCKETT, J., concurs in the concurring opinion of CROCKETT, C.J

"President Lincoln had declared the freedom of the slaves as a war measure, but when the war ended, the effect of the proclamation was ended, and so it was necessary to propose and to ratify the Thirteenth Amendment in order to insure the freedom of the slaves."

"The 11 southern states having taken their rightful and necessary place in the indestructible Union proceeded to determine whether to ratify or reject the proposed Thirteenth Amendment. In order to become a part of the Constitution, it was necessary that the proposed amendment be ratified by 27 of the 36 states. Among those 27 states ratifying the Thirteenth Amendment were 10 from the South, to wit, Louisiana, Tennessee, Arkansas, South Carolina, Alabama, North Carolina, Georgia, Mississippi, Florida, and Texas."

"When the 39th Congress assembled on December 5, 1865, the senators and representatives from the 25 northern states voted to deny seats in both houses of Congress to anyone elected from the 11 southern states. The full complement of senators from the 36 states of the Union was 72, and the full membership in the House was 240. Since it requires only a majority vote (Article I, Section 5, Constitution of the United States) to refuse a seat in Congress, only the 50 senators and 182 congressmen from the North were seated. All of the 22 senators and 58 representatives from the southern states were denied seats."

"Joint Resolution No. 48 proposing the Fourteenth Amendment was a matter of great concern to the Congress and to the people of the Nation. In order to have this proposed amendment submitted to the 36 states for ratification, it was necessary that two thirds of each house concur. **A count of noses showed that only 33 senators were favorable to the measure, and 33 was a far cry from two thirds of 72 and lacked one of being two thirds of the 50 seated senators."**

"While it requires only a majority of votes to refuse a seat to a senator, it requires a two thirds majority to unseat a member once he is seated. (Article 1, Section 5, Constitution of the United States) **One John P. Stockton was seated on December 5, 1865**, as one of the senators from New Jersey. He was outspoken in his opposition to Joint Resolution No. 48 proposing the Fourteenth Amendment. **The leadership in the Senate not having control of two thirds of the seated senators voted to refuse to seat Mr. Stockton** upon the ground that he had received only a plurality and not a majority of the votes of the New Jersey legislature. It was the law of New Jersey and several other states that a plurality vote was sufficient for election. Besides, **the Senator had already been seated. Nevertheless, his seat was refused**, and the 33 favorable votes thus became the required two thirds of the 49 members of the Senate."

"In the House of Representatives it would require 122 votes to be two thirds of the 182 members seated. Only 120 voted for the proposed amendment, but because there were 30 abstentions it was declared to have been passed by a two thirds vote of the House."

"Whether it requires two thirds of the full membership of both houses to propose an amendment to the Constitution or only two thirds of those seated or two thirds of those voting is a question which it would seem could only be determined by the United States Supreme Court. However, it is perhaps not so important for the reason that the amendment is only proposed by Congress. **It must be ratified by three fourths of the states in the Union before it becomes a part of the Constitution**. The method of securing the passage through Congress is set out above, as it throws some light on the means used to obtain ratification by the states thereafter."

"Nebraska had been admitted to the Union, and so the Secretary of State in transmitting the proposed amendment announced that ratification by 28 states would be needed before the amendment would become part of the Constitution, since there were at the time 37 states in the Union. **A rejection by 10 states would thus defeat the proposal."**

"By March 17, 1867, the proposed amendment had been ratified by 17 states and rejected by 10, with California voting to take no action thereon, which was equivalent to rejection. **Thus the proposal was defeated**."

"One of the ratifying states, Oregon, had ratified by a membership wherein **two legislators were subsequently held not to be duly elected**, and after the contest the duly elected members of the legislature of **Oregon rejected the proposed amendment. However, this rejection came after the amendment was declared passed."**

"Despite the fact that the **southern states had been functioning peacefully for two years and had been counted to secure ratification of the Thirteenth Amendment**, Congress passed the Reconstruction Act, which provided for the **military occupation of 10 of the 11 southern states. It excluded Tennessee from military occupation, and one must suspect it was because Tennessee had ratified the Fourteenth Amendment on July 7, 1866.** The Act further disfranchised practically all white voters and **provided that no senator or congressman from the occupied states could be seated in Congress until a new constitution was adopted by each state which would be approved by Congress, and further provided that each of the 10 states must ratify the proposed Fourteenth Amendment, and the Fourteenth Amendment must become a part of the Constitution of the United States before the military occupancy would cease and the states be allowed to have seats in Congress."**

"By the time the Reconstruction Act had been declared to be the law, three more states had ratified the proposed Fourteenth Amendment, and two—Louisiana and Delaware—had rejected it. Then **Maryland withdrew its prior ratification** and rejected the proposed Fourteenth Amendment. **Ohio followed suit and**

withdrew its prior ratification, as also did New Jersey. California, which earlier had voted not to pass upon the proposal, now voted to **reject the amendment. Thus 16 of the 37 states had rejected the proposed amendment."**

"By spurious, non-representative governments seven of the southern states which had theretofore rejected the proposed amendment under the duress of military occupation and of being denied representation in Congress did attempt to ratify the proposed Fourteenth Amendment. The Secretary of State on July 20, 1868, issued his proclamation wherein he stated that it was his duty under the law to cause amendments to be published and certified as a part of the Constitution when he received official notice that they had been adopted pursuant to the Constitution."

"Thereafter his certificate contained the following language:..."

"Congress was not satisfied with the proclamation as issued and on the next day passed a concurrent resolution wherein it was resolved *"That said fourteenth article is hereby declared to be a part of the Constitution of the United States, and it shall be duly promulgated as such by the Secretary of State."* Thereupon, William H. Seward, the Secretary of State, after setting forth the concurrent resolution of both houses of Congress, then certified that the amendment *"has become valid to all intents and purposes as a part of the Constitution of the United States."*

"The Constitution of the United States is silent as to who should decide whether a proposed amendment has or has not been passed according to formal provisions of Article V of the Constitution. The Supreme Court of the United States is the ultimate authority on the meaning of the Constitution and has never hesitated in a proper case to declare an act of Congress unconstitutional—except when the act purported to amend the Constitution. The duty of the Secretary of State was ministerial, to wit, to count and determine when three fourths of the states had ratified the proposed amendment. He could not determine that a state once having rejected a proposed amendment could thereafter approve it, nor could he determine that a state once having ratified that proposal could thereafter reject it. The court and not Congress should determine such matters. Consistency would seem to require that a vote once cast would be final or would not be final, whether the first vote was for ratification or rejection."

"In order to have 27 states ratify the Fourteenth Amendment, it was necessary to count those states which had first rejected and then under the duress of military occupation had ratified, and then also to count those states which initially ratified but subsequently rejected the proposal."

"To leave such dishonest counting to a fractional part of Congress is dangerous in the extreme. What is to prevent any political party having control of both houses of Congress from refusing to seat the opposition and then without more passing a joint resolution to the effect that the Constitution is amended and that it is the duty of the Administrator of the General Services Administration to proclaim the adoption? Would the Supreme Court of the United States still say the problem was political and refuse to determine whether constitutional standards had been met?"

"How can it be conceived in the minds of anyone that a combination of powerful states can by force of arms deny another state a right to have representation in Congress until it has ratified an amendment which its people oppose? The Fourteenth Amendment was adopted by means almost as bad as that suggested above."

"We have spoken in the hope that the Supreme Court of the United States may retreat from some of its recent decisions affecting the rights of a sovereign state to determine for itself what is proper procedure in its own courts as it affects its own citizens. **However, we realize that because of that Court's superior power, we must pay homage to it even though we disagree with it; and so we now discuss the merits of this case just the same as though the sword of Damocles did not hang over our heads.**"

I could not have outlined the problems with the ratification better than did Justice Ellett in this opinion of the court. With today's CSPAN cameras, cameras in court rooms, internet news, blogs and web pages, the wrangling of

Congress would be spread far and wide within minutes. If this type of maneuvering happened today, there would be an outrage. So why is it that almost 150 years after the 14th Amendment came into being, and almost 40 years after this court case, that this issue is known by less than 1% of our nation?. The Supreme Court is aware of it, and they do nothing! Congress is aware of it, and they do nothing! The people are the last resort—when they do nothing America will be lost.

With the ratification "scheme" completed, and the new citizenship order established, there were now two classes of citizens, but only one presumptive federal class that ruled everyone. The result of this, to the unsuspecting or unlearned, is a change from being a sovereign citizen of the State to a federal subject that resides (resident alien) in a state of the union.

When dealing with individuals within the confines of this country, the federal government presumes all citizens to be 14th Amendment citizens. If you were to write to your state election commissioner and ask the following: "I notice that in order to register to vote I must swear under penalty of perjury that I am a United States citizen. Knowing that Congress has assigned three different meanings to the term citizen, which definition of "citizen of the United States," as it is used, relates to voter registration?" More often than not the response will be a "14th Amendment citizen." This is their presumption, and by registering under that presumption, **you** have just verified that you are, indeed, a 14th Amendment citizen.

The second clause of Section 1 states: *"No state shall make or enforce any law which shall abridge the privileges or immunities of citizens of the United States."* This does not preclude the Federal Government from doing so, but only precludes the individual states from passing laws contrary to the federal laws against the new class of federal "citizens of the United States". This does not apply to the "regular" citizens, however, who lived in the various states. They have unalienable rights that the federal government could not touch. The federal government was making the same restrictions against the states that it made against the new federal citizen.

Did you know that you were a rebel? Did you register to vote in the federal elections? Then you are, by definition, a citizen of the United States; and you are participating in rebellion to your De Jour republic. Section 2 states:

> *"**But when the right to vote** at any election for the choice of electors for President and Vice-President of the United States, Representatives in Congress, the Executive and Judicial officers of a State, or the members of the Legislature thereof, **is denied***

> *to any of the male inhabitants of such State, being twenty-one years of age,* and citizens of the United States, or in any way abridged,* ***except for participation in rebellion, or other crime,*** *the basis of representation therein shall be reduced in the proportion which the number of such male citizens shall bear to the whole number of male citizens twenty-one years of age in such State."*

One of the techniques modern legal writers use in obfuscating a point, is to interject a lot of qualifying verbiage to muddy the issue. If we remove the "qualifying or expanding" phrases from above we get.

"But when the right to vote is denied, except for participation in rebellion, or other crime…"

Before the 14th Amendment, each state Citizen would vote; and the state would represent the people. After the 14th Amendment, the people were placed in rebellion to the state republics; and they now cast their vote to the new government, the federal. Since the "civil war", the new insurgent government has, by force, dominated the states into a democratic, federal society instead of the constitutionally guaranteed system of republics.

Therefore, one who has taken upon himself to rebel against the constitutional republics guaranteed for each state, by registering allegiance to the federal insurgent government and becoming a 14th Amendment citizen (with all rights and privileges, "granted" by the government) gives up all unalienable rights of true state Citizens.

If we look at the 9th and 10th Amendments, they grant all rights not enumerated to the federal government, to the states and the people. In order for the government to take over and install a democratic socialist society that would best serve the power elites; they had to usurp the states and individual rights. Thus enters the 14th Amendment, by an insurgent government, that wished to mandate its' will upon all the states of the union, regardless of the desires of the people. We have never returned to the rightful constitutional position we had before the civil war.

Prior to the civil war the United States was a federation of independent nation states. Each state stood independently, and each had the legal status as a nation. The Articles of Confederation and later the Constitution were put into place to provide a single voice when dealing with foreign governments and to handle disputes between states as well as protection from invasion. Much like Russia is a large single entity nation, and the former USSR was a confederation of individual countries with Russia as its protector and governing body, the "United States" was never designed as an independent nation. When the USSR fell the satellite countries gained independence from the mother Russia, and they were once again free to decide their own fate.

After the civil war, the insurgent federal government decided the states no longer had autonomous authority, and they could not cede from the Union. This was in contradiction to what was already agreed upon by the states. Part of that agreement was to allow the federal government certain powers from the states to facilitate the federal government's responsibilities. The true intent of the Fourteenth Amendment was to set up the "color of law" as justification for the new government to ensure (force) compliance between ALL the states. "Color of Law" is law that supplants or replaces the established, or root law, by a controlling government; to give the impression of legitimate authority. An example would be making a criminal out of an ordinary individual even though no harm has been committed (such as ticketing someone for not wearing a seat belt). The government has damaged the citizen, but the citizen has harmed no one. In the federal sense, it supplants law which overrides the once legitimate government, (the states), and makes them secondary to the federal, "by law", where no authority is vested.

The fourth Section of the amendment states:

> *"The validity of the public debt of the United States, authorized by law, including debts incurred for payment of pensions and bounties for services in suppressing insurrection or rebellion, shall not be questioned. But neither the United States nor any State shall assume or pay any debt or obligation incurred in aid of insurrection or rebellion against the United States, or any claim for the loss or emancipation of any slave; but all such debts, obligations and claims shall be held illegal and void."*

After removing all the qualifying statements, this says very simply "***The validity of the public debt of the United States… shall not be questioned.***" Does this sound like a government "of, for, and by the people"? Or, does it sound more like the communist manifesto or a statement of a conquering government? This is exactly the kind of language a government created under the "color of law" would enact in order to ensure compliance (by force). Then, of course, they would follow that up with the immunity clause, which would ensure there would be no legal response from the conquered masses.

At the beginning of this chapter I said that looking at the 14th Amendment was like looking at a picture inside a picture. Now I ask you, do you see the hidden picture? If the Constitution was the "**permanent**" law of the land, and the problem was to free the slaves and protect their rights, (which rights were already included in the Constitution), why go through the process of amending the Constitution for a small sub-set of society? An act of Congress could have done the same thing and would have carried the weight of law.

The answer is that they did not only want to free and protect the slaves, but they wanted to bring **all** people under the "control" of the federal government in order to preclude **another** "civil war" from ever happening again. They wanted to change the nature of the American citizen from that of a free man, to a nation of subjects, so the government could control society and engineer it to meet the needs of the collective.

Thomas Jefferson in 1821 said:

> "*It has long been my opinion, and I have never shrunk from its expression . . . that the germ of dissolution of our federal government is in the constitution of the federal judiciary; an irresponsible body—for impeachment is scarcely a scarecrow—working like gravity by night and by day, gaining a little today and a little tomorrow, and advancing its noiseless step like a thief, over the field of jurisdiction, until all shall be usurped from the States, and the government of all be consolidated into one.*
>
> "*To this I am opposed; because, when all government, domestic and foreign, in little as in great things, shall be drawn to Washington as the center of all power, it will render powerless the checks provided of one government or another,* ***and will become as venal and oppressive as the government from which we separated.*** " (Bold added.)

The U.S. Supreme Court in LAIRD v. TATUM, 408 U.S. 1 (1972), a case brought about by suspected violations of citizens rights by the military of our country. After the civil disorders in Detroit Michigan in the 60's, the military was called in to help the local police forces, which was challenged as being a blight on the rights of law abiding citizens. Justice Burger gave the opinion of the court saying:

> "*This case involves a cancer in our body politic. It is a measure of the disease which afflicts us. Army surveillance, like Army regimentation, is at war with the principles of the First Amendment. Those who already walk submissively will say there is no cause for alarm. But submissiveness is not our heritage.*

The First Amendment was designed to allow rebellion to remain as our heritage. The Constitution was designed to keep government off the backs of the people. The Bill of Rights was added to keep the precincts of belief and expression, of the press, of political and social activities free from surveillance. The Bill of Rights was designed to keep agents of government and official eavesdroppers away from assemblies of people. The aim was to allow men to be free and independent and to assert their rights against government. There can be no influence more paralyzing of that objective than Army surveillance. When an intelligence officer looks over every nonconformist's shoulder in the library, or walks invisibly by his side in a picket line, or infiltrates his club, the America once extolled as the voice of liberty heard around the world ***no longer is cast in the image which Jefferson and Madison designed, but more in the Russian image***... "(Bold added)

The present increase in the militarization of the nation's police force, especially since 9/11, has led to unprecedented sharing of intelligence and police powers involving the military. Police units now have specialized paramilitary units called SWAT, or some variation thereof, that use MOUT (military operations in Urban Terrain) training, which originated in the military and in many cases is taught **by** military instructors.

The authority for the broad governance of the people is based on the presumption that all Americans are 14th Amendment citizens and ALL citizens fall under the jurisdiction of the federal government. They would like you to believe that this is true; and most citizens do, but they are legally and morally wrong. We are so used to being led like sheep by our shepherd government, that most people do not know how to be true citizens. It makes most people uncomfortable and uncertain of the future not to have the "safety net" of big brother. Others are totally ignorant of what freedom truly is, and they are comfortable as long as they have a TV, a six pack, and a lazy boy.

The most dangerous aspects of the 14th Amendment are its' unintended consequences. From the day of their birth, the 14th Amendment placed all Federal citizens in shackles under the pretense of giving "privileges and immunities" to freed men. Unless we avail ourselves of our true heritage as free men, the government will treat all who are born on these shores as subjects. Until we know and demand our rights, we have only what we are given. Until we stand against evil, we will be ruled by evil. As English philosopher Edmund Burke once said, *'The only thing necessary for the triumph of evil is for good men to do nothing."* We have been doing nothing far too long.

Chapter 4
Executive Legislation

Executive legislation is the use of the presidential office to pass law. Much the same as a king would do when he announces a proclamation. I think most Americans would immediately notice that we do not have a monarchy, divine ruler, king, or magistrate in which we vest such singular power. That does not preclude, however, a president to think, or **act** as a king.

According to our constitution (see appendix) the Congress is the ONLY governmental body that has legislative power. It states in Article one, *"All legislative Powers herein granted shall be vested in a Congress..."* Notice the leading word, ALL. There seems to be little room for interpretation. It does not mean most legislation and it does not mean all legislation except what the President may have a whim to pass, it means **all**.

Black's Law Dictionary, Seventh Edition describes legislation as:

1. *The process of making or enacting a positive law in written form, according to some type of formal procedure, by a branch of government constituted to perform this process.*

If Congress is the **only** branch of government *"constituted to perform this process,"* then the executive branch is prohibited from doing so.

One of the earliest examples of a president using executive power to create law was on October 20, 1862. President Abraham Lincoln, in an attempt to replace the southern courts, ordered the establishing of a Provisional Court in Louisiana. This action was unconstitutional for two reasons. First, as mentioned above, ONLY Congress can pass legislation. Second, Article 1, Section 8 of the Constitution authorizes Congress as the only branch to *"constitute tribunals inferior to the Supreme Court."*

In January 1992, at the request of the Chairman of the Legislation and National Security Subcommittee, the National Security and International

Affairs Division of the General Accounting Office produced a report. The report was to, in part, *"determine whether national security directives (NSD), issued by the Bush administration through the National Security Council (NSC), have been used to make and implement US. Policy..."* In this report the committee stated: *"We also found that 116, or about half of the 247* (directives) *examined served three functions; they established policy, directed the implementation of policy, and/or authorized the commitment of government resources."*

It is lawful for the president to issue directives to his departments to communicate how he wants things run. It is another matter to issue directives that allow his departments to create statutes, or regulations that then have the "effect" of law. It is also unconstitutional for a presidential directive, or executive order that commits governmental resources/monies not appropriated by Congress.

In October 1999, the House of Representatives Committee on Rules, held hearings to determine ***"The Impact of Executive Orders on the Legislative Process: Executive Lawmaking"***. This is such an oxymoron! Executive Lawmaking! To be sure, the House had plenty to say concerning this issue. The following excerpts are from the hearing dated October 27, 1999.

Purpose of the hearings: *This hearing is designed to review an important and infrequently considered area of Executive/Congressional relations to raise awareness and promote vigilance and active oversight by the committees of Congress.* The phrase, "*an important and infrequently considered area*", struck me as being quite odd. If my position in government was to legislate, and another branch was doing so, however important I might think it to be, then why would it be only infrequently looked at? What happened to the checks and balances in government? What happened to the three branches of government with **separate and distinct powers**? This is the first Clue that something is amiss.

Another glaring admission: *"Executive orders by this (and any President) can have significant policy implications* ***and can encroach upon the lawmaking authority of the Congress.****"*(Bold added). Again, an encroachment of power should be thought of as grievous and should be dealt with immediately. Amazingly, the very next sentence reads, "*Congressional action to guard against this trend is constrained by the separation of powers...* " The separation of powers did not constrain the executive when it abused its' power, and Congress **does** have the power to investigate abuses of power.

The section continued: "*because the ability to issue an executive order confers enormous, unilateral power to the President...*" I don't remember reading anywhere in the Constitution where it states that the president has enormous and unilateral power. He is the head of the executive, and legally he can only give direction to those departments under his branch. He can make rules and regulations that guide **how** the executive will be constructed and operate; but he cannot pass legislation that affects the state or the people without congressional authorization (by way of legislation). If there is no law already in effect, legally he cannot create new law.

This next section, from the Rules Committee hearing, dealt with background.

> "*Article I of the Constitution states that "**All legislative powers** herein granted shall be **vested in a Congress** of the United States" while Article II states that "the executive power shall be vested in a President of the United States." The power of the Presidency was further defined to include the role of "Commander in Chief of the Army and Navy of the United States" **and empowerment to "take care that the laws be faithfully executed.**" The distinction between the authorities of the executive and legislative branches of our three-branch system of government has in practice, however, proven to be less clear-cut than the language the Framers suggested. The issuance of executive orders, proclamations and directives by the President is a practice not specifically enumerated in the Constitution, although it has been generally identified as flowing from the authorities vested in the President by Article II.*" (Bold Added)

Again, they have reiterated that all legislative powers are vested in congress, and the President has empowerment to "*take care that the laws are faithfully executed.*" There must be laws enacted BEFORE a president can ensure faithful execution of those laws. The Constitution does not give the president the authority to "enact" law. The last portion is of particular importance: "*The issuance of executive orders, proclamations and directives by the President is a practice **not specifically enumerated in the Constitution...***" How much clearer can this be? The Constitution is a limiting document, not an expansive document. If a power is not enumerated, it does not exist. The committee then went on to say that the issuing of executive orders came about by **establishment of precedent**. Congress is telling us that because previous presidents did this in the past, and they were not stopped, we have to let them keep doing it. The reason for checks and balances is to stop things like this from happening, or to correct them once they have been discovered. Because a prior criminal gets away with a crime, does that allow all those that follow to perpetrate that crime in the future? Of course not!

The next section of the report I have included in its entirety as it illustrates the depth to which we are mired:

> "On the other hand, in instances where the President issues an executive order that Congress does not oppose, but rather Congress wishes to exert its legislative authority in that area, Congress may seek by statute to sanction the action taken by the President. Similarly, the Congress may wish to sanction portions of an executive order, modify others and repeal others. Congress has the option, through the legislative process, of imposing its own stamp on a policy area staked out by executive order."
>
> "In his book, "Constitutional Conflicts Between Congress and the President" (Fourth Edition, Revised, University Press of Kansas, 1997), Louis Fisher outlines the tensions that exist between the legislative and executive branches when it comes to the practical application of the legislative power:
>
> *"The ambiguity of 'enumerated' and 'separated' powers is nowhere more evident than in the assignment of the legislative power.* ***Much of the original legislative power vested in Congress is now exercised, as a practical matter, by executive agencies****, independent commissions, and the courts.* ***The President's legislative power, invoked on rare occasions in the early decades, is now discharged on a regular basis throughout the year in the form of executive orders, proclamations, and other instruments of executive lawmaking.*** *In self-defense, Congress has developed a complex system that depends on procedural guidelines for agency action, judicial review, committee and subcommittee oversight, and a constantly evolving structure of informal, non-statutory controls."* (Page 118) (Emphasis added)

In essence Congress, has vacated its position as legislator, and has relegated is proper position within government to a servile role, beneath the executive. The executive, on the other hand, has usurped power from the legislature, and by that control, influences the judiciary, to the point of being a democratically elected "kingdom".

In the early years of the republic, there may have been the occasional instance that a president may have rightfully used executive directives. Today it is used as a matter of course to circumvent the checks and balances within the Constitution. The only saving grace Americans have is that there are Presidential term limits, and their replacements may not agree with their predecessors, or at least, they had their own pet projects to mark their time in office.

I wish to reiterate, there is **no** United States Constitutional provision that explicitly permits executive orders, aside from the vague grant of "executive power", given in Article II, Section 1, and the statement, "take Care that the Laws be faithfully executed", in Article II, Section 3. Remember what the 10th Amendment states: *"The* ***powers not delegated to the United States by the Constitution****, nor prohibited by it to the states,* ***are reserved to the states*** *respectively,* ***or to the people****."* If the Constitution does not specifically delegate a power to the government, it cannot be assumed. The power rests with the states or with the people, **period**.

The number of executive orders is staggering. Presidents have been writing "executive orders" since 1789, although in those early days they were called proclamations. Since 1929, we have had over 8,340, and still counting. Listed below are just a few executive orders, by number and title. As you read the brief description, ask yourself if this sounds like someone running an administration or someone is making law.

1863 Emancipation Proclamation—was, in effect, an executive order that only applied to the southern states, which were under military rule of law, occupied territory. (1863 is the year enacted, Executive Order (EO) numbers were not yet used)

6102 Franklin D. Roosevelt confiscated all privately held Gold in the United States on April 5, 1933. *There seems to be a problem, when the Constitution mandates only gold and silver may be used as money by our government and then by EO decree, the president says, no citizen may amass any gold.*

9066 FDR ordered creation of military exclusion zones, where no persons of Japanese decent may live, and they transported said exclusionary personnel to concentration camps for the duration of hostilities. *No due process of law, no criminal or treasonous acts were committed and there was no suspicious behavior, there were no trials, and no recourse. People lost entire life savings, homes, property, and possessions; none were returned or made whole again.*

9102 FDR ordered creation of a civilian agency to oversee the construction of the ten concentration camps for the relocation of persons of Japanese decent. *Remember EO's are done without Congressional approval; having budgetary impacts that were not approved by Congress as mandated by the Constitution.*

11110 On June 4, 1963, John F. Kennedy issued a silver currency order that directed the US Treasury to issue silver certificates against any silver bullion, silver, or standard silver dollars in the Treasury; bypassing the Federal Reserve Bank of New York. Five months after his assassination no more silver certificates were issued, and they are no longer valid. *This EO remains on the Federal Register and is still in effect.*

11921 Pres. Ford directed the Federal Emergency Preparedness Agency to develop plans to establish control over the mechanisms of production and distribution of energy sources, wages, salaries, credit and the flow of money in U.S. financial institutions in any **undefined** national emergency. *It also provides that when a state of emergency is declared by the President, Congress cannot review the action for six months.*

12170 Pres Carter, during Iran Hostage Crisis in Nov. 1979 allowed for freezing of Iranian Assets.

12333 Ronald Reagan, December 1981, extends the powers and responsibilities of U.S. intelligence agencies and directs federal agencies to cooperate fully with CIA requests for information. *This led to the unauthorized and illegal receipt of citizens IRS records to the foreign intelligence branch of the government.*

12810 G. Bush, June 1992, ordered the blocking of Property and Prohibiting Transactions with the Federal Republic of Yugoslavia (Serbia and Montenegro)

12986 President Clinton, Jan. 1996, mandated that the International Union for Conservation of Nature and Natural Resources would fall under the privileges and immunities act that provide a private organization immunity from suit.

13132 President Clinton, Aug. 1999, Federalism—after revoking Pres. Reagan's Federalism EO, Clinton instituted a similar EO with a more globalist feel. It speaks of laboratories of Democracy within the states, vice republics, and writing a new social contract, and other such socialist doctrine. *This is in direct opposition to the Constitution which guarantees each state a republican form of government.*

13158 President Clinton, May 2000, directed Marine Protected Areas, which appears to circumvent the existing procedures established under the Magnuson-Stevens Fishery Conservation and Management act and the National Marine Sanctuaries Acts. *The president in this EO is committing government resources without Congressional approval.*

13166 President, Clinton 2001, Improving Access to Services for Persons with Limited English Proficiency, establishes standards and requirements for mandating multi-language requirements. *Again, this creates law where none was legislated by Congress and commits governmental resources.*

13210 GW Bush, May 2001, President's Commission to Strengthen Social Security (commission) was terminated 30 days after their report was submitted. No enactments have been made to strengthen SS from this report. *Obviously this was more of a PR stunt with no intent to reform social security. To date, there have been no reform attempts by the Bush administration, just talk.*

13233 GW Bush, Nov. 2001, Further Implementation of the Presidential Records Act limits disclosure of Presidential correspondence and other information from the Freedom of Information Act for 12 years after the President leaves office (after all statues of limitation have expired). *Again, this is making law by proclamation of the "King" in direct opposition to the Freedom of Information Act passed by Congress.*

13338 GW Bush, May 2004, determines that the actions of the Government of Syria in supporting terrorism, continuing its occupation of Lebanon, pursuing weapons of mass destruction and missile programs, and undermining the United States and international efforts, with respect to the stabilization and reconstruction of Iraq, constitute an unusual and extraordinary threat to the national security, foreign policy, and economy of the United States. We hereby declare a national emergency to deal with that threat. *To date there has been no retaliation by Syria, no direct conflict from the country or any of its citizens, and no troop attacks. In fact, more deaths and destruction has been instigated by Pakistan than Syria; and no such declaration has been made concerning them. This is simply an attempt to utilize the War Powers Act and has little to do with an actual emergency.*

13397 GW Bush, March 2006, Responsibilities of the Department of Homeland Security with Respect to Faith-Based and Community Initiatives. Identify all existing barriers to the participation of faith-based and other community organizations, in the delivery of social and community services by the Department. These include, but are not limited to: regulations, rules, orders, procurement, other internal policies and practices, as well as outreach activities that unlawfully discriminate against, or otherwise discourage or disadvantage the participation of faith-based and other community organizations in Federal programs.

13398 GW Bush, April 2006, assists the International Independent Investigation Commission established pursuant to UNSCR April, 2005. Assist the Government of Lebanon in identifying and holding accountable, in accordance with applicable law, those persons who were involved in planning, sponsoring, organizing, or perpetrating the terrorist act in Beirut, Lebanon, on February 14, 2005. Take note of the Commission's conclusions in its report of October 19, 2005. It states that there is converging evidence pointing to both Lebanese and Syrian involvement in terrorist acts, that interviewees tried to mislead the Commission's investigation by giving false or inaccurate statements, and that a senior official of Syria submitted false information to the Commission. *In light of these determinations, and to take additional steps, with respect to the national emergency declared in Executive Order 13338 of May 11, 2004, to extend this "emergency" and allow certain actions to be taken against the Government of Syria.*

It is not a problem for a President to issue executive orders to his departments or to express his mandates or control over the executive branch. The problem comes in when executive orders are used to create agencies and departments, spend taxpayer dollars not appropriated by Congress, which then are given missions that require enactment of law in order to operate within the country (and especially the states). This has been happening with increased frequency and depth. Congress has the responsibility to provide the budget to operate the government, and falls into complicity with the executive every time it approves a budget which includes programs, departments, and other creations of the executive branch.

This trend of legislative lawlessness will someday exact a bitter price that our children will have to bare. When Truman integrated the Armed Forces by executive order, there was outcry. When Eisenhower desegregated public schools, there was outcry. These things were done to support a noble ideal, but they were wrongly enacted. It is the Congress' job to enact legislation, not the Presidents. It is the spineless, capitulating, self-serving, "professional" politicians who make this possible.

Today we live in a time when wars can be waged solely on executive order or decree, such as Kosovo, Bosnia, Korea, Viet Nam, or Iraq. Yes, we had people waging anti-war protests; but where was the judicial outcry demanding that Congress do its' job and declare war before sending soldiers into harms way? To be fair, the president did go to Congress to get a Congressional resolution for financial support. However, what choice did Congress have, and to what extent can the president exercise military power independent of Congress? These questions remain unresolved within constitutional authority.

The following are excerpts from a U.S. Department of Justice white paper dated January 19, 2006, on the President's decision to utilize NSA for internal (within the U.S.) wiretaps without a warrant.

> *"On September 14, 2001, in its first legislative response to the attacks of September 11th, Congress gave its express approval to the President's military campaign against al Qaeda and, in the process, confirmed the well-accepted understanding of the President's Article II powers. See Authorization for Use of Military Force (AUMF) § 2(a). In the preamble to the AUMF, Congress stated that "the President has authority under the Constitution to take action to deter and prevent acts of international terrorism against the United States," AUMF pmbl., and thereby acknowledged the President's inherent constitutional authority to defend the United States. This clause "constitutes an extraordinarily sweeping recognition of*

> *independent presidential constitutional power to employ the war power to combat terrorism."*

Notice that the logic jumps from our being a defender of the nation to "sweeping recognition of independent presidential constitutional power." Since when does any branch of government have independent power? All three branches require approval or oversight from one of the other branches.

> *"...In the context of the conflict with al Qaeda and related terrorist organizations, therefore, Congress has acknowledged a broad executive authority to "deter and prevent" further attacks against the United States."*

Next we have the "pending doom" scenario. Because we were attacked by Al Qaeda, the government, (in particular the president) has the authority to do away with constitutional restrictions and infringements on the rights of the citizens in the pretext of "deter and prevent". Why don't we then authorize door to door searches of every house, take away firearms, remove all objectionable literature, pass hate speech laws, ban meetings not authorized by the government, and station military personnel in every town to deter and prevent any further violence against our country? This was tried a couple of times in Russia and Germany, and we see how well that worked.

> *"The* (Authorization for the Use of Military Force) *AUMF passed by Congress on September 14, 2001, does not lend itself to a narrow reading. Its expansive language authorizes the President "to use* ***all necessary and appropriate force*** *against those nations, organizations, or persons* ***he determines*** *planned, authorized, committed, or aided the terrorist attacks that occurred on September 11, 2001." AUMF § 2(a) (emphases added). In the field of foreign affairs, and particularly that of war powers and national security, congressional enactments are to be broadly construed where they indicate support for authority long asserted and exercised by the Executive Branch.... Although Congress's war powers under Article I, Section 8 of the Constitution empower Congress to legislate regarding the raising, regulation, and material support of the Armed Forces and related matters, rather than the prosecution of military campaigns, the AUMF indicates Congress's endorsement of the President's use of his constitutional war powers. This authorization transforms the struggle against al Qaeda and related terrorist organizations from what Justice*

> *Jackson called "a zone of twilight," in which the President and the Congress may have concurrent powers whose "distribution is uncertain," Youngstown Sheet & Tube Co. v. Sawyer, 343 U.S. 579, 637 (1952) (Jackson, J., concurring), into a situation in which the President's authority is at is maximum because "it includes all that he possesses in his own right plus all that Congress can delegate," id. at 635. With regard to these fundamental tools of warfare—and, as demonstrated below, warrant-less electronic surveillance against the declared enemy is one such tool—the AUMF places the President's authority at its zenith under Youngstown."*

The primary impetus for the foregoing is that Congress can delegate its' authority to the president, adding to the powers he already had. What poppy cock! When the Constitution does not authorize a branch of government to do a thing, that action, or power cannot be assumed. If the Constitution states that Congress has the power or authority to do a thing, it is Congress who has it. By giving up that authority, they relinquish **all** authority, and they stand in treason to the nation. At a minimum the power would then revert back to the states or to the people. The powers of a branch of government is likened unto the soul of a man, the only way to give up your soul is to die. Congress cannot give away any power lawfully, by any act or compromise, and by doing so, it betrays the American people and the history of this great nation. Congress, without their enumerated powers is like a dead man, without soul and useless to society.

> *"It is also clear that the AUMF confirms and supports the President's use of those traditional incidents of military force against the enemy, wherever they may be—on United States soil or abroad. The nature of the September 11th attacks—launched on United States soil by foreign agents secreted in the United States—necessitates such authority, and the text of the AUMF confirms it. The operative terms of the AUMF state that the President is authorized to use force "in order to prevent any future acts of international terrorism against the United States," id., an objective which, given the recent attacks within the Nation's borders and the continuing use of air defense throughout the country at the time Congress acted, undoubtedly contemplated the possibility of military action within the United States. The preamble, moreover, recites that the United States*

> *should exercise its rights "to protect United States citizens both **at home** and abroad." Id. pmbl. (Emphasis added). To take action against those linked to the September 11th attacks involves taking action against individuals within the United States. The United States had been attacked on its own soil—not by aircraft launched from carriers several hundred miles away, but by enemy agents who had resided in the United States for months. A crucial responsibility of the President—charged by the AUMF and the Constitution—was and is to identify and attack those enemies, especially if they were in the United States, ready to strike against the Nation."*

Of the 75 people arrested in the aftermath of 9/11, only 1 has been charged, and all but six have been released. Because we activated our own missile defense system, and the defenses within the country, this gives the President authorization to do "whatever it takes" to secure our safety; the Constitution and unalienable rights of the citizen be damned! I don't believe the founding fathers would agree, and I doubt the majority of Americans would agree either.

The text of the AUMF demonstrates in an additional way that Congress authorized the President to conduct warrant-less electronic surveillance against the enemy. The terms of the AUMF not only authorized the President to "use all necessary and appropriate force" against those responsible for the September 11th attacks, it also authorized the President to "determine" the persons or groups responsible for those attacks, and allow him to take all actions necessary to prevent further attacks. AUMF § 2(a):

> *("The President is authorized to use all necessary and appropriate force against those nations, organizations, or persons he determines planned, authorized, committed, or aided the terrorist attacks that occurred on September 11th, 2001, or harbored such organizations or persons").*

Of vital importance to identifying the enemy and detecting possible future plots was the authority to intercept communications, to or from the United States, of persons with links to al Qaeda or related terrorist organizations. Given that the agents who carried out the initial attacks resided in the United States and had successfully blended into American society and disguised their identities and intentions until they were ready to strike, the necessity of using the most effective intelligence gathering tools against such an enemy, including electronic surveillance, was patent. Indeed, Congress recognized that the enemy in this conflict poses an "*unusual and extraordinary threat.*" (AUMF Pmbl.)

Now comes the cote de grate. Because the enemy lived among us, dressed like us, went to school with us, shopped at the mall, and used phones and email, the President decided that everyone and everything is now open to "*his determination*" as to what needs to be done and which rights are no longer valid. This comrade is how the communists do it. This is what the Russians told their people, and this is the logic Hitler used to convince his countryman to follow his grand plan. After all, according to President Bush, the Constitution is just a "*Goddamn piece of paper*", so he really does not care about the Bill of Rights or boundaries of power.

Over the past few years, presidents have become bolder in their steps to push the United States towards a new world order. I know this statement sounds like a conspiracy theory that you may read on the cover of one of the tabloids, but I would like you to consider this. Although the president is responsible for foreign affairs, any agreement or treaty that obligates the United States to perform actual or monetary support requires the approval of Congress. Any action by the president than obligates governmental resources, crates statutes or law is unconstitutional.

Since 2001 president Bush has signed the North American Free Trade Agreement (NAFTA), the Security and Prosperity Partnership Agreement (SPP), and in April of 2007 has signed the Transatlantic Economic Integration between the United States of America and the European Union. The latter agreement establishes a partnership that integrates the economies between the United States and the European Union, all without a single vote from Congress. The NAFTA and SPP agreements have committed funds, resources, man-hours, and created or expanded departments, of the executive branch, to support these efforts. All done without Congressional approval.

With NAFTA, and SPP programs already installed, the EU merger, in effect, will economically merge the northern American hemisphere with the European Continent. With the EU moving toward a "national" police and military force, for combined security, we have seen the nationalities of the European countries slowly start to deteriorate into the smelting pot of the United European States. None of which was shared with the people of the countries prior to entering into the agreement; it was supposed to be just a "*free trade agreement*". Now they have a parliament, a court system, and plans for police and military. Do you think this will change just because the U.S. has entered the mix? I think not!

European Commission President, José Manuel Barroso, at the signing of the Transatlantic Economic Integration Plan stated:

> *"It is a recognition that the closer that the United States and the EU become, the better off our people will be."*

He went on further to elaborate on the creation of the **Transatlantic Economic Council,** and that it is meant to be "*a permanent body, with senior people on both sides of the Atlantic.*"

As the EU started by simple free trade agreements, and has now morphed into a massive governing body, so too will this agreement, if we are not careful. At the rate this government is willing to, so easily, link the prosperity of this nation with the rest of the world, how easy it will be to turn over governance of its population, referred to in this agreement as nothing more than a "work force". The writing is on the wall, but too many of us, I fear, are illiterate.

I invite all to read the Presidents press release online at *http://www.whitehouse.gov/news/ releases/2007/04/20070430-4.html.* The press release shows that President Bush plans to have this done, and in place, before he leaves office in 2009; why such a rush? And why did he not push for congressional approval? And just as important; why is Congress allowing him to get away with this?

Robert A. Pastor, Vice President of International Affairs, and Professor of International Relations at American University, and member of the Council of Foreign Relations, provided testimony to the Subcommittee on the Western Hemisphere, U.S. Senate Foreign Relations Committee in June 2005 in which he stated:

> *"The U.S., Mexican, and Canadian governments remain zealous* ***defenders of an outdated conception of sovereignty*** *even though their citizens are ready for a new approach. Each nation's leadership has stressed differences rather than common interests. North America needs leaders who can articulate and pursue a broader vision."*
>
> *"I hope this Committee will pursue the North American agenda beyond the travel initiative considered here. On June 23rd, the three leaders promised to publish a report with specific recommendations on how to deepen* ***North American integration****. These should be reviewed together with Senator Richard Lugar's far-sighted bill for a "North American Cooperative Security Act" and Senator Cornyn's "North*

> *American Investment Fund." **The time has come for us to define a true North American Community. Our security and prosperity depend on it.**"* (Bold added)

With the amount of emphasis this government has placed on pushing NAFTA, SPP, and now the EU economic agenda, it leaves no doubt that the Council of Foreign Relations, of which G.H. Bush is also a member, has made great inroads towards removing individual nation sovereignty and ultimately the New World Order.

The frightening part of Presidents running awry of Constitution and of Law is not the increased frequency that it is being done, or the cost to our nations' skyrocketing debt; but it has become so routine that it barely gets mentioned.

Chapter 5
Judicial Legislation

We do not hear much about the judicial branch of government, especially in contrast to the executive and legislative, but they are the most powerful group of men in the entire nation. Appointed for life; they have the power to change the course of government and affect the people directly. They have not always had the extent of power they currently wield. This secretive group of nine justices make decisions and effect law from behind closed doors, without oversight or review. They have established "precedent" power that requires future justices to honor previous rulings regardless of whether they are right or wrong, and only change or reverse rulings in extreme circumstances. This is the only branch of government that does not have any constitutional means to correct their errors even when their motives are outright political. In this chapter we shall take a look at a brief history of the Supreme Court, their purpose, some of their decisions, and the scope of their current power, and determine just how constitutional our judicial branch has acted.

The judicial branch derives it's power from Article III, Section 1 of the Constitution, which states:

> *"The judicial Power of the United States shall be vested in one supreme Court, and in such inferior Courts as the Congress may from time to time ordain and establish. The Judges, both of the supreme and inferior Courts, shall hold their Offices during good Behaviour, and shall, at stated Times, receive for their Services a Compensation, which shall not be diminished during their Continuance in Office."*

In section 1 we see the initial creation of the court and find that no time limit is set for how long a justice may hold office. In fact, justices are appointed for life, or as stated above as long as they are in "good behaviour". This was done to ensure that rulings were not made due to political pressures or coercion. The justices also receive salary protection, again to ensure that their rulings were not coerced by threats of withholding or reducing pay.

Section 2, of Article 3, discusses the jurisdiction of the court, and states:

> *"The judicial Power shall extend to all Cases, in Law and Equity, arising under this Constitution, the Laws of the United States, and Treaties made, or which shall be made, under their Authority;—to all Cases affecting Ambassadors, other public Ministers and Consuls;—to all Cases of admiralty and maritime Jurisdiction;—to Controversies to which the United States shall be a Party;—to Controversies between two or more States;—between a State and Citizens of another State;—between Citizens of different States;—between Citizens of the same State claiming Lands under Grants of different States, and between a State, or the Citizens thereof, and foreign States, Citizens or Subjects."*
>
> *"In all Cases affecting Ambassadors, other public Ministers and Consuls, and those in which a State shall be Party, the supreme Court shall have original Jurisdiction. In all the other Cases before mentioned, the supreme Court shall have appellate Jurisdiction, both as to Law and Fact, with such Exceptions, and under such Regulations as the Congress shall make."*

The jurisdiction of the Supreme Court is divided into two parts, that of subject matter and that of parties to the litigation. The subject matter jurisdiction is identified in the opening statements of Section 2.

Section 2 starts with: *"The judicial Power shall extend to all* ***Cases****, in Law and Equity,* ***arising under this Constitution****, the Laws of the United States, and Treaties made, or which shall be made, under their Authority...*" This statement establishes the subject matter jurisdiction under which the Supreme Court may rule, which is only to the extent of the authority of the Constitution and the departments of government.

Before we go any further let's look at the term "case." Blacks Law Dictionary, Seventh Edition, defines case as *"A proceeding, action, suit, or controversy at law or in equity."* Sound familiar?

The remainder of this section deals with the parties of the litigation under which the Supreme Court has jurisdiction. They are:

- *"to all Cases affecting Ambassadors, other public Ministers and Consuls;"*

- *"to all Cases of admiralty and maritime Jurisdiction;"*
- *"to Controversies to which the United States shall be a Party;"*
- *"to Controversies between two or more States;"*
- *"between a State and Citizens of another State;"*
- *"between Citizens of different States;"*
- *"between Citizens of the same State claiming Lands under Grants of different States,"*
- *"and between a State, or the Citizens thereof, and foreign States, Citizens or Subjects."*

There are two classes of litigants missing in the preceding list that of a state and the federal or that of a Citizen of a state and the federal. And as the current federal government, as well as state governments, have stated they cannot be sued without their consent. This was written this way for a good reason. At the time of the creation of the Constitution, each state was an independent government with it's own Constitution and it's own laws. The Constitution did not replace the state governments or the laws of those states. Each state had the ability to govern it's Citizens as it saw fit. One state could not force a neighboring state to change it's laws. Realizing the problems of dealing with multiple governments with free and open exchange of citizens, the founders foresaw the need for the central government to play "referee" between the legal entities. The federal government did not have direct jurisdiction, however, over ANY Citizens of the several states, that has always been the jurisdiction of the states, with the exception of the above listed litigants.

The Constitution goes on to define the type of jurisdiction by stating:

> *"In all Cases affecting Ambassadors, other public Ministers and Consuls, and those in which a State shall be Party, the supreme Court shall have original Jurisdiction. In all the other Cases before mentioned, the supreme Court shall have appellate Jurisdiction, both as to Law and Fact, with such Exceptions, and under such Regulations as the Congress shall make."*

Notice that the only time the Supreme Court has "Original Jurisdiction" is for specific governmental offices and when a state is a party as we have already listed. That is it, all other cases the Supreme Court has only appellate jurisdiction. When we break down exactly where the Judiciary has jurisdiction we see that it was created with very limited scope and reach.

Alexander Hamilton characterized the judiciary as the weakest branch of government when he said, "*The Courts must declare the sense of the law; and if they should be disposed to exercise will instead of judgment, the consequences would equally be the substitution of their pleasure to that of the legislative body*." Meaning, that if the Supreme Court Justices were to act with their own interests, politics, or beliefs, as opposed to judging based upon strict constitutional understanding and merit, then they would be acting as legislatures (creating law) instead of interpreting law. I am certain, if you polled the average American, they would agree with Hamilton.

The Supreme Court has risen to a point of unrivaled power and partisanship, which is supported I might add, by Congress. Openly, in hearings to determine a justice candidacy, we hear questions as to whether this new justice will toe the line on what previous courts have ruled. If the court made a constitutional judgment then, isn't that all that can be asked? Should a justice follow precedence solely for precedence sake? Should he try not to make law but only adjudicate constitutionality?

Thomas Jefferson declared his wariness of the judiciary in 1823 in a letter to A. Coray stating:

> *"At the establishment of our Constitutions, the judiciary bodies were supposed to be the most helpless and harmless members of the government. Experience, however, soon showed in what way they were to become the most dangerous; that the insufficiency of the means provided for their removal gave them a freehold and irresponsibility in office; that their decisions, seeming to concern individual suitors only, pass silent and unheeded by the public at large; that these decisions nevertheless become law by precedent, sapping by little and little the foundations of the Constitution and working its change by construction before any one has perceived that that invisible and helpless worm has been busily employed in consuming its substance. In truth, man is not made to be trusted for life if secured against all liability to account."*

So, what happens when a question of law is presented and judges "rule" based on their political positions or pandering to a sect of government or society? This is called "judicial activism." There are some that would say that this does not happen, as there are nine different persons from different political views and affiliations, and they are honest and above reproach. This has not always been the case; and far too many times there have been 5 to 4 votes on extremely important decisions, where the motive for the decision is, at least, suspect. When one views the text of the Constitution there is very little to determine exactly how the Judicial Branch was to operate. Congress created two acts that established what the Supreme Court was to do, and what their composition was to be. They are known as the Judiciary Acts of 1789, and 1801.

During the Revolutionary War, the State of Georgia had purchased supplies from South Carolina native Alexander Chisholm. After the war, and after Chisholm's death, the administrators of Chisholm's estate went after Georgia to pay up what was owed. When officials refused to pay, Chisholm's heirs sued Georgia in federal court, but Georgia officials chose not to participate in the court proceeding, arguing that as a "sovereign" state, the federal courts were not permitted to rule on the case. The U.S. Supreme Court disagreed and ruled in favor of the Chisholm estate. The case created such uproar amongst the states that within a year, Congress proposes the 11th amendment, which provides that states cannot be sued in the federal courts unless they give permission to be sued. On March 4, 1794, Congress sent the proposed amendment to the states for ratification.

In 1795 the 11th amendment to the Constitution was ratified which altered Section 2. During the preceding years there arose a series of debts owed to British subjects by United States Citizens and even individual states in the case of Chisholm V Georgia. Due to defaults on these debts large confiscations of land began to occur with resulting court cases. Some argued as long as the states handled the case the federal had no jurisdiction to hear the cases. As we have just read above, when foreign states, Citizens or Subjects are involved, the Supreme Court has jurisdiction. Georgia, however, argued as a "sovereign" state the federal courts could not rule on the case. The Supreme Court ruled anyway and sided with Chisholm. This created an avalanche of protest from states and citizens alike. In order to "remedy" the situation the 11th Amendment was passed, which states: *"The judicial power of the United States shall not* ***be construed to*** *extend to any suit in law or equity, commenced or prosecuted against one of the United States by citizens of another state, or by citizens or subjects of any foreign state."* Although it does not say so directly, it has been interpreted that states cannot be sued in the federal courts unless they give permission to be sued. This has lead to the now broad reaching claim by all government agencies that a citizen cannot sue due to their "sovereign immunity."

Marbury v. Madison, 5 U.S. 137 (1803): In the last days of President John Adams' term in office, William Marbury was appointed as Justice of the peace for the District of Columbia. However, as Adams left and Thomas

Jefferson assumed office, Marbury realized his commission paperwork had not been delivered (as required) by the Secretary of State, John Marshall, who was by now no longer in office. Jefferson, through James Madison the new Secretary of State, refused to deliver the commission, therefore Marbury, and three others, petitioned the Court for a writ of mandamus to force the new administration to deliver the commission to Marbury. The court ultimately ruled that the Act which authorized the writ, overstepped the bounds as outlined in Article III of the Constitution; and therefore, the act was unconstitutional, and they did not have the authority to rule on this case. It was the opinion of the court, (though opinions carry no weight of law), that Madison should have provided the requested commission. Marbury was never seated as a Justice.

Although, at first blush, one would say this was the correct (or shall I say legal/constitutional) position. The unintended consequence was the establishment of the concept of judicial review. Judicial review is the power to invalidate legislation based on Constitutional grounds. After hearing of Justice Marshall's opinion in the case of Marbury V. Madison, Thomas Jefferson, in a letter to Abigail Adams, (September 11, 1804), warned that judicial review would be *"making the judiciary a despotic branch."* Further, nowhere is the power of judicial review mentioned in the Constitution and the courts can only offer inferences to substantiate so doing. I personally agree with having the capability to review congressional acts in the light of the Constitution. The problem arrives with the degree to which all branches of government have grown, by usurpation, to a point which would no longer be recognizable to the founders of our nation. Far too often we are reminded of our founders' vision and understanding of the nature of man. If there is any power deemed necessary by a branch of government that is not specifically enumerated the government must first amend the Constitution **before** utilizing that power. Only after such power is granted should any branch of government be able to act. Remember, if a power is not granted to a branch of government then it is reserved to the states or to the people, and it is the states and/or the people who must relinquish that power before it can rightly be assumed by the government.

The next case is arguably the pivotal case in America's history: ***Dred Scott v. Sandford***, [1] 60 U.S. (19 How.) 393 (1856). The Dred Scott case was years in the making. Scott, a slave, was moved about the country with his owners until 1843 when they moved to St. Louis, a non-slave state. It was here that Scott made an offer to buy his freedom, and was refused; so he decided to sue for freedom. His first two attempts were not fruitful; and finally in 1850, Dred Scott and his family were freed.

This verdict was appealed to the Missouri Supreme Court, which reversed the lower courts' decision; and pronounced that the Scott's were once again slaves. Scott then brought suit in federal court on various charges, but primarily to asses his position as a free man. The court heard arguments regarding jurisdiction and whether the previous decision was erroneous.

Finally, in March 1856, the Supreme Court gave its decision. The first part of their decision on jurisdiction was based on the Constitution and which involved the Citizens. It ruled: *"Consequently, no State, since the adoption of the Constitution, can by naturalizing an alien invest him with the rights and privileges secured to a citizen of a State under the Federal Government, although, so far as the State alone was concerned, he would undoubtedly be entitled to the rights of a citizen, and clothed with all the rights and immunities which the Constitution and laws of the State attached to that character."*

This ruling allowed the state to accept anyone under the state constitution and endow them with state citizenship and all to which it pertains. However, the definition of Citizen could never be anything more than what the founders meant it to be. The court ruled that Scott was not a Citizen, and therefore did not have jurisdiction to rule on the case.

This was also the pivotal case in our discussion of the 14th Amendment. The Federal Government could not declare Scott was a Citizen, because a "Citizen" was already defined. So, the 14th Amendment created another class of citizen, the 14th Amendment citizen, which is a legal term.

As Dred Scott upheld the meaning of the Constitution the next case flies in the face of it, ***Plessy v. Ferguson***, 163 U.S. 537 (1896). Mr. Plessy, a Louisiana man with $1/8^{th}$ black heritage, boarded a train car that was identified as whites only. Under Louisiana law you were considered black if you had $1/8^{th}$ percent mixed blood, and by law, such people had separate accommodations. Once identified as black, Mr. Plessy was asked to leave the "whites only" car, Mr. Plessy refused to leave. The police were called, and he was arrested and charged with violating the segregation law. At trial, Plessy argued violations of his 13th and 14th Amendment rights. The judge stated the state of Louisiana had the right to regulate rail lines within their state, and he found Mr.Plessy guilty and fined him $25.00.

Mr. Plessy, determined to fight against the charges, filed an appeal to the Supreme Court of Louisiana. The Louisiana court upheld the lower court verdict. He then appealed to the U.S. Supreme Court.

The Supreme Court, in a 7-1 decision, found in favor of the lower court decision. Justice Brown argued that the segregation laws did not violate the 13th amendment, and as there was no difference between the colored car and the white car, he could not see how the 14th Amendment was violated. He went on to admit, *"We consider the underlying fallacy of the plaintiff's argument to consist in the assumption that the enforced separation of the two races stamps the colored race with a badge of inferiority. If this be so, it is not by reason of anything found in the act, but solely because the colored race chooses to put that construction upon it."*, It would appear obvious that the cultural climate of the time played heavily into the courts decision; and by so doing, he allowed individual prejudices to overrule the constitutional protections. This was a clear case of judicial legislation.

Unfortunately our history is replete with examples of the Judiciary attempting to influence outside of its bounds. If we look at the rest of government, are we really surprised that they too attempt, and often do, try to expand their powers? Let's look at a few more cases. For brevity sake, I will not go into much court detail on these cases, but I encourage everyone to research these cases for a better understanding of the direction in which our judiciary is going.

Hans v. Louisiana—This is clearly a case of judicial activism. Hans was suing the state of Louisiana to secure the value of bonds he owned; and was worried about recent changes in state law that made the bonds worthless. The Supreme Court ruled that because of the 11th Amendment, he could not sue the state. This is in direct opposition to *Chisholm v. Georgia*, 2 U.S. 419 (1793), which ruled a Citizen could sue a state based on Article 3, Section 2 of the Constitution. The court ruled that Article 3 abrogated (abolished) the States' sovereign immunity, and granted the federal courts the affirmative power to hear disputes between private citizens and States. The 11th Amendment (see appendix) states that the Judicial power could not be used against one of the states by Citizens of **another** state. It does not mention Citizens of the same state, as it does in Article 3, Section 2, therefore, the Judiciary has created law outside of it's Constitutional ability to do so.

Lochner v. New York, 198 U.S. 45 (1905), is a landmark case which held that the 14th Amendment granted, by implication, the "right to free contract." This decision overturned a New York law which limited the hours that could be worked in a bakery due to health risks to the employees. The ruling stated that the existing law was *"unreasonable, unnecessary and arbitrary interference with the right and liberty of the individual to contract."* The ruling Sided with the business owners and the Citizens right to evaluate and decide contractual agreements between themselves and their employer. This case started a series of Lochner decision cases all of which relied on this decision (right to contract) for years to come. Today, however, the federal government interferes in many aspects of "right to contract" areas. They have again assessed limitations on maximum hours of work (for some professions), minimum wage levels, working conditions and standards, etc. overruling the state statutes.

Brown v. Board of Education, 347 U.S. 483 (1954), was a case of judicial review which sought and obtained desegregation of public schools. Its' earlier decision allowed for "separate but equal" status to be maintained within the states. By this decision, states throughout the country were forced to desegregate their schools; and in some cases, bus students from other areas miles away in order to provide a "desegregated school." Regardless of the "desired effect" sought by the Supreme Court; it is not within their power to create law. The power to create law only resides in the legislative branch of government, and then, only in limited, enumerated areas.

Chief Justice Earl Warren wrote for the unanimous Court: "*Today, education is perhaps the* ***most important function of state and local governments****. Compulsory school attendance laws and the great expenditures for education both demonstrate our recognition of the importance of education to our* ***democratic society****. It is required in the performance of our most basic public responsibilities, even service in the armed forces. It is the very foundation of good citizenship. Today it is a principal instrument in awakening the child to cultural values, in preparing him for later professional training, and in helping him to adjust normally to his environment. In these days, it is doubtful that any child may reasonably be expected to succeed in life if he is denied the opportunity of an education. Such an opportunity, where the state has undertaken to provide it, is a right which must be made available to all on equal terms"*

Benjamin Franklin was prophetic when he uttered the words, "A Republic, if you can keep it." Obviously our Justices believe we are now a democracy.

I agree that education is paramount to the success of any individual and thereby to the community and state in which he lives. There is no doubt about its importance to the state and local governments, and it should be there that it best defines the methodology. I want to point out that I do not agree with the "separate but equal" doctrine. I believe in giving all people the opportunity and access to education, but much more could be done without the federal bureaucracy we currently have. I do not disagree with the desegregation issue; I disagree, however, with the Supreme Court creating legislation to usurp power away from Congress or the states.

It is also well documented that the decision on Brown was greatly influenced by UNESCO's (United Nations Educational, Scientific, and Cultural Organization) 1950 statement, entitled *The Race Question*. This declaration denounced previous attempts to scientifically justify racism. This was a slow evolution away from the community and state to a central, all powerful, national government. This government had its' sights set on global governance and relying on the external dogma for guidance. Once again this shows the Supreme Courts true nature.

Mapp v. Ohio, 367 U.S. 643 (1961), Dollree Mapp's home was searched for a fugitive, without a warrant. A chest which contained pornographic material was discovered in violation of state law. She was subsequently arrested and charged. The lower and appellate courts found Ms. Mapp guilty of an obscenity charge; and her attorney appealed to the Supreme Court. Mapp's attorney argued a First Amendment free speech defense, which the court took into advisement. However, when the Supreme Court made its decision they chose to decide the case based on the legality of evidence and not the First Amendment question. Because the topic of pornographic material being covered by the First Amendment was such a hot topic, the courts chose to invalidate the evidence, calling it tainted evidence; and they did not give it due process as required by the Constitution. Within their decision, they also required that all states follow the tainted evidence ruling when dealing with court cases and Fourth Amendment issues. The Supreme Court has clearly overstepped the states' jurisdiction.

Roe v. Wade, 410 U.S. 113 (1973). Arguably, this is the most well know case of judicial legislation in U.S. history. In this case, the court decided that most laws restricting abortion violated a constitutional right to privacy under the Due Process Clause of the Fourteenth Amendment. The pertinent section of the Fourteenth Amendment states, *"nor shall any State deprive any person of life, liberty, or property, without due process of law."* The logic is founded in ones expectancy to privacy in ones dealings. The inference here is similar to that of the Fourth Amendment due process with the expectation of privacy in ones' dealings. Justice Blackmun, in writing the courts decision stated, the *"right of privacy, whether it be founded in the Fourteenth Amendment's concept of personal liberty and restrictions upon state action, as we feel it is,* *or, as the District Court determined, in the Ninth Amendment's reservation of rights to the people, is broad enough to encompass a woman's decision whether or not to terminate her pregnancy."* Note the **justice**, and I use that term lightly, did not say, "terminate the unborn child." The Fourteenth Amendment says the state shall not deprive any person of life. As there is controversy in determining when life begins, I would think we would want to support life and not death. A person may think and "decide" to act in any manner he may wish, and he will be free of governmental intrusion into his decision. When we allow life ending, life damaging, life altering decisions to be made without regard to protecting the innocence of life, we have damned a nation for the want of responsibility. I believe in pro choice, and pro responsibility; and the choice is made at the time of conception, not after. You may also note the assumption that the person in question was a Fourteenth Amendment citizen. As we have previously covered, this is an assumption on the government's part and may not be based, in any way, on fact.

Bush v. Gore, 531 U.S. 98 (2000). The Supreme Court, in a 5 to 4 decision, determined that a ballot recount being conducted in certain counties in the State of Florida was to be stopped due to Equal Protection issues arising from the lack of consistent standards across counties. Again this is a state issue being forced upon the people by the Federal Government.

Kelo v. City of New London, 545 U.S. 469 (2005). Kelo is a Supreme Court case involving the use of eminent domain to transfer land from one private owner to another to further economic development. The Court held in a 5 to 4 decision that the general benefits a community enjoyed from economic growth qualified such redevelopment plans as a permissible "public use" under the Takings Clause of the Fifth Amendment. This is a gross violation of property rights; and a misinterpretation of the Fifth Amendment, the consequence of this ruling; would be to benefit large corporations at the expense of individual homeowners. This action is quite common in most communist countries, comrade.

Roper v. Simmons, 543 U.S. 551 (2005). In this 5 to 4 Supreme Court decision which ruled that a person under the age of 18 a murder could not be put to death, regardless of how heinous or premeditated the crime. They based their decision on the 8th Amendment; cruel and unusual punishment clause. What about cruel and unusual murder! Justice Anthony Kennedy writes, *"It is proper that we acknowledge the overwhelming weight of **international opinion** against the juvenile death penalty."* We should consider "international opinion" when dealing with United States Constitutional issues? Who gives a flying leap what other countries "think?" Justices take an oath to defend the constitution not to care what other countries may think, period.

Justice Ginsberg and others stated that they hoped America would discard its "Lone Ranger" attitude when it came to interpreting our own Constitution; and they said that we should look at how other countries interpret their constitutions. How absurd!

West Coast Hotel Co. v. Parrish, 300 U.S. 379 (1937). This was a Supreme Court decision that upheld the constitutionality of minimum wage legislation overturning earlier decisions of the right to contract. Again, more legislation made by the courts which affected the American public.

Parker v. District of Columbia 311 F.Supp.2d 103 (D.D.C. 2004). Was a United States Court of Appeals case for the District of Columbia ruling, for the first time in American history, that a gun law was struck down on Second Amendment grounds. The case challenged the 31-year-old District of Columbia ban on handgun registrations to allow citizens to keep functional handguns in their District residences for personal protection. This ruling will certainly be appealed to the Supreme Court, and it is being touted by many on the left as judicial activism at its worst. The difference in this example is that the court is upholding the constitution exactly as it should. This is not activism but thoughtful, correct, constitutional thinking as it relates to 14th Amendment citizens.

The most recent Supreme Court case of judicial legislation was ***Massachusetts v. Environmental Protection Agency*** (case 05-1120) (APR. 07). In this case, twelve states and several cities, sued the Environmental Protection Agency (EPA) to force the federal agency to regulate carbon dioxide as a greenhouse gas. First of all, Congress passes legislation, not the Supreme Court; and secondly, the EPA, as part of the executive, upholds that legislation. If there is no law, then the Supreme Court has no authority to force or make law. Again, the Supreme Court is legislating from the bench.

As part of the decision, the majority report commented that "*greenhouse gases fit well within the Clean Air Act's capacious definition of air pollutant.*" Again, we are going back to justices relying on inference not rule of law. If the law does not say something specifically, then it must be returned to the legislature (Congress) to be modified, not to the courts.

As the primary greenhouse gas is carbon dioxide, breathing then can only consist of inhaling, as you emit CO2 when you exhale. Just when you thought you could breathe a sigh of relief...! Oops, more CO2. We're going to have to tax everyone an exhale tax to buy carbon offsets for polluting the air. This is a knee jerk reaction, based on emotion, not the facts; and expansion of law beyond the original scope of the law.

During the recent Justice Alito confirmation hearings, I was struck by the number of times both the panel and Judge Alito, stated the need to honor past court decisions. Is it improper to question a ruling of a prior Supreme Court case? Were they infallible beings of extraordinary wisdom and insight? I came away from the hearings with two very troubling concepts:

1. If the Supreme Court was to make a determination that resulted in creation or modification of "law," there was absolutely nothing that could overrule them unless the court decided to hear another case that would cause a reversal of the decision. We know how often that happens.
2. The Supreme Court views itself as the absolute law of the land. Their decisions carry the same weight and importance as the Constitution itself; and their decisions should never be changed or challenged. How arrogant is that? Even the Constitution can be amended, but not the decisions of the Court?

How do bad Supreme Court decisions get changed if Congress or the presidents hold no sway over the Court? The only way is to bring the court back into its primary function, the determination of constitutionality, not the making of law.

The role of the Judicial in the United States government is to make determinations of constitutionality. Judicial Activism involves mandating a certain course of action by a judge within the judiciary. A flagrant example is ***Goodridge v. Dept. of Public Health***, 798 N.E.2d 941 (Mass. 2003). In this case the Massachusetts Supreme Court ruled that Massachusetts may not "*deny the protections, benefits and obligations conferred by civil marriage to two individuals of the same sex who wish to marry.*" The court then gave the legislation of Massachusetts 180 days to change the law. This type of legislation from the bench is perhaps the most direct form of abuse because judges are "making" law rather than interpreting the law. Also, since the law was mandated by the judiciary, it is beyond the scope of the people to change it, as the judiciary is not staffed by elected officials.

One other point I'd like to make is that law is not about right and wrong. Laws are the rules upon which we agree to live by to bring order to our communities. Long before the issues of "gay rights" or "same sex anything," there was the institution of marriage,—the union between a man and a woman. This rule was in place long before this issue ever rose to adjudication, and its meaning cannot be changed. You can create a different "union" between same sex partners and call it a civil union (or what ever you want) and give it the same legal benefits in law; but it can never be a marriage. If someone has an elm tree in their front yard, but he wants an oak tree, just calling it an oak does not make it an oak tree. It can never be an oak because the word oak has a set meaning. Oak is oak, and marriage is marriage. The US Supreme Court has shown time and time again that they are willing to make law and change meanings to fit an agenda or purpose. Regardless of how noble or heartfelt their intention, it is unconstitutional and it is wrong. As we have seen the unintended consequences of good intentions have devastating effects that ripple throughout time and in the end hurt more than they help.

Chapter 6
Money

The Constitution and Coinage:

Daniel Webster wrote, *"Of all the contrivances devised for cheating the laboring classes of mankind, none has been more effective than that which deludes him with paper money."*

and

"We are in danger of being overwhelmed with irredeemable paper, mere paper, representing not gold nor silver, no sir, representing nothing but broken promises, bad faith, bankrupt corporations, cheated creditors and a ruined people."

Mr. Webster was obviously opinionated when it came to money, and with what he perceived would be our involvement with money today. To start this discourse on money, I would like to point out what our constitution and the founding fathers have to say.

Article I, Section 8, Clause 2, states that Congress shall have the Power *"To coin Money, regulate the Value thereof, and of foreign Coin, and fix the Standard of Weights and Measures."*

Article I, Section 10, Clause 1, states that **NO** State shall *"coin Money; emit Bills of Credit; make any Thing but gold and silver Coin a Tender in Payment of Debt."*

So Congress is to coin money (which means to create money or mint money) and regulate the value thereof. Regulate means to adjust, or in this case, to adjust the value. This would be the ability for the government to control inflation and regulate the economy, much as adjusting interest rates do now. Regulating value, however, adjusts wealth, whereas adjusting interest rates adjusts debt. In essence we have changed from a wealth based system to a debt based system.

The **Coinage Act of 1792** established the United States Mint and established **the dollar** as the unit of money in the United States, and it created a decimal system for U.S. currency.

The Act authorized production of $10.00 Gold Eagles, $5.00 Gold Half Eagles, $2.50 Gold Quarter Eagles, $1.00 Silver Dollars, $0.50 Silver Half Dollars, $0.25 Silver Quarters, $0.10 Silver Dimes, $0.05 Silver Half Dimes, $0.01 Copper Cents, and $0.005 Copper Half Cents.

The act further established a monetary equivalence between silver and gold of 15 to 1—15 units of silver would equal one unit of pure gold. However, they also used what was known as standard gold which equates to 11 parts pure gold to one part alloy (silver and copper); and standard silver, was 1485 parts pure silver and 179 parts copper alloy.

At that time a person could bring gold or silver bullion into the federal mint and exchange it for an equivalent value of coinage, minus a small exchange fee.

As an interesting side note, if you worked at the mint and were caught embezzling, the penalty was death. A second item of trivia is that the serrated edge of the coin was not done solely for its aesthetic value. It was a practice of the time, by unscrupulous people, to trim small amounts of gold from the edge of coins and melt them down, stealing from the weight of the original coin. The serrated edge allowed the receiver to know that he was getting the "full measure" of his payment and was not getting "short changed".

Between 1834 and 1862 there were a number of "coinage acts," which crated new coins and regulated the values, sizes, and purities; and it was the basis of our system between gold and silver. There were years when either gold or silver values fell below the commodity pricing and much of the coinage was melted down for bullion to fetch the higher commodity price.

From the time of the Civil War, the government flirted with paper in the form of Treasury Notes or bills of credit, as it was legal for the Congress to borrow on the credit of the country. These bills were never treated as legal tender, per se; and congress stated such by proclaiming, *"Nothing herein contained shall be construed to make any thing but gold and silver a tender in payment, of any debt due from the United States to individuals."* So even it's debt instruments acknowledge that only gold and silver was the only legal tender, as mandated in the constitution.

The Legal Tender Act of 1862 brought the first Legal Tender notes printed by the United States Department of the Treasury. They were printed in denominations of $1, $2, $5, $10, $20, $50, $100, $500, $1000, $5000, and $10,000, and they were issued directly into circulation. The notes were identified as obligations of the United States Government and they were limited by Congress to a total circulation of $300 million; however they were not backed by any reserve.

Now things start to get a little complicated. During this time, the government started printing "Interest notes" which, as its title says, paid interest. There were also gold certificates, which were backed by deposits of gold, and they were redeemable for gold coin.

Thus entered the first fiat currencies. Fiat currency is currency which is *made* legal tender by government declaration. It may or may not have backing in a precious metal. Today it does not. It circulates "as money," in that it can be bartered for products; and thus it derives its' true value. When you use the term "as money," it means that it is not real money, but it is used *instead* of money. Money has intrinsic value, as agreed upon by society. The paper money we have today is held up solely on the governments trust and the faith of those who accept it, nothing more. Gold and Silver, on the other hand, does not accept nor require trust and faith, as its' value is already agreed upon by the world.

Money derives its' value from what you can do with it. You can have all the money in the world; but if you're stuck in the middle of the desert, it won't do you much good. In society, the value of commodities has not changed very much in relation to gold and silver. For example, in the 1920's, you could buy a new custom-made suit, belt, shoes, tie, and a hat for 1oz. of gold. Today you can buy a custom tailored suit, belt, shoes, tie and a hat for 1 oz. of gold. The buying power of *real* money has not changed, what has changed is the value of paper money in relation to gold and silver. It now takes a lot more paper money for the same buying power that gold has maintained. This is not something that you would be taught in the government schools, as this could diminish the faith the government wants us all to have.

One of the problems the government had with issuing different types of notes is that some were interest bearing, some were not, some notes were backed by gold or silver, others were not. What if I gave you a federal note, which has no backing, in exchange for a gold certificate? I can redeem that certificate for real money—gold coin. The paper fiat money was only good if someone else accepted it. This could be a problem, and in fact, was a problem for some.

Andrew Jackson, in his farewell address in 1837, spoke on the topic of currency and banking:

> *"But when the charter of the Bank of the United States was obtained from Congress, it* ***perfected the schemes of the paper system and gave its advocates the position they have struggled to obtain from the commencement of the federal government*** *to the present hour. The immense capital and peculiar privileges bestowed upon it enabled it to* ***exercise despotic sway over the other banks*** *in every part of the country. From its superior strength it could seriously injure, if not destroy, the business of any one of them, which might incur its resentment; and it* ***openly claimed for itself the power of regulating the currency throughout the United States****. In other words, it asserted (and undoubtedly possessed) the power to make money plenty or scarce at its pleasure, at any time and in any quarter of the union, by controlling the issues of other banks and permitting an expansion or compelling a general contraction of the circulating medium, according to its own will."*

At the turn of the century, 1900 to 1935, a lot was happening in the government regarding banking, money, and taxes. We were about to embark on a new deal. What do you think of when you walk onto a car lot and the salesman says, "Have I got a deal for you!" That's the first sign that you should turn and run! FDR said, have I got a "New Deal" for you America; and we should have run.

Woodrow Wilson said: *"The growth of the nation ... and all our activities are in the hands of a few men ... We have come to be one of the worst ruled; one of the most completely controlled and dominated governments in the civilized world ... no longer a government of free opinion, no longer a government by conviction and the free vote of the majority, but a government by the opinion and duress of a small group of dominant men."* This statement was made three years after the initiation of the Federal Reserve. The dominant men spoken of by Woodrow Wilson are the leaders of the Federal Reserve, and the world bankers.

Horace Greeley, an author, journalist, and politician in the 1800's said: *"While boasting of our noble deeds, we are careful to control the ugly fact that by an iniquitous money system, we have nationalized a system of oppression which, though more refined, is not less cruel than the old system of chattel slavery."*

Anselm Rothschild, a member of the Rothschild banking family of Austria, said: *"Give me the power to issue a nation's money; then I do not care who makes the law."*

Andrew Jackson wrote:

> *"If congress has the right under the Constitution to issue paper money, it was given them to use themselves, not to be delegated to individuals or corporations."*
>
> *"The bold efforts that the present bank has made to control the government and the distress it has wantonly caused, are but premonitions of the fate which awaits the American people should they be deluded into a perpetuation of this institution or the establishment of another like it...* ***If the people only understood the rank injustice of our money and banking system there would be a revolution before morning."*** *[Emphasis added]*

Russell L. Munk, former Assistant General Counsel of the Department of the Treasury, said:

"Federal Reserve Notes are not dollars."

Article I, Section 10 of The Constitution For The United States Of America states: "No State shall enter into any treaty, alliance, or confederation; grant letters of marquee and reprisal; coin money; **emit letters of credit**; make any thing but gold and silver coin a tender in payment of debts; pass any bill of attainder, ex post facto law, or law impairing the obligation of contracts, or grant any title of nobility." (Emphasis added)

The U.S. Supreme Court in Craig v. Missouri, 4 Peters 410 1830, declared: "Emitting bills of credit, or the creation of money by private corporations, is what is expressly forbidden by Article 1, Section 10 of the U.S. Constitution." This is precisely the current form of "money" that we have in use today.

John Fiske, an American philosopher and historian of the 1800's, wrote:

> *"It was finally decided, by the vote of nine states against New Jersey and Maryland, that the power to issue inconvertible paper should not be granted to the federal government. An express prohibition, such as had been adopted for the separate states, was thought unnecessary. It was supposed that it was enough to withhold the power, since the federal government would not venture to exercise it unless expressly permitted in the Constitution." Thus,"* says Madison, in his narrative of the

> proceedings, *"the pretext for a paper currency, and particularly for making the bills a tender, either for public or private debts, was cut off." "Nothing could be more clearly expressed than this. As Mr. Justice Field observes, in his able dissenting opinion in the recent case of Juilliard vs. Greenman, "if there be anything in the history of the Constitution which can be established with moral certainty, it is that the framers of that instrument intended to prohibit the issue of legal-tender notes both by the general government and by the states, and thus prevent interference with the contracts of private parties." "Such has been the opinion of our ablest constitutional jurists, Marshall, Webster, Story, Curtis, and Nelson.* ***There can be little doubt that, according to all sound principles of interpretation, the Legal Tender Act of 1862 was passed in flagrant violation of the Constitution.***" (Emphasis added.)

GEORGE BANCROFT, American historian, statesman, and prior Secretary of the Navy, said:

> *"Madison, agreeing with the journal of the convention, records that the grant of power to emit bills of credit was refused by a majority of more than four to one. The evidence is perfect;* ***no power to emit paper money was granted to the legislature of the United States.***" (Emphasis added.)

As you can see from the litany of prominent men from the past, from our own Constitution, and even from the Supreme Court; our current money system is not only unconstitutional, it is a lie perpetrated on the American people by our own government.

We will next review the prime mechanism by which this fraud was able to flourish … the Federal Reserve.

The Federal Reserve (Fed):

The history and secrecy of the powerful men behind the creation of the Federal Reserve is both fascinating and foreboding, and it could not be better portrayed than in the book "The Creature from Jekyll Island, A Second Look at the Federal Reserve" (Written by G. Edward Griffin). This is a masterly depiction of the men, the times, and the methods used to enslave the American people in a blueprint for global monetary control. I highly recommend this book to anyone who has an interest in this topic.

As the history of how this came about has already been written, I will only review that history and the things prominent men have had to say regarding it. It will be left to your discretion to determine what this means to us today. In my opinion, the only difference between the slaves who were brought from Africa and the slaves we have become is that the slaves of old knew they were slaves. We have allowed our own country not only to enslave us, but to enslave our children—it is nothing less.

The Fed officially came into being by the enactment of the Federal Reserve Act of 1913. Because it was created by an act of Congress you might expect that it would be a government agency. You would, however, be wrong. The only thing federal about the Federal Reserve is the spelling of its name.

The Federal Reserve System, as it is now called, was the brain child of international bankers bent on centralizing our banking system; and it places the wealth of the country into the hands of those same bankers. During the turbulent banking era of the late 1800's, many banks failed due to corruption and mismanagement which caused panic across the nation.

For a number of years, congress and the banks have been pushing a central bank theory within Washington only to have it shot down. In 1907 another banking panic rocked the American landscape, and the motivation to push again for centralized banking began in earnest. In December 1910 a secret meeting, on Jekyll Island, Georgia, was arranged for the purpose of putting together what has become known as the greatest scheme ever perpetrated on the American people. This is thoroughly outlined, and documented Mr. Griffin's book.

Those in attendance at the meeting were Senator Nelson W. Aldrich, business associate to J.P. Morgan and father-in-law to John D. Rockefeller, Jr.; Abraham Piatt Andrew, Assistant Secretary of the U.S. Treasury; Frank A. Vanderlip, President of National City Bank of New York representing William Rockefeller and the international investment banking house of Kuhn, Loeb & Company; Charles D. Norton, president of J.P Morgan's First National Bank of New York; Benjamin Strong, head of J.P. Morgan's Bankers Trust Company; and Paul M Warburg, a partner of Kuhn, Loeb & Company, representative of the Rothschild's and brother to Max Warburg who was head of the Warburg Banking Consortium in Germany and the Netherlands.

This meeting would give birth to the plan by which the American people would be enslaved and the world would be drawn closer to a new world order. When Senator Aldrich first proposed this scheme to Congress, the Democrats blocked it. However, in 1913, Democrat Congressman, Carter Glass from

Virginia, proposed the same Jekyll Island scheme now known as the Federal Reserve Act, which **was** adopted.

Woodrow Wilson, who was President when the Federal Reserve Act was passed, said:

> *"A great industrial nation is controlled by its system of credit. Our system of credit is concentrated. The growth of the Nation and all our activities are in the hands of a few men. We have come to be one of the worst ruled, one of the most completely controlled and dominated governments in the world--no longer a government of free opinion, no longer a government of conviction, and vote of the majority, but a government by the opinion and duress, of small groups of dominant men."*

Just before President Woodrow Wilson died, he is reported to have said to friends that he had been "deceived;" and *"I have betrayed my Country,"* referring to the Federal Reserve Act.

CONGRESSIONAL RECORD, JUNE 10, 1932, p. 12595: *"The Federal Reserve Board and the Federal Reserve Banks are private Corporations."*

CONGRESSIONAL RECORD, MAY 11, 1972: *"Some people think the Federal Reserve Banks are United States government institutions, they are not government institutions, they are private credit monopolies."*

In essence, the Federal Reserve straddles the line between government, and Private Corporation. Their mandate is from the government, but their ownership is private, sort of. What I mean by that; is that all the member banks have ownership in the various Central Banks that make up the Federal Reserve. Each of the member banks in the nation belong to regional Central Reserve Banks. As members they have input into the reserve system and are protected by it. The regional Central Reserve Banks are members of the Federal Reserve Bank and vote to provide members to the Federal Reserve board. In essence; they make up a cartel of Americas banks.

Many believe that without the Federal Reserve there would be no need for the income tax. Both the Federal Reserve and the Income tax amendment were created in the same year, 1913. As President Franklin D. Roosevelt has pointed out, *"**In politics, nothing happens by accident. If it happens, you can bet it was planned that way.**"* Keep this in mind as we go through the rest of the book.

On the June 10th, 1932, in the House of Representatives, Representative Louis T. McFadden addressed the assembled members to discuss the then current banking crises and the depression. He states: (Taken from the Congressional Record, 1932, pages 12595 and 12596). (Bold added to highlight specific points of interest)

> *"Mr. Chairman, at the present session of Congress we have been dealing with emergency situations. We have been dealing with the effect of things rather than with the cause of things. In this particular discussion I shall deal with some of the causes that lead up to these proposals. There are underlying principles which are responsible for conditions such as we have at the present time and I shall deal with one of these in particular which is tremendously important in the consideration that you are now giving to this bill".*
>
> *"Mr. Chairman,* ***we have in this country one of the most corrupt institutions the world has ever known. I refer to the Federal Reserve Board and the Federal Reserve Banks.*** *The Federal Reserve Board, a Government board, has cheated the Government of the United States and the people of the United States out of enough money to pay the national debt.* ***The depredations and iniquities of the Federal Reserve Board has cost this country enough money to pay the national debt several times over****. This evil institution has impoverished and ruined the people of the United States, has bankrupted itself, and has practically bankrupted our Government.* ***It has done this through the defects of the law under which it operates****, through the maladministration of that law by the Federal Reserve Board, and through the corrupt practices of the moneyed vultures who control it."*
>
> *"Some people think the Federal Reserve banks are United States Government institutions. They are not Government institutions.* ***They are private credit monopolies*** *which prey upon the people of the United States* ***for the benefit of themselves and their foreign customers****; foreign and domestic speculators and swindlers; and rich and predatory money lenders. In that dark crew of financial pirates there are those who would cut a man's throat to get a dollar out of his pocket; there are those who send money into States to buy votes to control our legislation; and there are those who maintain international propaganda for the purpose of deceiving us and of wheedling*

us into the granting of new concessions which will permit them to cover up their past misdeeds and set again in motion their gigantic train of crime."

"These twelve private credit monopolies were ***deceitfully and disloyally foisted upon this country by the bankers who came here from Europe*** *and repaid us for our hospitality by undermining our American institutions."*

"... Mr. Chairman, last December, I ***introduced a resolution here asking for an examination and an audit of the Federal Reserve Board and the Federal Reserve banks*** *and all related matters. If the House sees fit to make such an investigation, the people of the United States will obtain information of great value. This is a Government of the people, by the people, for the people. Consequently, nothing should be concealed from the people.* ***The man who deceives the people is a traitor to the United States****. The man who knows or suspects that a crime has been committed and who conceals or covers up that crime is an accessory to it. Mr. Speaker,* ***it is a monstrous thing for this great Nation of people to have its destinies presided over by a traitorous Government board acting in secret concert with international usurers.*** *Every effort has been made by the Federal Reserve Board to conceal its power but the truth is the* ***Federal Reserve Board has usurped the Government of the United States****. It controls everything here and it controls all our foreign relations. It makes and breaks governments at will. No man and no body of men is more entrenched in power than the arrogant credit monopoly which operates the Federal Reserve Board and the Federal Reserve banks.* ***These evil-doers have robbed this country of more than enough money to pay the national debt****. What the National Government has permitted the Federal Reserve Board to steal from the people should now be restored to the people.* ***The people have a valid claim against the Federal Reserve Board and the Federal Reserve banks****. If that claim is enforced, Americans will not need to stand in the breadlines or to suffer and die of starvation in the streets. Homes will be saved, families will be kept together, and American children will not be dispersed and abandoned. The Federal Reserve Board and the Federal Reserve banks owe the United*

States Government an immense sum of money. We ought to find out the exact amount of the people's claim. We should know the amount of the indebtedness of the Federal Reserve Board and the Federal Reserve banks to the people and we should investigate this treacherous and disloyal conduct of the Federal Reserve Board and the Federal Reserve banks".

*"...**What is needed here is a return to the Constitution of the United States**. We need to have a complete divorce of Bank and State. The old struggle that was fought out here in Jackson's day must be fought over again. The independent United States Treasury should be re-established and the Government should keep its own money under lock and key in the building the people provided for that purpose. Asset currency, the device of the swindler, should be done away with. **The Government should buy gold and issue United States currency on it.** The business of the independent bankers should be restored to them. The State banking systems should be freed from coercion The **Federal Reserve districts should be abolished and the State boundaries should be respected**. Bank reserves should be kept within the borders of the States whose people own them, and this reserve money of the people should be protected so that the international bankers and acceptance bankers and discount dealers can not draw it away from them. The exchanges should be closed while we are putting our financial affairs in order. The **Federal Reserve act should be repealed and the Federal Reserve banks, having violated their charters, should be liquidated immediately**. Faithless Government officers who have violated their oaths of office should be impeached and brought to trial. Unless this is done by us, I predict that the American people, outraged, robbed, pillaged, insulted, and betrayed as they are in their own land, will rise in their wrath and send a President here who will sweep the money changers out of the temple."*

Mr. McFadden was a Republican member of the U.S. House of Representatives from the state of Pennsylvania. He served as treasurer and later as President of the Pennsylvania Bankers' Association. He served as Chairman of the United States House Committee on Banking and Currency. His obvious direct relation with the institutions and workings of the government, and banking in particular, makes him uniquely qualified to offer the preceding statement.

The Fed is a private corporate structure with foreign influence making the commerce decisions of this nation without any oversight from Congress. It is comprised of 12 regional Reserve Banks, which are corporations whose stock is held by commercial banks, which are members of the system. Each region has a board of 9 members whose job it is to implement the policy of the Board of Governors of the Fed. The Chairman of the Board of Governors is appointed by the President from a list provided to him from the Board of Governors of the Federal Reserve. They do not consult the government on Federal Reserve policy or the direction or goals of the Fed.

The Fed is not under governmental control, nor is it a common corporation where stockholders own voting shares. It is independent, and for all intent and purpose, is the cartel of the banking world, designed to serve *that end.* It is not operating in the best interest of the American people but for what is best for the cartel. It creates a debtor society where **debt** is monetized, fractionalized, and forced upon the unsuspecting public. It manages increased inflation by printing money as it sees fit, and at the demand of the Government, thus adding increased national debt, and inflation. This is the grossest tax of them all, as it is a hidden tax which robs from the weakest of the country. It encourages war, as that is when it makes its greatest gains; and at times, it finances both sides of the war. It destabilizes the economy to facilitate its own goals. Worst of all, it is an instrument for globalists new world order and totalitarianism.

Bob Prechter, an author and stock market analyst, stated:

> *"I cannot morally blame all Americans for allowing, for instance, the birth of the Federal Reserve System (a private cartel with full control over the issuance of national debt) and the money destruction that has followed. They are simply ignorant about it and don't know what happened or what is happening. They think that prices go up rather than that dollars go down. Unsound money imposes an environment of immorality, which in turn makes people behave in different ways for reasons they know not. Sometimes you can blame immorality for the imposition of bad structures (bad people do it with full knowledge of what they are doing), but sometimes it is simply stupidity. People revere democracy, but democracy ends in plunder by the majority. Are people immoral for supporting democracy? I think rather that they lack a deep understanding of its essence. At a very deep level, I would say that the reason*

such structures are created is due to both a lack of knowledge and a false morality, which in turn is due to a lack of knowledge."

This is not hard to imagine. The average person relies on the government as a protector. They have been told from the cradle that our country is the best on earth, that we are a free nation, a shining example to world. All this is true; and yet, we would be naïve if we think that fellow Americans would not take advantage of us. Harder still to image is that the government, which is sworn to protect and serve us, has betrayed us. Let us not fail due to a lack of knowledge. I hope, if nothing else, this book will spur you to investigate the claims it makes and that it will broaden your understanding of our country. If this is the only thing that happens; then my efforts will not have been in vain.

Alan Greenspan, former Chairman of the Federal Reserve and someone with an intimate knowledge of the Fed has said:

"The abandonment of the gold standard made it possible for the welfare statists to use the banking system as a means to an unlimited expansion of credit. In the absence of the gold standard, there is no way to protect savings from confiscation through inflation. There is no safe store of value... [Gold] stands as a protector of property rights. This is the shabby secret of the welfare statists' tirades against gold. Deficit spending is simply a scheme for the "hidden" confiscation of wealth. If one grasps this, one has no difficulty in understanding the statists' antagonism toward the gold standard."

If one of the principal roles of the Fed is the management of inflation, one has to wonder for whom it is being managed. In light of his previous statement, it does not seem to be for us.

Banking:

The next step in our look at money and government is the banking industry.

Sir Josiah Stamp, a former president of the Bank of England, stated:

"The modern banking system manufactures money out of nothing. The process is perhaps the most astounding piece of sleight of hand that was ever invented. Banking was conceived in inequity and born in sin... Bankers own the earth. Take it away from them but leave them the power to create money, and, with a flick of a pen, they will create enough money to buy it back again... Take this great power away from them, or if you

want to continue to be the slaves of bankers and pay the cost of your own slavery, then let bankers continue to create money and control credit."

Banks work on a principal called fractional reserve banking. This is a system in which banks only need keep a fraction of the total deposits kept in reserve. This is facilitated in America by the Federal Reserve Board, which determines a deposit multiplier. Banks then use this multiplier, times its reserves, to come up with its total deposits.

You might think that that would not amount to very much. Most people put money in the bank, and within a few weeks, it's gone—paid out to creditors for living expenses. But what is not known is that banks monetize debt; or more simply, they create money from debt. According to backing theory, as long as every new issue of money is matched by an equal increase in bank assets (IOUs and cash), the value of money is unaffected by a change in its quantity. These IOU's are created every time we make a loan; the debt we incur becomes an asset to the bank. This then allows the bank to increase its loan capability, and thus, an endless supply of money.

The following quote comes straight from the Federal Reserve Bank, New York: *"Because of 'fractional' reserve system, banks, as a whole, can expand our money supply several times, by making loans and investments." "Commercial banks create checkbook money whenever they grant a loan, simply by adding new deposit dollars in accounts on their books in exchange for a borrower's IOU."—*

Concerning our banking, Thomas Jefferson said; *"I believe that banking institutions are more dangerous to our liberties than standing armies. Already they have raised up a money aristocracy that has set the government at defiance. The issuing power should be taken from the banks, and restored to the people to whom it properly belongs."*

Today, banking has become an essential comfort in our modern life. When used as a tool, it allows us to go about our daily activities without the need for large amounts of cash on hand; and it gives us the ease to make purchases at the speed of electrons. But at what cost?

The problem is that the banking "service" has many hidden costs. The ease of debt makes even the most stalwart citizen a slave to the debtors whip. When we reflect on the 3 to 4 percent tax against which we rebelled with England, it is astounding that we readily sign on to 15% credit cards and mortgages of 5 to 10 %. Twenty years ago we financed a car for three to four thousand dollars, now we pay $24,000 and think that it's a good deal.

All of this has been made possible by our banking system and the Fed. Was this the America the signers of the Constitution gave us? I don't think so; but that does not mean that we cannot have a gold and silver standard, and still pass electrons back and forth to show ownership. The difference is the currency would have value. Not like the fiat currency we have today.

FDR, in a letter to Colonel E. Mandell House, on November 21, 1933, stated: *"The real truth of the matter is, as you and I know, that* ***a financial element in the large centers has owned the government of the U.S. since the days of Andrew Jackson.*** *"*

In an article in the May/June 2007 issue of "Foreign Affairs", a publication of the Council on Foreign Relations, a magazine read by governments and world leaders of commerce and nations, stated:

> *"It is only since 1971, when President Richard Nixon formally untethered the dollar from gold that monies flowing around the globe have ceased to be claims on anything real. All the world's currencies are now pure manifestations of sovereignty conjured by governments. And the vast majority of such monies are unwanted: people are unwilling to hold them as wealth..."*

This is not a new concept in the world of banks and nations, but to come out and make a clear announcement to the world is another thing, and a sign of the state of our currency. They go on to say:

> *"But the dollar's privileged status as today's global money is not heaven-bestowed. The dollar is ultimately just another money* ***supported only by faith*** *that others will willingly accept it in the future in return for the same sort of valuable things it bought in the past. This puts a great burden on the institutions of the U.S. government to validate that faith.* ***And those institutions, unfortunately, are failing to shoulder that burden.*** *Reckless U.S. fiscal policy is undermining the dollar's position even as the currency's role as a global money is expanding..."*
>
> *"...Today, with* ***money no longer bound to any material substance****, it is worth asking whether the world even approximates the* ***"ideal social order"*** *that could sustain a fiat dollar as the foundation of the global financial system.* ***There is no way effectively to insure against the unwinding of global imbalances*** *should China, with over a trillion dollars of reserves, and other countries with dollar-rich central banks come to fear the unbearable lightness of their holdings."*

The article went on to say that the world needs to reduce its currencies to one of three, the U.S. dollar, the Euro, or the Pan Asia currency. Although the United States, in the last 70 years, has managed to reduce the value of it's currency to the point of failure, and as there is no backing to this currency (fiat), then logic would dictate that by moving the world to the same failing mechanism, would doom the entire globe!

The preceding does not paint a very good picture of the financial prosperity for our children, or even for us baby boomers, as I fear this will proceed fast enough to impact this entire generation.

If we just researched a single issue, some might conclude this was a conspiracy theory. However, when we look at item, after item, after item, we have to stop and think that perhaps there is substance to what is being said. I was skeptical when I first began to research certain historical and legal positions regarding money as they came to my attention. I have spent nearly my entire life in the service of this country's military and intelligence community. My trade is to research things, to tie pieces of information together, and to draw a logical conclusion. The more I researched, the more I became convinced that we are no longer living in the republic our forefathers created.

Chapter 7
Income Tax

Let me say right up front, I am not a lawyer; and this section is not meant to give you legal advice. Your decisions are between you, your God, and your lawyer. The information presented here is for educational purposes only; and it is provided to help you understand the intricacies regarding Federal Income Taxes.

What I wish to impart to you in this chapter is some history, some court cases, and some IRS code, which operates the tax machine. I will also include writings from former presidents and our founding fathers concerning the income tax. It is my position that the income tax laws, as written today, are valid and 100% constitutional. It is my contention that in violation of the constitution, the government has overstepped its bounds in the implementation of the tax laws on its' citizens who otherwise would not be liable for such taxes and they are being forced to pay such taxes under the threat of arms, the loss of freedom, and the confiscation of property outside of the rules set by the Constitution.

President Andrew Jackson said:

> "***Congress has no right under the Constitution to take money from the people*** *unless it is equipped to execute some one of the specific powers entrusted to the government…and in such a case it is unquestionably the duty of the government to reduce them, for no circumstances can justify it in assuming a power not given to it by the Constitution* ***nor taking away the money of the people when it is not needed for the legitimate wants of the government.***" (Emphasis added.)

He went on to speak of the corruption of government, and especially when dealing with taxation of the people He said:

"The result of this decision has been felt in the rapid extinguishment of the public debt and the large accumulation of a surplus in the treasury, notwithstanding the tariff was reduced and is now very far below the amount originally contemplated by its advocates. But, rely upon it, the design to collect an extravagant revenue and ***burden you with taxes beyond the economical wants of the government*** *is not yet abandoned. The various interests which have combined together to impose a heavy tariff and to produce an overflowing treasury are too strong and have too much at stake to surrender the contest. The corporations and wealthy individuals who are engaged in large manufacturing establishments desire a high tariff to increase their gains. Designing politicians will support it to conciliate their favor and to* ***obtain the means of profuse expenditure for the purpose of purchasing influence*** *in other quarters; and since the people have decided that the federal government cannot be permitted to employ its income in internal improvements,* ***efforts will be made to seduce and mislead the citizens*** *of the several states by holding out to them the deceitful prospect of benefits to be derived from a surplus revenue collected by the general government and annually divided among the states; and if, encouraged by these fallacious hopes, the states should disregard the principles of economy which ought to characterize every republican government, and should indulge in lavish expenditures exceeding their resources,* ***they will before long find themselves oppressed with debts which they are simply unable to pay****, and the temptation will become irresistible to support high tariff in order to obtain a surplus for distribution. Do not allow yourselves, my fellow citizens, to be misled on this subject.* ***The federal government cannot collect a surplus for such purposes without violating the principles or the Constitution and assuming powers which have not been granted.*** *It is, moreover,* ***a system of injustice****, and if persisted in will inevitably lead to corruption, and must end in ruin. The surplus revenue will be drawn from the pockets of the people—from the farmer, the mechanic, the laboring classes of society; but who will receive it when distributed among the states, where it is to be disposed of by leading state*

> *politicians, who have friends of favor and political partisans to gratify? It will certainly not be returned to those who paid it and who have most need of it and are honestly entitled to it.* ***There is but one safe rule, and that is to confine the general government rigidly within the sphere of its appropriate duties. It has no power to raise a revenue or impose taxes except for those purposes enumerated in the Constitution, and if its income is found to exceed these wants it should be forthwith reduced and the burden of the people so far lightened."***

Of all the freedoms lost, this topic will encompass the most far reaching depths of our society. Here we will touch on citizenship, property, due process, education, and personal enslavement. The old adage of death and taxes is applicable; but its not what you would think. Many of you may have seen the movie, "The Matrix," which portrayed unwitting humans as batteries that supplied the machine masters with electrical power generated by their bodies. Today, it is unwitting humans who supply the machine of the government with power generated by our labor in the form of taxes.

Before I go any further, I would like to acknowledge someone who I feel is a scholar and a man of honor, Mr. Dave Champion. I have listened to his radio show and read the articles on his web page, www.originalintent.org; and it is due to his example of living up to his duty as a patriot, that I have undertaken the endeavor of writing this book. In this book I acknowledge his teachings and insight.

The next few pages will be filled with statements which you may find hard to believe, but everything I present here will be backed by law, the founding fathers, and IRS statutes. As a matter of fact, the majority of my evidence will be IRS documents, Supreme Court Cases, the Constitution, and federal law. I may provide my own opinion; but when I do, it will be straight forward and serve more as a guide to help you through the maze of obfuscation that has been written intentionally into the code. If the governments were to put the law simply and plainly for all to read and understand, then everyone would realize they are not liable for income taxes, and that they have been lied to their entire lives. However, the government has become too accustomed to the cash flow from these taxes to stop now and will do anything, even at the point of a gun, to keep the money flowing.

Let's first take a look at where the income tax laws were derived. When our country was first created, there was no income tax at all. It would be over 100 years before our government would attempt to pass any personal income tax laws.

I believe we would all agree that any action or law created by the federal government must be in line with the federal Constitution in order to be valid. The same holds true with the state governments; any laws passed must conform to the individual state constitution.

There are two types of federal taxes allowable within the framework of the federal constitution, direct and indirect. Remember from earlier; Article 1 Section 8 of the Constitution provides Congress with the power t*o "lay and collect* ***taxes*****,** ***duties*****,** ***imposts*** *and* ***excises****...*". There is no mention here of direct and indirect taxes. However, it is generally understood that the first term for "taxes" was meant to be direct taxes, or taxes paid directly to the government. Indirect taxes are comprised of duties, imposts, or excises—items not paid directly to the government, such as sales tax.

Black's Law Dictionary, Seventh Edition, defines direct tax as: *"A tax that is imposed on property, as distinguished from a tax on a right or privilege. Ad valorem"* (according to the value) *"and property taxes are direct taxes."* An indirect tax is defined as: "*A tax on a right or privilege such as an occupation tax or franchise tax."*

The Supreme Court has also defined direct taxes in Knowlton v. Moore, 178 US 41 (1900), in which they state: "*Direct taxes bear upon persons*, upon possessions, *and enjoyment of rights*." There is also a stipulation placed on all direct taxes by Article 1, Section 9 of the Constitution which reads: *"No Capitation, or other direct, Tax shall be laid, unless in Proportion to the Census or Enumeration herein before directed to be taken."* This amendment has never been repealed, and it is still valid today. To be constitutional any direct tax must be done in proportion to the census; meaning, whatever the total amount to be required by each state will be assessed based on its census to give a per capita amount. There is argument that the 16th Amendment changed this, but as you will see, it does not.

Before continuing let's discuss the term "legal definition" and the use of words and terms within the law. The *common* understanding of certain words or terms may not be what is meant in the law. The term 'individual', to a lay person, would be understood as a singular person without reference to gender. However, in government, the term might include corporations, partnerships, or other *legal fictions*. (A legal fiction is an assumption something is true, in law, even though in reality it is not; to alter how a legal rule operates.) In short, a word means exactly what the law defines it to mean, regardless of the common usage. The IRS tax code is chock full of defined terms that expound on common usage; and in some cases, it goes completely contrary to common usage. Always ask yourself, when reading any law text, what does this specific word mean in this instance? If the law text does not specify a meaning, then it may be presumed to mean the common definition. In the legal community, there exists a law dictionary; and though it carries no weight *as* law, its definitions are used to support positions *in* law. I'm sure that's as clear as mud.

Every word in a law has meaning, and is not there by accident. Each word means what it says; but in order to "understand" what is meant, you must know the "legal" meaning of the words. For example, the word "employee" has a totally different meaning than is generally understood, and without knowing the "legalese" you would have an erroneous understanding of the law as it applies to you.

Compare the following definitions for employee:

1. Webster's New Collegiate Dictionary, 1977 Edition: *"One employed by another usually for wages or salary and in a position below the executive level."*
2. Blacks Law Dictionary, Seventh Edition: *"A person who works in the service of another person (the employer) under an express or implied contract of hire, under which the employer has the right to control the details of work performance."*
3. IRS Tax code, title 26 USC, section 3401(c): "employee—*For purposes of this chapter, the term "employee" includes an officer, employee, or elected official of the United States, a State, or any political subdivision thereof, or the District of Columbia, or any agency or instrumentality of any one or more of the foregoing. The term "employee" also includes an officer of a [federally owned or controlled] corporation."* (Emphasis added.)

Notice how very closely the dictionaries follow the "understood" meaning of the word "employee". But, as I have already said, Congress can give its own meaning to words. In this case, the term has absolutely no resemblance to either of the dictionary terms. In fact, the IRS' own definition, and this is their *only* definition for employee, does not describe the majority of workers within the United States. Read number 3 again and see if you are one of those identified as an employee. With this information in hand, let's take a look at some of the history and cases that have evolved into the current tax system we have today.

Congress passed the Income Tax Act of 1894, and it assessed taxes on *"rents or income of real estate."* In 1895 the Supreme Court ruled the act unconstitutional, as it was not significantly different from a tax on the property itself. Therefore, it was a direct tax requiring apportionment among the several States. The court did not rule that all income was immune from direct taxation; and as we have previously discussed, the exact definition is required to understand what was meant by income.

In 1913 Congress passed the 16th Amendment which states: "*The Congress shall have the power to lay and collect taxes on incomes, from whatever source derived, without apportionment among the several States, and without regard to any census or enumeration.*"

To complicate things a bit more, we need to determine exactly what income the 16th Amendment is really talking about. We know that prior to this, rents or income of real estate, was said to be direct taxes and must be apportioned; but is that all the 16th Amendment was concerned with?

The court ruled in *Helvering v. Edison Bros. Stores,* 133 F.2D 575 (1943), that *"The Treasury Department cannot, by interpretive regulations, make income out of that which is not income within the meaning of the revenue acts of Congress,* ***nor can Congress, without apportionment, tax as income that which is not income within the meaning of the 16th Amendment.***"

We must try to determine what the 16th Amendment means by "income". The IRS claims the 16th Amendment is the constitutional grant of income tax authority, so identification of the income gives us the basis to understand WHO is made liable to pay the income tax. Since the only income that can be taxed directly without apportionment is the 16th Amendment income, let's examine what the law says.

In Corn v. Fort, 95 S.W.2d 620 (1936), the court ruled: *"The individual, unlike the corporation, cannot be taxed for the mere privilege of existing. The corporation is an artificial entity which owes its existence and charter powers to the state; but* ***the individuals' Right to live and own property are natural rights for the enjoyment of which an excise cannot be imposed.***" Aha! This says there is a separation of incomes between corporate and individual. They cannot be lumped together because the individual has a right to property (your income is your property). The corporation owes its existence to the state, and therefore, is taxable.

Now we know that direct tax can only apply to property/income, if apportioned among the states, other than 16th Amendment Income. We also now know that there is a difference between ordinary income and 16th Amendment income, as the courts have pointed out. And we also know, as the last court case shows, ordinary income/property cannot be taxed as an excise.

Congress passed a new Corporate Tax Act in 1909; and in 1913, the Supreme Court in *Stratton's Independence, LTD. v. Howbert*, 231 US 399, 414 (1913), stated: *"As has been repeatedly remarked, the corporation tax act of 1909 was not intended to be and is not, in any proper sense, an income tax law. This court had decided in the Pollock case that the income* ***tax law of 1894 amounted in effect to a direct tax upon property, and was invalid because not apportioned according to populations, as prescribed by the Constitution.*** *The act of 1909 avoided this difficulty by imposing not an income tax [direct],* ***but an excise tax [indirect] upon the conduct of business in a corporate capacity, measuring however, the amount of tax by the income of the corporation".***

As in the Corporate Tax Act of 1909 the court ruled that an excise tax (indirect tax) was a tax on the privilege, enjoyed by the shareholders, of doing business. It was not a tax on property. As income is property, it cannot be taxed directly without apportionment.

Another example of indirect tax is described in *Tyler v. United States*, 281 U.S. 497, at 502 (1930): *"A tax laid upon the happening of an event, as distinguished from its tangible fruits, is an indirect tax."*

In order for the laws concerning income to have meaning, the term "income" must have the same meaning in ALL the tax acts of congress. This was brought out in Merchants' Loan & Trust CO. v. Smietanka, 255 U.S. 509 (1921) stating:

> *"It is obvious that these decisions in principle rule the [255 U.S. 509, 519] case at bar* ***if the word 'income' has the same meaning in the Income Tax Act of 1913 that it had in the Corporation Excise Tax Act of 1909****, and that it has the same scope of meaning was in effect decided in Southern Pacific Co. v. Lowe, 247 U.S. 330, 335 , 38 S. Sup. Ct. 540, where it was assumed for the purposes of decision that there was no difference in its meaning as used in the act of 1909 and in the Income Tax Act of 1913 (38 Stat. 114).* ***There can be no doubt that the word must be given the same meaning and content in the Income Tax Acts of 1916 and 1917 that it had in the act of 1913.*** *When to this we add that in Eisner v. Macomber, supra, a case arising under the same Income Tax Act of 1916 which is here involved, the definition of 'income' which was applied was adopted from Stratton's Independence v. Howbert, supra, arising under the Corporation Excise Tax Act of 1909, with the addition*

> *that it should include 'profit gained through sale or conversion of capital assets,'* ***there would seem to be no room to doubt that the word must be given the same meaning in all of the Income Tax Acts of Congress that was given to it in the Corporation Excise Tax Act, and that what that meaning is has now become definitely settled by decisions of this Court."***

The constitution cannot have transient meanings. The Supreme Court has said the income determined in the Income Tax Acts must have the same meaning throughout all income tax acts as the meaning given in the **Corporation** Excise Tax Act. So what exactly did the court definitely settle this to be?

The supreme court told us in Doyle v. Mitchell Brother, Co., 247 US 179 (1918): *"Whatever difficulty there may be about a precise and scientific definition of 'income,' it imports, as used here, something entirely distinct from principle or capital either as a subject of taxation or as a measure of the tax; conveying rather the* ***idea of gain or increase arising from corporate activities.*** *"* (Emphasis added.) Let me reiterate; "the idea of gain or increase arising from CORPORATE activities." Even the names of these tax bills included the name "corporate."

On August 15, 1909, Congress passed "The Corporation Tax" law (Ch. 6, 36 Stat. 11). This act was written in clear, concise language. It describes the activity, the "carrying on or doing business", and the exercise of the *privilege* which is the subject of the tax. Section 38 of the Act reads, in part, as follows: "*That every corporation, joint stock company or association organized for profit and having a capital stock represented by shares, and every insurance company ... shall be subject to pay annually a special excise tax* **with respect to the carrying on or doing business by such corporation, joint stock company or association, or insurance company,** *equivalent to one percentum upon the entire net income over and above five thousand dollars received by it from all sources during such year...*" (Emphasis added.)

The Supreme Court and Congress have both decided that income is the gain or increase arising from corporate activities; and congress must use the same definition in all its acts.

However, even as late as 1984, in a report by the Congressional Research Service, authored by Howard Zaritsky, an attorney for the research service, stated: "*The Supreme Court, in a decision written by Chief Justice White, first noted that the Sixteenth Amendment did not authorize any new type of tax, nor did it repeal or revoke the tax clauses of Article I of the Constitution... Direct taxes were, notwithstanding the advent of the Sixteenth Amendment, still subject to the rule of apportionment and indirect taxes were still subject to the rule of uniformity." (Report 84-168A)*

The 16th Amendment did not authorize any new taxing authority; and as we have seen in previous court cases, the 16th Amendment was an excise against business. The CRS report went on to say: "*Therefore, it can be clearly determined from the decisions of the United States Supreme Court that the income tax is an indirect tax, generally in the nature of an excise tax.*"

Therefore, individuals cannot be taxed via excise (privilege) on property, and any direct tax must still be apportioned through the many states.

Again, returning to *Merchants Loan & Trust v. Smietanka*, 255 US 509 (1921), it ruled that income "*must be given the same meaning, in all the Income Tax Acts of Congress that it was given in the Corporate Excise Tax Act, and what that meaning is has become definitely settled by the decisions of this court.*"

"In determining the definition of the word 'income' thus arrived at, this court has consistently refused to enter into the refinements of lexicographers or economists, and has approved in the definitions quoted, what it believes to be the commonly understood meaning of the term ***which must have been in the minds of the people when they adopted the Sixteenth Amendment to the Constitution****."* The very next line referenced *Doyle v. Mitchell Brother, Co.*, 247 US 179 (1918) which, concerning income, stated "***...gain or increase arising from corporate activities.***"

Let's take another look at the 16th Amendment. "*The Congress shall have the power to lay and collect taxes on incomes, from whatever source derived, without apportionment among the several States, and without regard to any census or enumeration.*" When the lay person first reads this, they initially think of a direct tax. Notice there is no language that says it modifies or repeals any other part of the Constitution. Therefore, the laws of apportionment and uniformity must still be in place. And you would be right. As a matter of fact, shortly after this amendment was passed, two cases came before the Supreme Court that would challenge this. They were *Brushaber v. Union Pacific R.R. Co.*, 240 U.S. 1 (1916) and *Stanton v. Baltic Mining Co.*, 240 U.S. 103 (1916).

Most people may find reading court cases dry and boring, but I rather enjoy reading them. I think they are fascinating. However, reading Brushaber is like reading a book that has been typed on the back of worms and stuck in a can. All the words are there, but it's hard to piece it all together. So hard in fact, that both sides of the tax argument have used the same case to support their own side. Fortunately for us the Stanton case can help us out. Justice White in the Brushaber case stated:

> *"The various propositions are so intermingled as to cause it to be difficult to classify them. We are of the opinion, however, that the* ***confusion*** *is not inherent, but rather arises from the* ***conclusion*** *that the Sixteenth Amendment provides for a hitherto unknown power of taxation, that is, a power to levy an income tax which although* ***direct*** *should not be subject to the regulation of apportionment applicable to* ***all other direct taxes****. And the far-reaching effect of this* ***erroneous assumption*** *will be made clear by generalizing the many contentions advanced in argument to support it, as follows: (a) The Amendment authorizes only a particular character of* ***direct*** *tax* ***without apportionment****, and therefore if a tax is levied under its* ***assumed*** *authority which does not partake of the characteristics exacted by the Amendment, it is outside the Amendment and is void as a direct tax in the general constitutional sense because not apportioned ...* (Emphasis added.)

Notice that he uses the negative approach when stating the assumption that the 16th Amendment provides an unknown power of taxation or a power to levy an income tax, not subject to apportionment, **is an erroneous assumption**.

As the previous paragraph was the easiest section of Brushaber to understand, I will not attempt to relate the entire Brushaber text here for two reasons. First, entire discourses have been written on the meanings of this case that are still argued about to this day and it is beyond the scope of this book. Secondly, the Stanton decision, written by the same Justice White, gives us a much easier version to use.

In *Stanton v. Baltic Mining Co.*, 240 U.S. 103 (1916) Justice White references the Brushaber case and states: "*...by the previous ruling it was settled that the provisions of the 16th Amendment conferred* ***no new power of taxation****, but simply* ***prohibited*** *the previous complete and plenary power of* ***income taxation*** *possessed by Congress from the beginning* ***from being taken out of the category of indirect taxation to which it inherently belonged*** *...*" As we can see, therefore, the 16th Amendment *does not* provide for direct taxation as others have argued.

We now know that income is property, and property cannot be taxed directly; but as we have discussed, it can be used as the basis for a tax amount when dealing with an indirect tax. Therefore, income tax is not a tax on income; but rather, it is an excise tax with respect to doing an activity or privilege, and it uses the amount of income as a gauge to the level of taxation. Doing business under the protection of a corporation is a privilege. Contracting for labor/skill/employment is a right. The former can be legally taxed for the privilege of doing business; the later cannot be legally taxed as it is a right not a privilege.

I would love to think that our congressmen are vying for our best interest, but I have to wonder when the *House Congressional Record*, March 27, 1943, page 2580 states: *"The income tax is, therefore, not a tax on income as such. It is an excise tax with respect to certain activities and privileges which is measured by reference to the income which they produce. The income is not the subject of the tax: it is the basis for determining the amount of tax."*

And guess who determines what activities are a privilege and therefore taxable? Right, it is the very same congressmen who want you to send in your hard earned dollars. What are the activities that require taxation? According to United States Code, the following are the taxable activities which are "revenue liable":

1. *The **distiller or importer of distilled spirits** shall be **liable for** the taxes imposed thereon by section 5001(a)(1). 26 U.S.C. § 5005(a)*
2. *The **manufacturer or importer of tobacco products and cigarette papers and tubes** shall be **liable for** the taxes imposed thereon by section 5701. 26 U.S.C. § 5703(a)(1)*
3. *"**Each person who is engaged in the business of accepting wagers** shall be **liable for** and shall pay the tax under this subchapter on all wagers ..." 26 U.S.C. § 4401(c)*
4. "There shall be imposed a special tax of $500 per year to be paid by **each person who is liable for the tax imposed under section 4401 or who is engaged in receiving wagers for or on behalf of any person so liable.** *26 U.S.C. § 4411(a)*

Do you see how clearly and accurately the law states exactly what activity and who is "liable for" an activity which is taxable. Reading this, one would have to assume that if you are not doing these activities you would not have to pay an income tax. You would be right, and yet wrong, as far as the IRS is concerned, and we'll get into that shortly.

What have we learned so far?

1. We have learned that there are direct and indirect taxes. Direct taxes apply directly to the taxpayer and cannot be avoided by normal

activity. Indirect taxes are applied towards a privilege or excise. You only need to avoid doing the taxable activity, to avoid paying the tax.

2. The definition of income as stated in the Corporate Tax Act of 1909 must be used by congress in all its income tax acts.
3. 16th Amendment income, as defined by the Supreme Court, is the basis upon which a tax amount is determined and it is not the subject of the tax.
4. The definition of "income" as used in the 1909 *Corporate* Tax Act is the same definition that the Supreme Court has said must be used when applying it to the 16th Amendment.

From a constitutional perspective, when we see the number of citizens that have gone to jail for tax related offenses, we have to ask "what the heck is going on?" It is not the 16th Amendment that has become the problem; but it is the implementation of the tax law that has gone astray. Even the tax code supports what we have just learned. It is the misapplication of that law that has gotten so many citizens into trouble.

In reality, most people who otherwise would not be required to pay taxes, volunteer to pay. We are presumed to be taxpayers either by outright agreement or by our actions, we volunteer to pay taxes. When you fill out and sign a W-4 form, you are agreeing that you **are** a taxpayer, and you wish to have "taxes" withheld. Most people, of course, do not know that they do not need to submit a W-4 if they are a non-taxpayer.

Do you think the government would allow its' citizens to 'volunteer' to be a taxpayer?

Do you think the government would let you assume that you're a taxpayer even if you were not one?

And, don't you think that even if you 'volunteered,' (or the government assumed you to be a taxpayer), and they suspected that you may have cheated on your taxes, that they would not come after you like a starving coyote on a hen house?

If you answered yes to all three questions; you would be right!

I am now going to spend the next few pages discussing the IRS code. Many fear the code, few have read it, and fewer still have understood what they read. Remember; when dealing with law text, the paramount issue is context. A term used in one section may have a totally different meaning when defined within another section, or even within sub-sections. So attention must be made to ensure correct context is applied within each section.

The Internal Revenue Service is responsible for administrating the United States governments' Internal Revenue Code (IRC), also known as "Title 26" of the United States Code. The Code is broken down into 11 sections called "subtitles," and has an appendix at the end. The subtitles range from 'A' through 'K,' and they are as follows:

Subtitle A—Income tax
Subtitle B—Estate and Gift tax
Subtitle C—Employment tax
Subtitle D—Miscellaneous Excise taxes
Subtitle E—Alcohol, Tobacco, & Certain Other Excise taxes
Subtitle F—Procedure and Administration
Subtitle G—Joint Committee on Taxation
Subtitle H—Financing of Presidential Election Campaigns
Subtitle I—Trust Fund Code
Subtitle J—Coal Industry Health Benefits
Subtitle K—Group Health Plan Requirements

Of primary concern to most of us are Subtitles A and C; and possibly at some point in our lives Subtitle B. But the two we will focus on here are A and C, Income and Employment tax respectively. Each subtitle above is a separate tax code dealing with the subject content. Subtitle A is separate from Subtitle C, however, definitions may be shared by any of them or may solely refer to the section defined. Again, context is very important in understanding the impact of the code.

Subtitle A, or Income Tax, is probably the one that most of us are familiar with. You will find that things will not be "as an open book" when reading IRS code. This is done for a specific reason; and that is obfuscation, (to make opaque what would otherwise be clear). But once you have learned 'how' to read this material, it does become easier. It's like driving for the first time or riding a bike; it becomes easier with practice. The difference is if you make a mistake driving you might get a ticket, if you make a mistake with the IRS, it could ruin your life.

I told you earlier that the IRS does not deal with non-taxpayers, and that you would not find code that deals with non-taxpayers. *Economy Plumbing and Heating Co. v. United States*, 470 F. 2d 585 (1972), states: *"The revenue laws are a code or system in regulation of tax assessment and collection.* ***They relate to taxpayers, and not to nontaxpayers****. The latter are without their scope.* ***No procedure is prescribed for nontaxpayers****, and no attempt is made to annul any of their rights and remedies in due course of law.* ***With***

them Congress does not assume to deal, and they are neither of the subject nor of the object of the revenue laws".

There are two points I wish to emphasize. First, there are, by admission of the Supreme Court, both TAXPAYERS and NONTAXPAYERS. Secondly, no procedure is prescribed for nontaxpayers. Why would that be? Congress does not assume to deal with them.

If there are taxpayers and nontaxpayers, how can you tell the difference? If you look up under US Code Title 26, Subtitle F, Chapter 79, Section 7701 Definitions, subparagraph a, item 14, we find: *"The term "taxpayer" means any person* **subject to** *any internal revenue tax."*

If you notice from the contents outline above, Subtitle F is entitled "Procedure and Administration". So why don't they have the definition for taxpayer under the obvious chapter of "Income Tax?" Hmmmm! Believe me; it does not get any better as we progress.

Now we know that some people are "subject to" internal revenue tax, which means some people are not "subject to" internal revenue tax. We determined earlier that the 16th Amendment did not authorize a direct tax on property, in particular, your income. We also have determined that unless you were involved in one of the activities that made you "liable for" a tax, then you would not be subject to that tax.

The next question you should ask is, how do you make yourself subject to the internal revenue code? How many times have you been asked for your Social Security Number (SSN), and you just give it out? Only taxpayers use SSN's. When you signed on with your employer and he asked you to fill out a W-4, and you filled it out and signed it (under penalty of perjury) stating that you are indeed a taxpayer. Why should the government think you are anything but a taxpayer, subject to all the benefits, privileges, laws, and enforcement of the internal revenue code?

It is my personal belief that many, if not most of the IRS investigators and leadership, have a thorough understanding of the law and know that it is unconstitutional and misapplied. By using force upon unsuspecting citizens, using unconstitutional and illegal methods to force compliance, knowing its illegality, the IRS is guilty of extortion and racketeering. It is no different than if they were the mob. At least the mob does not try to make itself look legitimate.

It is by our own actions, and by the actions of those with whom we do business, that we announce ourselves to be taxpayers. Honestly, most people just are ignorant of the truth, and have been taught their entire lives that all

Americans are taxpayers. It is only when we remove ourselves, through enlightenment and purposeful action, that we can declare that we are not taxpayers. As you will see this is easier said than done, and not everyone has the resolve to accomplish this, especially in today's society.

Let's go back to the employer who asks you to submit a Social Security Number and fill out a W-4 (backup withholding form) during your hiring process. Remember, all tax codes operate on the presumption that whatever is being done is taxable because the tax code does not deal with the non-taxable. When looking at the IRS code, you will not see code that states person X or person Y are not required to file (or be taxed), that is beyond their scope. With this in mind, if the employer gives you a W-4 and you fill it out and sign it; you're telling the employer that you are a taxpayer, because only taxpayers fill out these forms. The employer cannot determine your tax status because that would be against the law. He can only request your status; and to be honest, most people do not know their correct status, and thus they claim themselves to be taxpayers. It should be noted that there is no law requiring an employer to demand a Social Security Number from a prospective employee, prior to employment.

26 CFR 301.6109-1(c)—*If the person making the return* **[employer information returns]** *does not know the taxpayer identifying number of the other person, such person must request the other person's number. A request should state that the identifying number is required to be furnished under authority of law. When the person making the return, statement, or other document does not know the number of the other person, and has complied with the request provision of this paragraph, such person must sign an affidavit on the transmittal document forwarding such returns, statements, or other documents to the Internal Revenue Service, so stating.* (Bold added]

There is no place in the preceding code where it demands your Social Security Number, it only requests one. If the employer does not receive a number from you, all he does is submit an affidavit stating so. There is no prerequisite to provide a Social Security Number before being hired. It is not a mistake in the language of the code section above when it only 'requests' a number. The problem is that giving out our Social Security Number has become so common that many employers do not understand what the law actually says. What is even worse is that there are employers who ***do*** know; and they still will not obey the law. I believe they are complicit in robbery and extortion, nothing less.

I also want to point out that there is no regulation that allows for the firing, or the refusal to hire someone based on the refusal to provide a taxpayer identification number. However, there are exceptions to this, for instance, when dealing with jobs which make one liable for taxes (as we have mentioned above), or if you're a government employee. We'll delve deeper into this a little later.

Did you know that having monies withheld from your pay is voluntary, and is established because YOU desired to do so? Let's take a look at what the IRS states in its own regulations:

> *26 CFR 31.3402(p)–1 "Voluntary withholding agreements. (a) In general. An employee and his employer* ***may*** *enter into an agreement under section 3402(b) to provide for the withholding of income tax..."* (The operative word here is **may** enter into an agreement, not must enter into an agreement. An agreement is something both parties agree to do.)
>
> 26 CFR 31.3402(p)–1 "Voluntary withholding agreements. (b), (ii) In the case of **an employee who desires to enter into an agreement** under section 3402(p) with his employer, if the employee performs services (in addition to those to be the subject of the agreement) the remuneration for which is subject to mandatory income tax withholding by such employer, **or if the employee wishes to specify that the agreement terminate on a specific date,** the employee shall furnish the employer with a request for withholding which shall be signed by the employee, and shall contain—
>
> > (a) The name, address, and social security number of the employee making the request,
> >
> > (b) The name and address of the employer,
> >
> > (c) A statement that the employee desires withholding of Federal income tax, and applicable, of qualified State individual income tax (see paragraph (d)(3)(i) of § 301.6361–1 of this chapter (Regulations on Procedures and Administration)), and
> >
> > (d) **If the employee desires that the agreement terminate** on a specific date, the date of termination of the agreement.
>
> (Notice the bold items above all deal with an employee who desires or wishes to enter into an agreement. Also notice the ability of an employee to terminate any such agreement simply by notifying the employer of the specific date of termination.)

> ***26 CFR 31.3402(p)–1 "Voluntary withholding agreements.*** *(2) An agreement under section 3402 (p) shall be effective for such period as the* ***employer and employee mutually agree upon.*** *However,* ***either the employer or the employee may terminate the agreement*** *prior to the end of such period by furnishing a signed written notice to the other.* (Here again we see the volunteer nature withholding is supposed to have. An agreement that is mutually agreed upon can only be so if BOTH parties agree. If one of the two parties does not agree, then there is no agreement. All that is required to terminate the agreement is a signed notice to the other party.)

Here's the way I see it. If you honestly believe that the money you are going to be receiving in exchange for your time and talents is not subject to a taxing authority, then you should not provide a number. By providing a number, you are telling the employer and the taxing authority, under good faith belief, that you **are liable to** the taxing authority.

An interesting observation here is that nowhere in the "income tax" code will you find a definition for "income". There is "gross income", "adjusted income", "adjusted gross income", "taxable income", "non-taxable income", "ordinary income", and "community income"; but nowhere will you find the definition for just plain income. That is because it has already been settled by the courts and the constitution, as stated above.

Another question to ask yourself is, "Do you get paid wages?" The IRS code is very specific about wages. It says: *"For purposes of this chapter, the term "wages" means all remuneration (other than fees paid to a public official)* ***for services performed by an employee for his employer****, including the cash value of all remuneration (including benefits) paid in any medium other than cash; except that such term shall not include remuneration paid—."* (TITLE 26 Subtitle C CHAPTER 24 § 3401 Definitions) Did you notice the bold in the middle of the sentence you just read? When you first read this, it sounds pretty convincing. Maybe I do earn wages?

Also notice, the wages spoken about are only for "service performed by an employee". What do they mean by "employee"? Just a little further down the page, in the same section, 3401, we find the definition for Employee, which says: *"For purposes of this chapter, the term "****employee****" includes an officer, employee, or elected official of the United States, a State, or any political subdivision thereof, or the District of Columbia, or any agency or instrumentality of any one or more of the foregoing. The term "employee"* *also includes an officer of a corporation."* Does this description fit you and your job?

To cover our bases, let's take a look at what an employer is. *"For purposes of this chapter, the term "employer" means the person for whom an individual performs or performed any service, of whatever nature, as the employee of such person, except that—*

> ***(1)*** *if the person for whom the individual performs or performed the services does not have control of the payment of the wages for such services, the term "employer" (except for purposes of subsection (a)) means the person having control of the payment of such wages, and*
>
> ***(2)*** *in the case of a person paying wages on behalf of a nonresident alien individual, foreign partnership, or foreign corporation, not engaged in trade or business within the United States, the term "employer" (except for purposes of subsection (a)) means such person."* ***(Subsection (a) is the section on wages from above)***

I want to point out two things: First, is that the government can give any word or phrase in its code a definition. An example would be the word "person." Most of us are probably pretty sure what the word "person" means; and we definitely know when we see one. A person is a flesh and blood personage like we meet on the street. In the IRS code, however, a person can also be an individual, a trust, an estate, a partnership, an association, a company, or a corporation. I don't know about you, but I haven't seen too many corporations or estates at the dinner table. Secondly, we cannot take anything for granted. We must always check the meaning of each and every word used.

Now we know that we don't have 16th Amendment income, we don't earn wages, and we are not employees. We earn a living by exchanging property, or our time and talent, for equal property, money or other item of value. For instance, if you made a footstool and your neighbor liked it, and he offered you $100 dollars for your footstool. You think that's a fair trade for your time and talents, and you make the trade. Where is the gain or income? There is essentially no difference between this and agreeing to trade your time and talents with a company in your town. It is an exchange of property for an agreed upon value. The company wants your time and talents; and you, in "exchange," agree to receive a sufficient monetary amount, as an equitable trade.

The constitution, corroborated by the Supreme Court, guarantees that a persons' "unalienable rights" cannot be violated or infringed upon, with the exception of a tax on property that is direct and apportioned among the many states. One of the greatest rights we have is the ability to contract for our labor. Our labor is our property; and as of this writing' Congress has not imposed a direct tax on our labor, nor would it be constitutional. Article I, Section 10 of the Constitution states: *"No State shall pass any law impairing the obligation of contracts."* In my opinion, taxing the contract of labor is a definite impairment.

If you think it is just us old folk sitting around the kitchen table who are concerned with the overstepping of taxation, read what Congressman Ron Paul (Texas) said: *"Strictly speaking, it probably is not necessary for the federal government to tax anyone directly—it could simply print the money it needs. However, that would be too bold a stroke, for it would then be obvious to all what kind of counterfeiting operation the government is running. The present system combining taxation and inflation is akin to watering the milk: too much water and the people catch on."*

Congressional house records do not carry the weight of law, but they are useful to establish legal finding in respect to a congressional position. House Congressional Record from March 27, 1943, pages 2579-2580 states: *"The income tax is, therefore,* ***not a tax on income*** *as such.* ***It is an excise tax*** *with respect to certain activities and privileges which is measured by reference to the income which they produce. The income is not the subject of the tax: it is the basis for determining the amount of tax."* (Written by F. Morse Hubbard, former legislative draftsman in the Treasury Department).

If income is not the tax, but only the basis for determining the amount of tax, and it is an excise tax, which is synonymous with a privilege tax, what then is the privilege that is being taxed? Is it a privilege now to have a job and earn a living? Is this a breathing tax for the privilege of being alive? Or maybe it's a citizen tax for the privilege of just being an American.

The Second Plank of the Communist Manifesto, written by Karl Marx and Frederick Engels, states: "A *heavy progressive or graduated income tax."* It seems the farther we move away from the enlightened guidance of our founders, the closer we get to a new world order where the masses are controlled by the elite few. They called America the *New World*, a world of hope and freedom. From that freedom will we announce to the world a "New World" Order where none will dare to make afraid or oppress the weak, to be controlled by the elite who will ensure peace upon all the land.

This is not some fairy tale mutterings, but a theme that has been building its' mantra stronger with each passing year. From the late 1800's and early 1900's with the stealing of Americas treasure, the forcing of worthless paper currency upon the world, to the financial enslavement of its people paying over 1/3rd of their wages to the government; to the announcement by George H.W. Busch in 1991: *"Now, we can see a new world coming into view. A world in which there is **the very real prospect of a new world order.** In the words of Winston Churchill, a "world order" in which "the principles of justice and fair play ... protect the weak against the strong ..." **A world where the United Nations, freed from cold war stalemate, is poised to fulfill the historic vision of its founders.** A world in which freedom and respect for human rights find a home among all nations."* Like father like son! It is G.W. Bush's plan to bring the Middle East into the central banking scheme, which is governed by international law, owing no allegiance to any nation, to bring the force of the world armies to enforce the New World Order!

I would like to make note of the, apparent, confusion within the law, as it pertains to taxation. The ruling comes from the Supreme Court case of GOULD v. GOULD, 245 U.S. 151 (1917), in which the court ruled: *"In the interpretation of statutes levying taxes it is the established rule not to extend their provisions by implication beyond the clear import of the language used, or to enlarge their operation so as to embrace matters not specifically pointed out. **In case of doubt, they are construed most strongly against the government and in favor of the citizen.**"*

In practice this decision is followed a lot less that it should be; but in all fairness, I don't know how many cases actually cite this as part of their taxation defense. If the language is confusing, and beyond the clear import of the text, the courts are to rule in favor of the citizen over the government. This does not happen often. In fact, there is a case where the judge would not allow "law" to be argued in front of the jury, and where the jury was told by the judge, and that he would tell the jury what the law is and no one else. Obviously the defendant was convicted, for how can you argue a case based in law if you cannot argue the law? The point made here is that the court system is part of the government system, ruling on a government position. There is bias, and it may not be blind justice.

Another item people find confusing is the SS-FICA line on their pay stub. If you asked 100 people to explain FICA, 99 would probably say this is their social security deduction. They would all be right—But wrong. It is "entitled" FICA, or Social Security. But remember what we said above, the government can define anything they want. In fact, what you will learn next is that it is just more "income tax." Just like before, they use the same definitions we have just discussed; but as with the other "so called" income taxes, they overstep and misapply those taxes to everyone. What makes this even more egregious is that the IRS gets private companies to do their evil bidding for them.

As we mentioned earlier in the book, next to income tax, social security, is probably the second biggest RICO scheme ever perpetrated on the American citizen. The Social Security Act was enacted by FDR as another of the New Deal reconstruction acts under title 42 Health and Welfare, Chapter 7, Social Security. However, there are no provisions within title 42 for the collections of monies to fund Social Security. Instead you have to go to Title 26, Chapter 21, subtitle C: Federal Insurance Contributions Act or FICA.

We will first look at the code that imposes this tax, referring to the above, Subtitle C, Section 3101(a) states: *"Old-age, survivors, and disability insurance: In addition to other taxes, there is hereby* ***imposed on the income*** *of every individual* ***a tax equal to the following percentages of the wages*** *(as defined in section 3121 (a)) received by him with respect to employment (as defined in section 3121 (b)"* (Bold Added)

A common misconception is that FICA tax is a savings program; it is not. As the wording above clearly shows, FICA is just another income tax that uses wages as its basis. This is very important, as it relates to how the money can be used. Many people I have talked to believe that FICA taxes are assigned to an account, and all the money paid into it during our working life is what funds our Social Security payments when we retire. As we shall see this is completely false.

Another popular delusion is that we have a contractual arrangement between ourselves and the government concerning FICA. It is NOT a contract, but a "political" promise which Congress could renege on at any time. Monies disbursed by the Social Security Administration must be appropriated each year as needed. Since there is no contractual obligation and therefore no mandate, other than the fact that there would be 300 million pissed off citizens, and congresses own greed for power. The impact, however, is that Congress is required to appropriate funds each and every year to pay for Social Security from the general coffers.

FICA states that it is based on a percentage of "wages" earned. If wages are the basis of the tax, then how does the IRS define wages? Section 3121 defines wages as: *"For purposes of this chapter,* ***the term "wages" means all***

***remuneration for employment**, including the cash value of all remuneration (including benefits) paid in any medium other than cash; except that such term shall not include...* " Therefore, wages are remuneration for the activity called employment.

How does Section 3121 define employment? It states: *"For purposes of this chapter, the term "employment" means any service, of whatever nature, performed*

> ***(A) by an employee** for the person employing him, irrespective of the citizenship or residence of either,*
> ***(i)** within the United States, or*
> ***(ii)** on or in connection with an American vessel or American aircraft under a contract of service which is entered into within the United States or during the performance of which and while the employee is employed on the vessel or aircraft it touches at a port in the United States, if the employee is employed on and in connection with such vessel or aircraft when outside the United States..."*

We have wages earned by an employee within the United States. First, remember, congress can define the words used within its code to mean whatever they want it to mean as long as they specifically define its meaning. Secondly, the Supreme Court, in Gould V Gould, cited above says, "*not to extend their provisions by implication beyond the clear import of the language used.*" Wages means only what it says it means, and by implication it cannot mean anything else. The term employee was not redefined for this section so the original definition we cited earlier still stands.

How does Section 3121 define the term United States? Surprisingly, most of us would think of it as the collection of member states of the union; but the Internal Revenue Code for this section says it means: *"The term 'United States' when used in a geographical sense includes the Commonwealth of Puerto Rico, the Virgin Islands, Guam, and American Samoa."* It can only mean what it is defined to mean, and nothing else.

You might be thinking that this definition is only meant to "include" these other areas within the commonly used term "United States". However, law is very precise, and it cannot function under conjecture. To support my view on this is Code section 4612, which defines the term United States as it relates to a tax on crude oil, as: *"the FIFTY STATES, the District of Columbia, the Commonwealth of Puerto Rico, any possession of the United States, the Commonwealth of the Northern Mariana Islands and the trust territory of the*

Pacific Islands." As you can see, when Congress means to include the "Fifty States," they expressly do.

Remember in our discussion of the Constitution; that the federal government was limited to its' possessions. The Internal Revenue Code, in section 7655, cross references the term "United States", in respect to both the self-employment tax imposed in chapter 2 of the Internal Revenue Code, as well as the FICA tax imposed in chapter 21, as:

> ***(a) Imposition of tax in possessions***
>
> *For provisions imposing tax in possessions, see—*
>
> ***(1)** Chapter 2, relating to self-employment tax;*
>
> ***(2)** Chapter 21, relating to the tax under the Federal Insurance Contributions Act.*

So, we can see here that the code associates the term of "United States" as the possessions; meaning the federal possessions. In the areas identified as federal possessions the U.S. Government has complete legislative control and can directly tax its' people. With this in mind it makes perfect sense that the federal government would identify the tax for its possessions to include the self-employment and FICA taxes, as these are the persons to whom the tax is imposed.

The FICA code places the tax directly on the employee. It is a direct tax, but it is not unconstitutional, as it is written. My contention is the unconstitutional enforcement of FICA tax on those to whom it does not apply. Remember, the Federal government has unlimited scope and power when it comes to Washington D.C. and its' territories, and it can apply taxes directly to those who derive the privilege of working there. However, that is the extent of their defined power. Their usurped power, on the other hand, seems to be boundless—unless we stop it.

I mentioned earlier, that Congress can give a word whatever meaning they want it to have.

Occasionally a term will have limitations applied to it such as "for the purposes of this Chapter" or "for the purposes of this section." However, there are other definitions which have no limitations made; and therefore, none can be granted. Any term so defined "must" have the same meaning when used elsewhere in the code.

Title 26, Subtitle C, Chapter 24 entitled "*Collection Of Income Tax At Source On Wages*," Section 3401, (Definitions), gives definitions to a broad range of terms. The terms **employee** and **employer** have been used throughout the chapter; and like many other words and terms used, the

Internal Revenue Code provides a specific meaning, which may not be the same as the traditional or commonly used meanings.

In this section, (3401), the term **employee** has been defined as: *"**Employee**—For purposes of this chapter, the term "employee" includes an officer, employee, or elected official of the United States, a State, or any political subdivision thereof, or the District of Columbia, or any agency or instrumentality of any one or more of the foregoing. The term "employee" also includes an officer of a corporation."* According to this definition, are you an "**employee**"? Not many people are.

Within the IRS code the words **includes** or **including** have been used. Some within the government may state that this is an "enhancing phrase" which adds to the meaning of the word or phrase to which it applies. The Supreme Court has also ruled, in Montello Salt Co. v. Utah, 221 U.S. 452 (1911), that this **is not** the case, and it states that the term adds limitations to that which is identified. Therefore, the word **employee** can not have any other definition than the one just mentioned.

In the very next paragraph the word **employer** is again defined as: *"For purposes of this chapter, the term "employer" means the person for whom an individual performs or performed any service, of whatever nature, as the employee of such person..."* Notice how the code identifies the employee as a government worker, but its description of the employer is obfuscated by stating the employer is one for whom the employee works. This means that the meaning of the term **employer** is limited to those entities described in the **employee** definition. Therefore, the term **employer** does not apply to any non-government employer outside of the federal "possessions", over which Congress has direct authority.

Now, based on these two definitions alone, most workers within the states of the union are not subject to the withholding provisions of this chapter.

And as we discussed earlier; the definitions of **employee** and **wages**, this section is limited to activities of the possessions of the federal government and not to the 50 states in general.

We have determined, thus far, that wages are income earned in one of the possessions of the federal, and that the employee/employer relationship is that of government employee and government; but sneaky lawyers thought of a catch-all for those who don't fall into the *word trap* by adding Section 3402, paragraph (p), **"**Voluntary withholding agreements", sub paragraph 3, entitled "Authority for other voluntary withholding". The pertinent items read: *"The Secretary is authorized by regulations to provide for withholding—*

> ***(A)*** *from remuneration for services performed by an employee for the employee's employer which (without regard to this paragraph) does not constitute wages, and*
>
> ***(B)*** *from any other type of payment with respect to which the Secretary finds that withholding would be appropriate under the provisions of this chapter,* ***if the employer and employee, or the person making and the person receiving such other type of payment, agree to such withholding****. Such agreement shall be in such form and manner as the Secretary may by regulations prescribe..."*

Many are under the mistaken belief that the deduction and withholding of money for taxes is required by law. Reading the code plainly shows this to be untrue. The Fifth Amendment states that no person shall be deprived of property, such as having pay withheld, without due process of law—meaning a court ruling.

Where does the corporation that you work for get its' authorization to withhold money from you? It gets its' authorization from the Federal Regulations and from you. Federal Regulation Number 31.3402(p)-1 entitled "Voluntary withholding agreements" reads:

> *"(a) In general.* ***An employee and his employer may enter into an agreement*** *under section 3402(b) to provide for the withholding of income tax upon payments of amounts described in paragraph (b)(1) of §31.3401(a)–3, made after December 31, 1970.* ***An agreement*** *may be entered into under this section only with respect to amounts which are includible in the gross income of the employee under section 61, and must be applicable to all such amounts paid by the employer to the employee. The amount to be withheld* ***pursuant to an agreement*** *under section 3402(p) shall be determined under the rules contained in section 3402 and the regulations thereunder. See §31.3405(c)–1, Q&A–3 concerning agreements to have more than 20-percent Federal income tax withheld from eligible rollover distributions within the meaning of section 402.*
>
> *(b) Form and duration of agreement. (1)(i) Except as provided in subdivision (ii) of this subparagraph, an* ***employee who desires*** *to enter into an agreement under section 3402(p)* ***shall furnish his employer with Form W–4*** *(withholding exemption certificate) executed in accordance with the provisions of section*

3402(f) and the regulations thereunder. The ***furnishing of such Form W–4 shall constitute a request*** *for withholding.*

(ii) In the case of an ***employee who desires*** *to enter into an agreement under section 3402(p) with his employer, if the employee performs services (in addition to those to be the subject of the agreement) the remuneration for which is subject to mandatory income tax withholding by such employer, o****r if the employee wishes to specify that the agreement terminate on a specific date, the employee shall furnish the employer with a request for withholding which shall be signed by the employee,*** *and shall contain—*

- *(a) The name, address, and social security number of the employee making the request,*
- *(b) The name and address of the employer,*
- *(c) A statement that the employee desires withholding of Federal income tax, and applicable, of qualified State individual income tax (see paragraph (d)(3)(i) of §301.6361–1 of this chapter (Regulations on Procedures and Administration)), and*
- *(d) If the* ***employee desires*** *that the agreement terminate on a specific date, the date of termination of the agreement.*

If accepted by the employer as provided in subdivision (iii) of this subparagraph, the request shall be attached to, and constitute part of, the employee's Form W–4. An ***employee who furnishes his employer a request*** *for withholding under this subdivision shall also furnish such employer with Form W–4 if such employee does not already have a Form W–4 in effect with such employer.*

(iii) No request for withholding under section 3402(p) shall be effective as ***an agreement between an employer and an employee*** *until the employer accepts the request by commencing to withhold from the amounts with respect to which the request was made."*

Whew! Did you notice how throughout this entire section there were **no** demands, directives, or requirements, but only requests, and desires that you enter into the agreement. Also it provides for the ability to terminate such withholdings simply by a request from the employee. If the law required the withholding of tax from your pay, no permission or request form would be needed!

What have we learned about the income tax?

1. The income tax acts prior to the 16th Amendment were repealed as unconstitutional because they were not apportioned among the many states of the union.
2. The 16th Amendment was passed to correct an area of *corporate* taxation
3. The income referenced in the 16th Amendment means, and has always meant, income from doing business
4. The Supreme Court ruled the 16th Amendment added no new power of taxation to Congress, and the requirements to abide by apportionment for direct taxes were still valid.
5. That the majority of workers in America today do not fall under the definition of a taxpayer and they owe no taxes on their labor.
6. Income is property, labor is property; and neither can be legally taken from you without due process, as guaranteed by the 5th Amendment
7. The IRS routinely takes the property of citizens in violation of the due process clause.
8. There is a probability that the 16th Amendment was never ratified.
9. Social Security is voluntary, and most people are coerced into participating out of fear of losing their jobs or freedom.
10. FICA tax is not a tax on wages but is another form of income tax.
11. That there is no "Social Security account" holding the monies withheld from you
12. FICA taxes are withheld and placed into the general fund, and they are used as the government sees fit.
13. There is no contract with the government that insures they will have to pay you any Social Security, should they so decide.

Commenting on the complexity of the Income Tax Act during the house debates in 1913, Senator Elihu Root stated: *"I guess you will have to go to jail. If that is the result of not understanding the Income Tax Law I shall meet you there. We shall have a merry, merry time, for all of our friends will be there. It will be an intellectual center, for no one understands the Income Tax Law except persons who have not sufficient intelligence to understand the questions that arise under it."* This was spoken before the very first income tax act was passed and it has gotten ten times more complicated since then.

IRS Intelligence Activities

The next section, though not directly related to income tax, shows the depth of unconstitutional behavior and treachery that is inherent in our government. This information comes directly from hearings before the Select Committee to Study Governmental Operations with Respect to Intelligence Activities of the United States Senate, dated April 26, 1976.

The opening paragraph reads:

> *"The **Internal Revenue Service functions as an intelligence agency** in two respects. First, through its Intelligence Division, it both collects general intelligence about possible tax violators and investigates specific allegations of tax fraud to secure evidence for criminal prosecution. Second, the IRS accumulates vast amounts of information about the financial and personal affairs of American citizens from the **tax returns and supporting information which Americans voluntarily submit each year**. As a rich deposit of intelligence and an effective intelligence gatherer, the IRS is a powerful tool which other agencies of government, including Congress and the executive branch, have periodically sought to employ **for purposes other than tax law enforcement**. This report is primarily an exploration of the reasons these **uses of the IRS have led to serious and illegal abuse of IRS investigative powers and to a compromise of the privacy and integrity of the tax return**."* (Bold Added)

Not only do they admit to being an intelligence collector, but they admit that returns submitted are voluntary. Isn't that interesting? The tax form has a signature block at the bottom that says you are signing the form under penalty of perjury; and when you look this up in the instructions, it tells you that your information could be used by law enforcement against you. Here it also says that it can be used for purposes *other* than law enforcement.

Were you ever so advised? Under the law, when submitting official documents, they must reveal EVERYTHING to you they will be using your information for. Providing information to federal agencies to spy on Americans is unconstitutional, and breaks a myriad of laws.

The Select Committee study ends the opening statement saying they are investigating serious and illegal abuse of IRS investigative powers. There's a shock! But the real question is why the American public has never heard of the testimony? You would think this would be big news to every taxpayer and business in America.

The report goes on to discuss the size of the intelligence division of the IRS, and the number of armed agents. Why an intelligence division would require arms against its' own people is interesting in and of itself, and it places into context how the government views its' own citizens. We are the enemy! Because of this intelligence capability, agencies within the government including Congress, the FBI, and even the White House, has sought to direct the efforts of the IRS against groups and individuals.

The report continues stating: *"The use of IRS intelligence collection capability to achieve desirable* ***non-tax objectives*** *has resulted in* ***loss of control over investigative techniques****, and a loss of the capacity to limit the scope and nature of information gathered to that which is related to tax enforcement.* ***Operation Leprechaun****, for example, was an effort to employ IRS investigative power to combat political corruption. The operation* ***led to the collection of details on the personal and sexual lives of certain Florida political figures*** *and to illegal acts on the part of IRS informants."* (Bold added) It makes you feel all warm and fuzzy knowing the government is there to help, doesn't it?

Further problems were highlighted as follow:

> *"The use of the IRS for non-tax purposes requires "unbalanced enforcement," where the target group is selected for reasons other than the significance of the tax compliance problem it presents.* ***Unbalanced tax enforcement has given rise to a combination of elements which have produced abuse:***
>
> *(1) the subordination of tax criteria to achieve a concentration of enforcement resources* ***creates an atmosphere within the IRS which encourages excessive zeal*** *and departure from other normal criteria of IRS operation;*
>
> *(2) the pursuit of* ***non-tax objectives through selective tax enforcement*** *by the IRS Intelligence Division has historically involved the use of techniques such as paid informants, electronic surveillance, and undercover agents, all of which are* ***prone to abuse****;*
>
> *(3) because the IRS decentralized organizational structure is designed to achieve tax objectives and is, by design, resistant to pressure from above, in order to bring about the desired imbalance in the enforcement program, the*

IRS has generally found it necessary to ***bypass its normal organizational structure;***

(4) in doing so, the IRS has ***bypassed the normal administrative mechanisms which check excess and abuse at the lower levels"***

We have an entire division of the IRS with extreme powers to affect the individual citizen who have no oversight, who are performing non-tax objectives, and who are outside the normal organizational structure. Now remember, as with any other criminal activity, only a very small percentage of are ever caught. If we are seeing this type of admitted activity, the "actual" depth must be much greater.

One line that demands separate focus is the following: *"Both the FBI and the CIA have had virtually unrestricted access to any tax information they sought for any purpose."*

Those who have worked in the intelligence community will notice a couple glaring problems with this statement. First, and foremost, the CIA is a **foreign** intelligence service and it is unlawful for them to access data on US citizens without express oversight consent and it must be documented. Secondly, for anyone outside the IRS or for use other than that which is tax related, access must be done under the rules of due process requiring a warrant. According to this statement, the information was available for "any purpose." This is egregious!

The report found that the IRS, itself, had glaring problems: *"The most important facts the staff found were:*

(1) The IRS has not required either the CIA or the FBI to state the specific purpose for which it needed tax return information.

(2) In the absence of such a specific statement, the ***IRS could not judge whether the request met the regulatory criteria for release*** *of the information. In effect, IRS had delegated the determination of the propriety of the request to the requesting agency.*

(3) Further, in the absence of a statement of the specific, reason the tax return is needed, there is ***no basis upon which to limit the subsequent use of the return*** *to the purpose for which it was initially released.*

(4) As a result of these weaknesses in the disclosure mechanism, the ***FBI has had free access to tax informatio****n for improper purposes. The FBI obtained tax returns, for example, in an effort*

> *to disrupt the lives of targets of its COINTELPRO operations, by causing tax audits. The* ***FBI used as a weapon against the taxpayer the very information the taxpayer provided pursuant to his legal obligation to assist in tax collection*** *and, in many cases,* ***on the assumption that access to the information would be restricted to those concerned with revenue collection and used only for tax purposes.*** *"*

The report goes on to detail the broad range of illegal activities the IRS used to collect information against citizens, to include:

1. "unlawful electronic surveillance by IRS agents"
2. "IRS efforts against "activism" and "ideological" organizations and individuals"
3. "reviewed the tax status of groups and individuals in the absence of specific evidence of tax violations"
4. "IRS Intelligence Division perceived a need to improve its' ability to gather and retrieve intelligence beyond the scope of investigations of specific allegations of tax fraud."
5. "no clear standard for deciding who should be investigated."
6. "CIA obtained tax return information on at least thirteen occasions through unofficial channels. There was no written authority for the informal disclosure of tax return information to the CIA, and, according to the IRS, there is no basis upon which any of the disclosures could be considered legal."

It is obvious to me that the U.S. government operates in a similar manner against its own citizens as it would against a foreign enemy. It utilizes the same networks and processes as it would for prosecuting a war effort. It is of little wonder that we have such a divide between the political machinery and the people from who so much has been taken.

The way the IRS enacts illegal levies further shows the level of obfuscation and in some cases outright deceit they use to bilk the citizens of their funds. When a notice of deficiency is sent to a "taxpayer," and no response is received within the allotted 10 days, the IRS may send out a Notice of Levy (form 668-W) to banks or employers to initiate withholding of funds. These funds are then transferred to the IRS.

At this point, the IRS has not gone to a court and has bypassed the due process of law; but they have still taken your money. The instructions on the back of the Notice of Levy states the authority and duties to be performed are: (US Code, Title 26, Subtitle F, CHAPTER 64, Subchapter D, PART II)

Sec. 6331. LEVY AND DISTRAINT.

"(b) ***Seizure and Sale of Property.****–The term "levy" as used in this title includes the power of distraint and seizure by any means. Except as otherwise provided in subsection (e), a levy shall extend only to property possessed and obligations existing at the time thereof. In any case in which the Secretary may levy upon property or rights to property, he may seize and sell such property or rights to property (whether real or personal, tangible or intangible)."*

"(c) ***Successive Seizures.****–Whenever any property or right to property upon which levy has been made by virtue of subsection (a) is not sufficient to satisfy the claim of the United States for which levy is made, the Secretary may, thereafter, and as often as may be necessary, proceed to levy in like manner upon any other property liable to levy of the person against whom such claim exists, until the amount due from him, together with all expenses, is fully paid."*

This may sound all well and good, and seems to be pretty forthright, except, the section starts with paragraph **(b)**. Why would they not start with paragraph (a)? If they did, they would not get anyone to honor the levy. Here is what paragraph (a) says: (Ibid)

(a) Authority of Secretary

"If any person liable to pay any tax neglects or refuses to pay the same within 10 days after notice and demand, it shall be lawful for the Secretary to collect such tax (and such further sum as shall be sufficient to cover the expenses of the levy) by levy upon all property and rights to property (except such property as is exempt under section 6334) belonging to such person or on which there is a lien provided in this chapter for the payment of such tax. ***Levy may be made upon the accrued salary or wages of any officer, employee, or elected official, of the United States, the District of Columbia, or any agency or instrumentality of the United States or the District of Columbia, by serving a notice of levy on the employer (as defined in section 3401(d)) of such officer, employee, or elected official.*** *If the Secretary makes a finding that the collection of such tax is in jeopardy, notice and demand for immediate payment of such tax may be made by the Secretary and, upon*

> *failure or refusal to pay such tax, collection thereof by levy shall be lawful without regard to the 10-day period provided in this section."*(Bold added)

The opening statement puts fear into the reader when it says "any person liable to pay any tax." You might automatically think, "Hey I'm a person." However when you read the explanation further, where they define whom and what may be levied, it says: "***any officer, employee, or elected official, of the United States, the District of Columbia, or any agency or instrumentality of the United States or the District of Columbia".*** Well now, isn't that special! They just forgot to include that on the instruction sheet. I think that might be some pretty welcome information to know. So why do you think they omitted that from the form? I'll give you a hint, so they can more easily steal your money!

The issue throughout this chapter has not been that Congress does not have the power to tax. The Constitution clearly provides that Congress does have such power. It is not that the laws are unconstitutional, but only the misapplication of the laws against Citizens who are not liable for those taxes. It is egregious that a government that has shown, by it's own documents and reports, that it knows that the majority of Americans are not liable for this tax, and yet continues to support the misapplication of those laws. This is nothing short of criminal.

Chapter 8
War Powers

When the Constitution was drafted and ratified there was only one body of the federal government that had the power to declare war—Congress. That power was delineated in Article 1, Section VIII, and provides that Congress shall have power:

> "***To*** *declare War, grant Letters of Marque and Reprisal, and make Rules concerning Captures on Land and Water;*
> **To** raise and support Armies, but no Appropriation of Money to that Use shall be for a longer Term than two Years;
> **To** provide and maintain a Navy;
> **To** make Rules for the Government and Regulation of the land and naval Forces;
> **To** provide for calling forth the Militia to execute the Laws of the Union, suppress Insurrections and repel Invasions;
> ***To*** *provide for organizing, arming, and disciplining, the Militia, and for governing such Part of them as may be employed in the Service of the United States, reserving to the States respectively, the Appointment of the Officers, and the Authority of training the Militia according to the discipline prescribed by Congress;*"

As with all other duties and responsibilities of the Congress, these responsibilities cannot be traded, given away, ignored, delegated, or otherwise done away with. Items within the Constitution are designed to ensure a balance of power that protects our nation from despotic, power-hungry men who would use their positions as a means to advance their own selfish agendas. So when the Constitution says, the "*Congress shall have power to …*," then that is exactly what it means. Nowhere does it say that Congress can give away any power as it sees fit. It is a matter of responsibility to the nation, and more importantly a responsibility to you and me, and when they fail or give away power they fail us and the nation. It is the responsibility of the people of this nation to hold our leaders to those responsibilities; and if necessary, we should rise up and take back a government that has failed its' responsibility, **by whatever means necessary**.

During this chapter we will look at what the Constitution says about war powers for both the President and Congress. We will touch on Title 50 of the U.S. Code, entitled "War and National Defense," as well as what the founding fathers envisioned for those who would have power to send our troops into harms way and place our nation into war. We will also look at how the Supreme Court has viewed this topic, and what their decisions mean for us as citizens.

Under Article I, section 8 of the Constitution, the Congress has the power to declare war, and to raise and support the armed forces. Under Article II, section 2, the President is to be the Commander in Chief of the armed forces. The Commander in Chief has the authority to repel attacks against the United States. Should Congress **declare war,** the president is authorized to direct the armed forces to initiate such a war. Nowhere in the Constitution does it grant the **President** the power to instigate a war or to perform "acts of war," against another nation, **without consent of Congress under a declaration of war**.

Over the veto of President Nixon, The War Powers Resolution was enacted in a 1973 response to what Congress felt was a predilection by prior Presidents to involve American forces in hostilities that may lead to war without congressional approval or declaration. The intent of the Resolution was to establish procedures for making decisions which might get the United States involved in war. Since the Korean War, Various Presidents, had involved the armed forces in hostilities abroad without a declaration of war or other congressional authorization. Congress wanted to reign in what it perceived to be an assumed power by the President.

Section 2 of the War Powers Resolution states its' purpose as: *"insure that the collective judgment of both the Congress and the President will apply to the introduction of United States Armed Forces into hostilities, or into situations where imminent involvement in hostilities is clearly indicated by the circumstances, and to the continued use of such forces in hostilities or in such situations."* However, in practice, the resolution has given the power to the President to place American troops into hostilities by merely "consulting" with Congress prior to sending troops. This is a far cry from the intent of the resolution, which is to receive Congressional authority prior to engagement.

Presidents have utilized the War Powers Resolution after "consulting" with congress, and then they have ordered troops into hostilities without congressional authorization.

The resolution also sets down the requirement for reporting to Congress prior to and during hostilities, and/or other key events, such as substantial increases in troop strength abroad. The stated objective for the reporting requirements was to *"ensure that the Congress by right and as a matter of law will be provided with all the information it requires to carry out its constitutional responsibilities with respect to committing the Nation to war and to the use of United States Armed Forces abroad."* Had Congress had the intestinal fortitude to do its' job, and to rein in presidents who abuse the power of their positions; this would not have been required. It does not state in the Constitution that the Congress has the power to declare war "with the permission of the President" or that the President need only consult the Congress prior to committing troops to acts of war. There is a reason for separating the consent to go to war from the command and control of the war machine. It was to prohibit a single person, the President, from acting unilaterally and committing acts of war without proper authority.

The Constitution gives the President and Congress specific roles in dealing with armed conflict. The President was given a defensive role to protect the nation from invasion and to lead the armed forces during times of war. Congress was given the authority to declare **when** we would become engaged in armed conflicts against other nations.

It appears that some presidents see Congress as merely the purse strings that restrain the President from leading the troops as Commander in Chief. Many have inferred that the mantle of Commander in Chief gives inherent powers to the President to lead the nation and troops as he sees fit. This would include using the troops to enforce foreign policy, a political police force if you will. This view of the presidential authority is in the least dangerous; and ultimately, *despotic*.

The resolution states that the Commander in Chief has specific and *limited* powers when it comes to introducing the forces into hostilities. It states: *"exercised only pursuant to (1) a declaration of war, (2) specific statutory authorization, or (3) a national emergency created by attack upon the United States, its territories or possessions, or its armed forces."* The executive branch, by decree, and executive orders, has responded by authorizing the President to use forces in a much broader definition than the Constitution allows, to include: rescuing American citizens abroad, rescuing foreign nationals, protecting U.S. Embassies, suppressing civil insurrection, or any other of a myriad of agreements, treaties, or security commitments involving the United States.

A requirement of the War Powers resolution requires the President to report to Congress, in writing, whenever he has activated the resolution. One of the most problematic provisions of the Resolution is the automatic withdrawal provision which requires the President to withdraw U.S. forces from hostilities within 60-90 days after his report is submitted, under section 4(a)(1). In the past, Presidents have been reluctant to submit a report, and thereby, start the clock on the removal of troops. In some cases, Presidents have not reported at all. This presented a larger, more far reaching problem than Congress realized. Since Congress provided that the President had independent authority to use armed forces in certain circumstances, on what basis can Congress seek to terminate such independent authority? Could it be by the mere passage of time? By congressional resolution to limit the executive, Congress, in effect, gave greater power and latitude to the President than he had before.

Another major contention with the War Powers Resolution is the use of American forces by the United Nations. Since the resolutions enactment, we have provided troops under the auspices of the UN to Kuwait, Iraq, Somalia, the former Yugoslavia/Bosnia, and Haiti. Under what circumstances should Congress approve U.S. troops to participate in UN actions?

There is a portion of the UN Charter that authorizes the President to negotiate with the UN Security Council: *"which shall be subject to the approval of the Congress by appropriate Act or joint resolution...."* Once these agreements have been concluded, there would be no further congressional authorization needed. However, no such agreement has yet to be finalized, and yet we still provide troops and supplies to conflicts without congressional provision. The War Powers Resolution does not speak specifically to the UN charter or regarding the provision of troops in its' actions; but it does speak to treaties. Section 8(a)(2) states that authority to introduce U.S. Armed Forces into hostilities shall not be inferred from any treaty unless it is implemented by legislation specifically authorizing the introduction. It is intended to constitute specific statutory authorization within the meaning of the resolution.

On October 16, 2002 the President signed into law the "Authorization for Use of Military Force against Iraq Resolution." In the Presidents' remarks concerning the passing of this resolution he stated: *"the United States speaks with one voice on the threat to international peace and security posed by Iraq." ... "Iraq will either comply with all U.N. resolutions, rid itself of weapons of mass destruction, and ... its' support for terrorists, or will be compelled to do so."* The President noted that: *"...my request for it did not, and my signing this resolution does not, constitute any change in the long-standing positions of the executive branch on either the* ***President's constitutional authority to use force to deter, prevent, or respond to aggression*** *or other threats to U.S. interests or on the constitutionality of the War Powers Resolution."*

Notice that this finely crafted verse does not limit the area where he President perceives this threat to be. The Constitution allows him to repel invasion, nothing more. Iraq did not invade, or support the invasion of the terrorists on September 11, 2001. Was Saddam an evil, despicable excuse of a man who did not deserve to breath? Sure! Does that give the President the power to invade another sovereign nation? No. Could the President have gone to Congress with the evidence that was presented to the UN in support of building a coalition and make a case for declaration of war against Iraq? Definitely! Would that have been the correct and constitutional way to go to war? Most emphatically, yes!

What did the founding fathers have to say on the separation of the war powers between the President and Congress?

In 1788, in the Federalist #69, Alexander Hamilton compared the war powers, stating: *"The President is to be commander-in-chief of the army and navy of the United States. . . . It would amount to nothing more than the supreme command and direction of the military and naval forces, as first General and Admiral of the Confederacy; while that of the British king extends to the declaring of war and the raising and regulating of fleets and armies,—all of which by the Constitution under consideration, would appertain to the legislature."* He went on to say: *"... 'The Congress shall have the power to declare war'; the plain meaning of which is,* ***that it is the peculiar and exclusive duty of Congress, when the nation is at peace, to change that state into a state of war****..."* The act of war is by nature, a declaration of war, and it was NEVER meant to be in the hands of one man, even if he be President.

In a letter to Thomas Jefferson in 1798, James Madison stated: *"The constitution supposes, what the History of all Governments demonstrates, that* ***the Executive is the branch of power most interested in war, and most prone to it. It has accordingly with studied care vested the question of war***

to the Legislature." Even the question of war is vested in the legislature. The wisdom to ensure that one man does not have the ability to thrust a nation into war has shown to be prophetic.

In a letter to Congress in 1805, Thomas Jefferson stated: *"Considering that Congress alone is constitutionally invested with the power of changing our condition from peace to war, I have thought it my duty to await their authority for using force in any degree which could be avoided."* Again, it is Congress who has the power to place the nation at war, not the President.

As early as 1793 George Washington said: *"The constitution vests the power of declaring war in Congress;* ***therefore no offensive expedition of importance can be undertaken until after they shall have deliberated upon the subject and authorized such a measure****."* Again, no OFFENSIVE action can be undertaken without the express authorization of Congress.

James Wilson (who helped frame and ratify the Constitution) said: *"This system will not hurry us into war; it is calculated to guard against it.* ***It will not be in the power of a single man,*** *or a single body of men, to involve us in such distress; for the important power of declaring war is vested in the legislature at large..."* Remember, the United States is a collection of *individual* states/governments united together. Congress, consisting of the House and the Senate, are those governments' representatives, and the consent of those states are required before subjecting their Citizens to war.

And even the Supreme Court in *United States* v. *Smith,* 27 Fed. Cas. 1192, no. 16,342 (C.C.D.N.Y. 1806), Supreme Court Justice William Paterson stated: **"...It is the exclusive province of congress to change a state of peace into a state of war**."

Since the passing of the War Powers Act, Congress has issued "authorizations for the use of force" instead of actually declaring war. This may be a result of the flower power days in the seventies, when this resolution was passed. We fell into a state of negative testosterone, where being a "man" (or having the guts to stand up and say what you actually believed) went to the wayside. Instead, we decided it was better to be "politically correct" or Heaven forbid we should act aggressively!

War is a very serious act, and it should not be gone into lightly or for transient reasons. Because of this, the Constitution gave Congress power to declare acts of war. The executive was given authority over homeland security, the defense of nation, and to repel invasion. Nothing more was granted unless it came by way of the legislature.

In my view, Congress needs to grow some intestinal fortitude and take back its' rightful position. It should tell the executive where "the bear does its thing." Today Congress spends twenty percent of its time worrying about the nation, and eighty percent worrying about retaining their jobs on the next voting cycle. If it were up to me, there would be term limits just like the executive branch.

I feel that all authorizations for the use of force or any other contrivance that deals with sending troops to conduct military operations, should be repealed. All this is covered in the Constitution. If it's an emergency to repel an invasion, a national disaster, or to save American lives, then the President can send in the Calvary. If it is anything else, he can go to Congress and get the authorization he needs.

Since the cold war, every major action of war has ended in dividing the nation. In my estimation, this is because we went in half assed by signing some resolution. If we are hell bent to take on another nation, then we should have the guts to openly declare war, if that is what we intend to do. Then there is no equivocation about why we are there and what our goals are; we become a United States, not a country of the President.

There are some in the patriot movement who believe the republic is lost. They believe nothing short of civil war will restore us to our rightful government. The more I see and learn, the more I may have to agree. In 1789, when discussing the power of the Congress to declare war, Thomas Jefferson said: *"...one effectual check to the dog of war, by transferring the power of letting him loose from the Executive to the Legislative body, from those who are to spend to those who are to pay."*

We have learned here that both the executive and the legislative bodies of our government are broken. The Congress has given away more and more of it's responsibilities until it is a shell, having only the color of law and no substance. The executive has usurped more and more power until it has become a despotic ruler at the expense of the American people, their rights and freedoms.

The executive was never meant to have the power to use military force offensively without the consent of Congress. The executive's military power was one of defensive protection of the nation; and to go on the offensive demands a declaration of Congress, for **all** offensive military actions against another nation are "acts of war".

Chapter 9
The Militia

Lately there has been much debate about the militia. What is it? What is its' purpose? How does it relate to the government (state and federal)? The complexity of this subject is based, in large part, on its' simplicity. Because the militia was so common, during the time when the Constitution was written, there was little reason to explain it. Every man, woman, and child knew what the militia was and what role it played in the communities of the early Americans.

I will first attempt to describe what the militia is and what it is not. Second, I will attempt to convey the importance to all Americans of the militia mentality, its lifestyle, and dedication to responsible citizenry. And lastly, I will attempt to convey what the militia should mean to every community and citizen in this nation, as it could mean the very salvation of our nation.

Contrary to popular 21st century belief, the militia is not a group of anti-government yahoos who are out on the back forty of uncle Jebs' farm shooting and playing army. No disrespect to uncle Jeb. In the early years of this nation, the militia was made up of every able-bodied man in the area. When cattle rustlers made off with part of the herd, a posse of militia was gathered from among the locals, and they set off to bring the scoundrels back. The sheriff could then present him to the judge, find them guilty, and "hang em."

When our nation was threatened by the British, the Continental Army could in no way resist the might of the Empire. It was the ordinary citizenry who gathered their own arms and responded to the call of the nation. They fought in every major battle, and many minor ones, all the way through the civil war. There were entire units made up of only militia "volunteers". The very essence of the militia is the community, for one is more apt to fight harder for his neighbor than for a stranger.

In the latter years of our government, the legislature has attempted to redefine the meaning of the term "militia" with indifference to how it was used in the Constitution. Title 10 of the United States Code, Chapter 13 entitled The Militia reads:

> *"(a) The militia of the United States consists of all able-bodied males at least 17 years of age and, except as provided in section 313 of title 32, under 45 years of age who are, or who have made a declaration of intention to become, citizens of the United States and of female citizens of the United States who are members of the National Guard."*
>
> *"(b) The Classes of the militia are –*
>
> 1. *the organized militia, which consists of the National Guard and the Naval Militia; and*
> 2. *the unorganized militia, which consists of the members of the militia who are not members of the National Guard or the Naval Militia."*

As we have seen previously, when reading government statutes, that what is being said is not what one would think, using standard definitions. In this case, the government starts off with *"The militia of the United States"*. Reading this one would be lead to believe they are speaking of the Second Amendment "militia"; this would be in error. The Constitution does not define the "militia of the United States", and the only true *Constitutional* Militia would be "the Militia of the several States". This militia can only be "employed in the service of the United States" or "called into the actual Service of the United States."

An important point to remember is that the Militia was not created by the Constitution. It was in place before the Constitution as the body of the nation—We the People of the United States. We the People established the Constitution to provide the framework and limitations on the new government. The Militia was part of the framework that dealt with law, order, and defense. During times of specific need the "Federal Government" could call up the Militia to defend the country, enforce it's laws, and to suppress rebellion. But make no mistake, it is not part of the "Federal Government", it is part of the establishing government, it is "We the People."

Regardless of bureaucratic meandering, the original militia is not associated with today's National Guard. The National Guard is an extension of the standing army of the United States, and it is considered a part of the national reserves. They are paid from federal coffers, they fall under federal military regulation, and they have missions that directly support full-time military operations. They are under the command of the Governor of the state for use as he sees fit until needed by the federal government. At that point, Congress orders the National Guard to active duty, and they no longer fall under the jurisdiction of the Governor. The Constitutional militia is something entirely different.

Some call this the difference between organized (reserves) and unorganized (militias). I say that we cannot go back in time and change the meaning of the word as it was originally written. What the word militia meant, when written, is exactly what it means now, nothing more, and nothing less. Is it possible that the original militia was never thought to last? Sure. Was it possible that adding the militia phrases to the Constitution were an appeasement to the anti-federalists? Definitely! Do either of these two assumptions change the definition of the word militia, as it was written? Absolutely not! The term was antecedent to the constitution, and it had a place within the culture of the American colonies and early states. Its' purposes were many and varied, as we shall see, but it was designed to ensure that the people had a means with which to confront tyranny.

For the first 150 years of our country the militia was set up exactly as it was from the beginning, that is, it was made up of all able bodied men between the ages of 16 and 60. Their job was to aid in defense of the community from Indians, invaders, and even took part in the revolutionary war. During the times of federal service the "militia of the several states" became know as units of the National Guard, as distinguished from the regular army soldiers. In 1903 the government increased the role of the "National Guard" as a Reserve force for the U.S. Army. Thus changing it's status from a militia of the several states to a reserve force of the government. The rest of the populace became, the reserve militia or unorganized militia, at least by government definition. Thus the government, by deception and color of law, tries to rewrite the Constitution without a constitutional amendment, and the federal encroachment on states powers increases.

The meaning of the word militia, which was penned by the founding fathers, did not change with the federalization of the "new militia" or National Guard. Make no mistake; the Constitutional militia literally was all able bodied male citizens. The newly formed "organized" militia, or National Guard, was no longer **the** "militia". As soon as the government federalized the troops, they changed the definition, and therefore the meaning of the term militia.

Could the federal government call upon the militia of the states? The answer is an emphatic yes. The government could call to arms all able-bodied citizens for any lawful, Constitutional purpose. However, short of a formal call to arms, the militia of the several states does not come under the direct control of any state or official jurisdiction. The militia is the Constitutional authority and power of the people over its' government. It is, by design, the peoples last defense against a government that has turned against its' people and against the Constitution which they swore to defend.

The Declaration of Independence reads (in part):

> *We hold these truths to be self-evident, that all men are created equal, that they are endowed by their Creator with certain unalienable rights, that among these are life, liberty and the pursuit of happiness. That to secure these rights, governments are instituted among men,* ***deriving their just powers from the consent of the governed.*** *That whenever* ***any form of government becomes destructive to these ends, it is the right of the people to alter or to abolish it****, and to institute new government, laying its foundation on such principles..." "... and accordingly all experience hath shown that mankind are* ***more disposed to suffer, while evils are sufferable, than to right themselves*** *by abolishing the forms to which they are accustomed."*
>
> *"But when a long train of abuses and usurpations, pursuing invariably the same object evinces a design to reduce them under absolute despotism,* ***it is their right, it is their duty, to throw off such government, and to provide new guards for their future security****."*

The founders of our nation insured that their posterity had the means to right a government which had gone astray. This was to have an armed populace with the duty and responsibility to correct that government. The Second Amendment states: "*A well regulated Militia being necessary to the security of a free State, the right of the people to keep and bear Arms shall not be infringed.*" There are those that try to separate this statement either to support collective or individual rights. Instead we should understand how these are tied together. The main idea is that they are not separable. The militia *is* "We the People". To have a militia that is unarmed, is to not have a militia. If the people are unarmed, it is the same. In essence it is a responsibility of citizenship to own, train, and be ready to support, when called upon, to defend this nation. To not support the militia, and to be unarmed, is to turn ones back on ones civic responsibility. And yes, I would even say, it would make us bad citizens.

I know I have said this before, and I will repeat this several more times before the end of this book. The Constitution is not the **origin** of our rights; our rights were antecedent (pre-dated, came before) to the Constitution. The Constitution was created to place restrictions and limitations on the government with regard to its dealing with the "the People," and to protect our rights from infringement. Even if that infringement was the government, this is why we have the militia. Otherwise, we would be as chattel, slaves to the whim of rulers.

If we, "the People," had our rights granted to us by the creator, and "we the People," created the government to uphold and defend those rights, by what means do the citizens have to regain or force the government back to compliance with the Constitution? The answer is the Militia.

Today we hear the many stories of "militia" groups that build large compounds and participate in paramilitary training. Some groups calling themselves the militias are actually racists or separatists, or some form of religious affiliations, while others simply share a common communal value, however they all call themselves "militia". The question presented here is, are they militia? The short answer is yes... and no. Yes they are militia, as they are made up of able bodied men who are not part of the standing army or the reserve (which includes the National Guard). For that matter, every citizen of the nation, except a small number of government officers or the standing military, are members of the militia. However, the militia is no respecter of persons, other than citizens. Any group which calls itself a militia but excludes others from participation based on race, gender, political affiliation, or any other exclusionary measure, would not be a part of the constitutional militia. It would more correctly be identified as a private army or other paramilitary group going by the name of "militia". But as the government defines terms contrary to the common usage, so do rogue groups trying to add an air of legitimacy to their cause.

Can a group of citizens go out and hone their shooting and tactical skills? Definitely, and all should be encourage to do so. I liken this to the Boy Scout motto of "Be Prepared," or to paraphrase an oft quoted phrase, "It is better to have and not need, than to need and not have." We expect everyone who gets behind the wheel of a car to know how to drive. Before you get behind the stick of an aircraft you have to prove you can fly. It's just common sense that as citizens, whose ultimate responsibility it is to defend this nation if invaded, should do all we can to prepare ourselves and our communities. We have lost our sense of civic responsibility which was so prevalent in past generations. As Americans, we very well may be paying for this in future generations.

We have established who and what make up the militia. Let's look at the responsibilities of the militia from a constitutional point of view.

When dealing with a corrupt government the Declaration of Independence charges it's citizens that: *"... it is the right of the people to alter or abolish it..., it is the right, it is their duty, to throw off such government..."* The second and fifth amendments also speak of our responsibilities to come to the aid of the country in times of war, and insurrection, to repel invasions, and public danger, and to enforce the constitutional laws of the union.

From the Militia Act of 1792 Section 1: **"That whenever the United States shall be invaded, or be in imminent danger of invasion from any foreign nation or Indian tribe, it shall be lawful for the President of the United States, to call forth such number of the militia..."** Section 2: *"That whenever the laws of the United States shall be* ***opposed or the execution thereof obstructed****, in any state, by combinations too powerful to be suppressed by the ordinary course of judicial proceedings, or by the powers vested in the marshals by this act... to call forth the militia of such state to* ***suppress*** *such combinations, and to cause the laws to be duly executed."*

The militia stands as a bulwark to those who value freedom and justice against those who would spread the disease of communism or the "New World Order." The work of ensuring that our republic stands firm goes not to the militia alone but to all levels of our society from the local politicians, police and fire, community response teams (CERT), our church's as well as civic groups. All have a dynamic roll in building a patriotic spirit that binds and unifies all citizens and which stands as the moral compass for all that is good, right, and lawful.

From the teachings of our founders and the Courts, we find the following quotes in reference to the militia:

> Tench Coxe, an American political economist, said in 1788: *"Who are the militia? Are they not ourselves? Is it feared, then, that we shall turn our arms each man against his own bosom?* ***Congress shall have no power to disarm the militia.*** *Their swords, and every other terrible* ***implement of the soldier****, are the birth-right of an American... The unlimited power of the sword is not in the hands of either the federal or state*

> *governments, but where I trust in God it will ever remain, in the hands of the People."*

Knowing that the militia is the people, this could also read: Congress shall have no power to disarm the people. Yet when we look at the thousands of gun laws and the banning of all types of firearms, and most notably the assault weapons ban, we must wonder what our government is really trying to do. The Militia is supposed to carry the type of weapon commonly used by the current soldier.

> In **Cockrum v. State**, 24 Tex. 394 (1859) the Hon. John Gregg said: *"The right of a citizen to bear arms, in the* ***lawful defense of himself or the state, is absolute****. He does not derive it from the state government, but directly from the sovereign convention of the people that framed the state government. It is one of the "high powers" delegated directly to the citizen, and "is excepted out of the general powers of government." A law cannot be passed to infringe upon or impair it, because it is above the law, and independent of the law-making power."* (Bold added)

Although this speaks more to the right to bear arms, of particular import here is the "lawful defense of ones self or the state". This clearly aligns the responsibility of citizens to come to their own defense, as well as that of the state. As important is the courts recognition that this right is absolute. Black's Law Dictionary describes absolute right as: "*A right that belongs to every human being, such as the right of personal liberty; a natural right."* If this is truly so then why are so many citizens banned, licensed, regulated, and forced to pay high fees to exercise this right? Any action that can be banned, licensed, regulated, and fees imposed has been relegated to a privilege rather than a right.

During a floor debate over the second Amendment on August 17, 1789, Representative Edbridge Gerry of Massachusetts (statesman and signer of the Declaration of Independence), (Annals of Congress, 750) stated: *"What, Sir, is the use of a militia? It is to prevent the establishment of a standing army, the bane of liberty. ... Whenever Governments mean to invade the rights and liberties of the people, they always attempt to destroy the militia, in order to raise an army upon their ruins."*

Whereas the Constitution has declared the responsibility of every able bodied man as a member of the militia, our government has branded any person who even associates with the militia as an enemy of the state and as a suspected terrorist. In a September 2001 GAO report, entitled Combating

Terrorism, Selected Challenges and Related Recommendations, which discusses terrorist incidents in the United States, reads:

> *"The FBI broadly defines terrorism as "the unlawful use of violence, committed by a group of two or more individuals against persons or property to intimidate or coerce a government, the civilian population, or any segment thereof, in furtherance of political or social objectives." The FBI includes in its annual reports on terrorism in the United States acts such as bombings, arson, kidnapping, assaults, and hijackings committed by* ***persons who may be suspected of associating with militia groups****, animal rights groups, and others."* (Bold added)

Any group, especially a paramilitary group, may call itself a militia; but a name does not make it so. There are many militia groups whose only reason for training is to be of value to the community, the state, and the nation, in a time of need. Any other groups who espouse violence are not the militia, and they should not be lumped in with the true militia. The identification of citizens who associate with patriotic like-minded individuals, whose only goal is to support the nation in a time of need, should not be identified as terrorists.

One final point concerning the militia and arms is that in order for the government to fulfill it's obligations to the constitutional militia; is that it cannot abide by the bans of the items necessary to field that militia. This would include weapons, ammunition, or military gear. Nor can the government allow tax, licensing, registration, limiting, or confiscating any of this items that would be used by the militia as that infringes on the ability of the people to function as a militia.

As the militia is the means to ensure the American people would never again be oppressed by tyrannical governments, invaders from other nations, or insurrection from within, it is vitally crucial that all citizens have free access at all times to their equipment to fulfill their right and obligation to defend this nation from all enemies foreign and domestic. It is right, it is honorable, and it is constitutional.

CHAPTER 10
2ND AMENDMENT

When it comes to the inalienable rights of American citizens, we normally do not try and establish proof that they have a particular right *before* they are allow to exercise that right. If a person is presumed, or has shown themselves, to be a citizen we should not mandate registration of that individual in order to use that right. To do so, transforms a right into a privilege, and is an affront to the Constitution and to the citizen. Do we require citizens to take a legalized reading class, and obtain a license before they are able to purchase a book? Do we require a 12-hour class in organized religion, and then demand a $150.00 licensing fee in order to attend church? Would we think it right and proper if we were required to take a speaking exam and to register all talks with the government before being allowed to offer an opinion?

Do the foregoing questions seem absurd and ridiculous? Of course they do. Logically speaking, if something were a right then you would not be able to tax, license, register, or charge a fee to participate in that right. As it makes no sense to require licensing, registration, or paying taxes and fees for any other right, why do feel it is okay to do so with the right to keep and bare arms? And as the Constitution does not require or give power to the government to restrict our rights, there is no requirement or power for them to do so with the Second amendment.

Premise: One of the basic tenets of American history is the belief in "Life, Liberty, and the pursuit of happiness."

Premise: Fundamentally, we believe each person has the right to defend themselves from an attacker—the right to life.

Observation: A right without the tools to that right is a denial of that right. For instance, to deny ownership of religious materials is in effect denial of the right to worship. To deny printing presses, or electronic print medium, is to deny free press. To deny firearms is to deny personal defense.

In other words, it is absurd to deny citizens the tools which are required to fulfill a right.

The Constitution created a government established by "We the People." The government was granted power by the people. If the people did not have the power to self defense it could not grant that power to the government to defend the nation. If "We the People" are the creators of the government, and the government are authorized arms, then in order for the people to maintain their position, in relation to the government, they to must be armed. If the servant government (servant of the people) has arms, and the people do not, then the roles are reversed for the people can not resist a government that has become tyrannical.

This same logic applies to self defense. If the law abiding citizen does not have the means to resist a lawless adversary, then the adversary becomes the law. Our Congress has formally passed an "assault weapon" ban. The stated goal was to remove the arms used by gangs, drug smugglers, and extremists. How many of us really believe that anyone in any of the aforementioned groups, who owned an "assault weapon", would get rid of those weapons, just because the Congress passed a law? However, many law abiding citizens did, in fact, give up their arms so as to remain "law abiding". The end result is no change for the criminal element and a disarming of the citizen. This has happened, without exception, with EVERY gun law passed by Congress. In this regard, every gun law, by definition, aids the criminal and penalizes the law abiding citizen.

The Second Amendment, arguably the most contentious of all the Bill of Rights amendments, however, is the least tried in the Supreme Court. It simply states:

> "*A well regulated Militia being necessary to the security of a free State, the right of the people to keep and bear Arms shall not be infringed.*"

It may be a small amendment, but, it carries the weight and guarantee for all other rights. For without the capability of the people to defend themselves, to prepare as a militia, or to reign in a tyrannical government, we all become serfs and subjects.

I often hear people referring to the rights *OF* the Constitution, or of their *Constitutional* rights. Let me be as clear as I possibly can be. Outside of the Fourteenth Amendment, the Constitution does not *grant* anyone *any* rights. The Constitution was created to form a limited government and to provide the bounds within which the government was to operate. It specifically enumerates the things the government could and could not do in relation to its' citizens. The rights enjoyed by the citizens, of the many states, were endowed, by their creator, prior to the creation of the Constitution and therefore could not be granted by it.

The last chapter dealt with the militia, where we learned that the militia was comprised of the citizenry of every state. Now coupling that knowledge with the second half of this amendment, it makes sense that the right of "the people" to keep and bear arms is directly related to the role of the militia. The citizenry needs to be armed in order for the militia to have value.

There are those wayward souls who espouse the thought that the militias are the only ones who are to be armed. If they believe that all citizens are members of the militia, then they would be correct. If they are of contrary opinion, then they would be totally ignorant, and completely lacking in historical content and devoid of rational thought. It has been proven that the drafters of the Constitution knew the English language; they were fluid in its usage, and knowledgeable of it's construction and meanings; and whenever the term "the people" is used, it is used to denote the individual citizen.

For instance, let's take a look at the 1st Amendment, which in part says: *"...the right of* ***the people*** *peaceably to assemble, and to petition the government for a redress of grievances."* Using the collectivist point of view, the *people* would have had to **all** be together in order to be allowed to assemble. Or, all citizens had to come together to petition the government. That really does not make sense, does it? What about freedom of press or freedom of speech? Is it only the "collective voice" who has this freedom or is it the individual? Obviously "the people" means the individual, not the group as a whole.

To further emphasis this point please read the following: *"The people who enter the building are hereby subject to search."* Does this mean that the entire building will be vacated en masse from the building, and they will undergo a group search? Or does it mean that any individual who enters the building is subject to search? Obviously it is the individual.

The Supreme Court has also spoken on the collective issue in U.S. v. Emerson, 46 F.Supp.2d 598 (N.D.Tex. 1999), in which it states: *"Collective rights theorists argue that addition of the subordinate clause qualifies the rest of the amendment by placing a limitation on the people's right to bear arms. However, if the amendment truly meant what collective rights advocates propose, then the text would read "[a] well regulated Militia, being necessary to the security of a free State, the right of the States*

to keep and bear Arms, shall not be infringed." However, that is not what the framers of the amendment drafted. ***The plain language of the amendment, without attenuate inferences therefrom, shows that the function of the subordinate clause was not to qualify the right, but instead to show why it must be protected.*** *The right exists independent of the existence of the militia. If this right were not protected, the existence of the militia, and consequently the security of the state, would be jeopardized."*
"...The Court has also held that given their contemporaneous proposal and passage, the amendments of the Bill of Rights should be read in pari materia, and amendments which contain similar language should be construed similarly. Patton v. United States, 281 U.S. 276, 298 (1930), cited by David Harmer, Securing a Free State: Why the Second Amendment Matters, 1998 BYU L. REV. 55, 61 (1998). The Court's construction of "the people" as used in the Second Amendment supports a holding that the right to keep and bear arms is a personal right retained by the people, as opposed to a collective right held by the States. ***Thus, a textual analysis of the Second Amendment clearly declares a substantive right to bear arms recognized in the people of the United States.*** *"* (Bold Added)

As the foregoing statement clearly shows, there is one aspect of this amendment which is based in the collective thought, and that is collective safety. The Second Amendment prohibited the government from infringing on an individuals right in order to protect a collective **purpose**. This individual right does not translate into a collective right; it solely restrains the government from attacking a collective (states) power by means of infringement of the individual right. If the federal could disarm the populace, then the states would have no effective militia and no means to defend itself. This is why there is such a strong tie between the militia and the people.

In the Dred Scott case and its importance on the 14th Amendment, the direct language leaves little doubt as to meaning of the term "the People." It reads: *"The words* ***'people of the United States' and 'citizens' are synonymous terms****, and mean the same thing. They both describe the political body who, according to our republican institutions, form the sovereignty, and who hold the power and conduct the Government through their representatives. They are what we familiarly call the 'sovereign people,' and every citizen is one of this people, and a constituent member of this sovereignty. The question before us is, whether the class of persons described in the plea in abatement compose a portion of this people, and are constituent members of this sovereignty? We think they are not, and that they* *are not included..." (Dred Scott v. Sandford, 60 U.S. 393 [1856])* The question here was whether Scott, a black man, was a citizen. Was he a person? Yes. Was he a citizen? No. He was not a citizen until the 14th Amendment was ratified. This is when the government attempted to bestow rights to the newly formed class of citizen, the 14th Amendment citizen.

"...The right of the people to keep and bear arms shall not be infringed." We already know that the Bill of Rights was written to place limitations on the federal government in it's dealings with the people. What does it mean to be infringed? From the Merriam-Webster New Collegiate Dictionary, 1977 edition it reads: *"1. obsolete: defeat, frustrate. 2. To encroach upon in a way that violates law or the rights of another. Synonymous with trespass."* Based on this definition any action which attempts to make guns obsolete, or to defeat the ability of ownership, or frustrates the keeping and bearing of arms is infringing on the rights of the citizens and is an affront to the Constitution.

Remember, the constitution and "Bill of Rights" are there to *restrain the government*; not the people. This was an instruction to the government to leave the peoples' guns alone. They could not trespass on or encroach upon our right as citizens to own and bear arms. If we look at the enforcement of federal laws and the cost government has placed on the American people I think we must conclude that infringement has and is occurring. The federal government has the right to regulate its' jurisdictions outside of the state jurisdiction; but I will show that the en***force***ment of those laws is where they have violated the Constitution.

So let's do a quick recap:

- The militia consists of all the people.
- The people are guaranteed the right to arms to ensure the ability of the militia could not be usurped.
- The government is prohibited from trespassing against these rights by the 2nd Amendment.
- The people's right to arms is not granted by the 2nd Amendment, only protected by it. The people have always had the right.
- The Supreme Court has upheld the individual right to keep and bear arms.

In 1833 Justice Story, a Supreme Court Justice appointed by James Madison in 1811, penned "Commentaries on the Constitution of the United States." Regarding the Second Amendment he wrote:

"The next amendment is: "A well regulated militia being necessary to the security of a free state, the right of the people to keep and bear arms shall not be infringed." "

"The importance of this article will scarcely be doubted by any persons, who have duly reflected upon the subject. ***The militia is the natural defence of a free country*** *against sudden foreign invasions, domestic insurrections, and domestic usurpations of power by rulers. It is against sound policy for a free people to keep up large military establishments and standing armies in time of peace, both from the enormous expenses, with which they are attended, and the facile means, which they afford to ambitious and unprincipled rulers, to subvert the government, or trample upon the rights of the people.* ***The right of the citizens to keep and bear arms has justly been considered, as the palladium of the liberties of a republic****; since it offers a strong moral check against the usurpation and arbitrary power of rulers; and will generally, even if these are successful in the first instance, enable the people to resist and triumph over them. And yet, though this truth would seem so clear, and* ***the importance of a well regulated militia would seem so undeniable****, it cannot be disguised, that among the American people* ***there is a growing indifference*** *to any system of militia discipline, and a strong disposition, from a sense of its burthens, to be rid of all regulations. How it is practicable to keep the people duly armed without some organization, it is difficult to see.* ***There is certainly no small danger, that indifference may lead to disgust, and disgust to contempt; and thus gradually undermine all the protection intended by this clause of our national bill of rights.*** *"*

In the early years of our nation, it was common sense and historically imperative that the people be armed. They were armed not only for self defense, but as defense against invasion from nefarious nations as well as from "ambitious and unprincipled rulers" who would look to remove their rights and to enslave the nation.

The last line, highlighted above, could have been written today, as it reflects the current position of many on the political left. The growing apathy of the citizens of our nation, who are unwilling to stand up for what is right, will lead to further encroachment upon the liberties for which our fore fathers fought and died. It is my fear that someday soon there will be too few true patriots left, and this nation of cowards will be led willingly to their slaughter or enslavement. My only hope is that I will not live to see it.

United States Representative Ron Paul, from the 14th District in Texas, stated in a November 6th, 2006 article entitled "Gun Control on the Back Burner":

> *"The Second amendment is not about hunting deer or keeping a pistol in your nightstand. It is not about protecting oneself against common criminals. It is about preventing tyranny. The Founders knew that unarmed citizens would never be able to overthrow a tyrannical government as they did. They envisioned government as a servant, not a master, of the American people. The muskets they used against the British Army were the assault rifles of that time.* ***It is practical, rather than alarmist, to understand that unarmed citizens cannot be secure in their freedoms."*** (Bold added) You can read this entire article and more on his official web site at www.house.gov/paul/tst/tst2006/tst110606.htm.

Recent news dealing with high school and college shootings, in which the schools were announced to be "gun free zones," should act as a barometer for the nation on what could happen if the populace were disarmed. If we announce to all criminals that we are gun free, and we have no means to stop the criminal, we are telling them that they are free to wreak havoc as they see fit, because no one will have the means to stop the criminal, and he knows it. In my estimation when a public or private organization removes your ability to protect yourself, they, by default, are liable and should be open to full prosecution by anyone harmed while under their care.

In February of 1982, The Subcommittee on the Constitution of the United States Senate, of the Ninety-Seventh Congress, Second Session, produced a report on "The Right to Keep and Bear Arms" which was published by the Government Printing Office. It is amazing to me how little press this research paper, written by prominent legislators, has received. The forward, written by a number of the members, wrote stirring articles that place great weight on this amendment and this right. The following is part of the forward written by Senator Orrin G. Hatch, (Utah) on January 20 1982. It states:

> *"In my studies as an attorney and as a United States Senator, I have constantly been amazed by the indifference or even hostility shown the Second Amendment by courts, legislatures,*

and commentators. James Madison would be startled to hear that his recognition of a right to keep and bear arms, which passed the House by a voice vote without objection and hardly a debate, has since been construed in but a single, and most ambiguous Supreme Court decision, whereas his proposals for freedom of religion, which he made reluctantly out of fear that they would be rejected or narrowed beyond use, and those for freedom of assembly, which passed only after a lengthy and bitter debate, are the subject of scores of detailed and favorable decisions. Thomas Jefferson, who kept a veritable armory of pistols, rifles and shotguns at Monticello, and advised his nephew to forsake other sports in favor of hunting, would be astounded to hear supposed civil libertarians claim firearm ownership should be restricted. Samuel Adams, a handgun owner who pressed for an amendment stating that the "Constitution shall never be construed . . . to prevent the people of the United States who are peaceable citizens from keeping their own arms," would be shocked to hear that his native state today imposes a year's sentence, without probation or parole, for carrying a firearm without a police permit."

Senator Hatch goes on to tell about the process by which James Madison drafted the language of this most important amendment. It was gone over many times and trimmed for brevity and succinct clarity. Senator Hatch continues writing:

"*The proposal finally passed the House in its present form: "A well regulated militia, being necessary for the preservation of a free state, the right of the people to keep and bear arms shall not be infringed." In this form it was submitted into the Senate, which passed it the following day. The Senate in the process indicated its intent that the right be an individual one, for private purposes, by rejecting an amendment which would have limited the keeping and bearing of arms to bearing "For the common defense"*."

The Senator goes on to denounce the thought that the National Guard is our modern militia by the following:

"*Subsequent legislation in the second Congress likewise supports the interpretation of the Second Amendment that creates an individual right. In the Militia Act of 1792, the second*

> *Congress defined "militia of the United States" to include almost every free adult male in the United States. These persons were obligated by law to possess a firearm and a minimum supply of ammunition and military equipment. This statute, incidentally, remained in effect into the early years of the present century as a legal requirement of gun ownership for most of the population of the United States. There can by little doubt from this that when the Congress and the people spoke of a "militia", they had reference to the traditional concept of the entire populace capable of bearing arms, and not to any formal group such as what is today called the National Guard. The purpose was to create an armed citizenry, which the political theorists at the time considered essential to ward off tyranny. From this militia, appropriate measures might create a "well regulated militia" of individuals trained in their duties and responsibilities as citizens and owners of firearms."*

The Senator also goes on to repudiate the stance of the left that says gun laws reduce crime when he states:

> "*If gun laws in fact worked, the sponsors of this type of legislation should have no difficulty drawing upon long lists of examples of crime rates reduced by such legislation. That they cannot do so after a century and a half of trying — that they must sweep under the rug the southern attempts at gun control in the 1870-1910 period, the northeastern attempts in the 1920-1939 period, the attempts at both Federal and State levels in 1965-1976 — establishes the repeated, complete and inevitable failure of gun laws to control serious crime."*

He ended his comments with a sentiment of honor, courage, and devotion to the founding principles that have made this great nation a shining beacon for the world when he states:

> "*Both as an American citizen and as a United States Senator I repudiate this view."* (That gun laws stop crime). *"I likewise repudiate the approach of those who believe to solve American problems you simply become something other than American. To my mind, the uniqueness of our free institutions, the fact that an American citizen can boast freedoms unknown in any other land, is all the more reason to resist any erosion of our individual rights. When our ancestors forged a land "conceived in liberty",*

they did so with musket and rifle. When they reacted to attempts to dissolve their free institutions, and established their identity as a free nation, they did so as a nation of armed freemen. When they sought to record forever a guarantee of their rights, they devoted one full amendment out of ten to nothing but the protection of their right to keep and bear arms against governmental interference. Under my chairmanship the Subcommittee on the Constitution will concern itself with a proper recognition of, and respect for, this right most valued by free men." (Comment added)

I may be cast a heretic; but the fact of the matter is, laws are not meant to stop crime. In many cases laws create crime where none existed. An example would be what I call the stupidity laws, such as mandatory helmet wearing on motorcycles or seat belts in cars etc. These "laws" tell us that the government knows what is best for you, and they will en***force*** their will upon you by writing laws to protect you from yourself. This is EXACTLY the mentality of a communist and brute force is EXACTLY the methodology a communist would use to make you do what they know is best for you.

In general, Laws are made to codify certain unwanted behavior and to establish acceptable behavior in society. However, as soon as you transfer this mechanism to inanimate objects, this logic fails. To illustrate, I think we would all agree that a criminal who steals, rapes, or murders is doing wrong. The tools he **may** use in that action do not change the act. "Ah", says the liberal/communist, "but you remove the ability for him to get the tool, now he cannot accomplish the act." If only that were true. I look at the genocide that has taken place in African states; the mutilation by means of machete; where limbs were severed and people left to bleed to death. Whole villages where women were raped, breasts removed, children hacked to death. Evil will do what evil does by whatever means is at their disposal. To assume the morally bankrupt of our society would stop a behavior by solely passing a law against an instrument he *may* use in the commission of a heinous crime is naïve at best. Added to this is the undercurrent of black market supplies of weapons, around the world and here in America. The criminal does not obey laws, and he is prohibited to obtain weapons, yet he still gets them. Thus the net effect is to disarm the victims, making them unable to lawfully protect themselves.

The law abiding citizen is, by definition, not the problem. The problem is the criminal, because by definition, he does not obey the law. As importantly, is that the government is treating ALL citizens by the standards of the criminal. For instance, a criminal uses a handgun in the commission of a robbery. Another criminal uses an ice-pick to commit the same crime. A third uses a baseball bat. With the logic of the gun control advocates the mere possession of a gun, an ice-pick, or a baseball bat should be outlawed. The root of the problem, however, is not the objects with which they perpetrate their crime; it is their willingness to commit the crime. The item used to aid that crime is merely the tool. And as every tool used to commit a crime has a peaceful use, outlawing the tool ONLY infringes on the person who would **not** use it for nefarious reasons.

Using the above example of the three criminals, the only constant that runs through all scenarios is the criminal. As the criminal is the human being, then we must draw the conclusion that the defect is the human being, as the gun, ice-pick, and baseball bat cannot act of their own volition and cannot act alone; we are left with the conclusion that we must outlaw the human being. Ok, I can hear the groans, this is of course absurd, we all know there are good humans who would not think of acting is such immoral ways. So in the end we must trust that most of us humans are good people and stop passing laws as if everyone is a criminal and focus on the *behavior* of the human being, that is where the decision to do evil is located not in inanimate objects.

The gun control advocates would have us believe the following:

First: Gun control laws curb criminal behavior.

Second: If gun availability is lessened there would be a decrease in gun crimes.

Third: More gun control means safer streets, schools, homes, etc.

All three statements would be true, in a vacuum or in a totally controlled environment. If we add the human element into the equation, these statements become false. First, as we have already discussed, the criminal does not obey the law and therefore does not care about legally purchasing or owning firearms. Do we really believe that someone who is capable of rape or murder cares one whit about registering a firearm or submitting for a license? Of course not! He does not obey the law; therefore no law will curb his behavior. Second, in every state where handguns are freely permitted to be carried there has been a lessening of overall violent crimes.

In every country where massive gun confiscation and control has been enacted, they have seen an increase in gun related crime. It does seem to follow, "if you outlaw guns, the only people who will have guns will be the outlaws." Third, the city with the most stringent gun control laws is the city with the highest gun crime, Washington D.C.

So why doesn't gun control work? It is really quite simple, laws are meant to control "behavior" not objects, a set of standards, if you will, that says these things we do not do, and if you do them there will be consequences.. Legal systems are designed to provide a framework of acceptable "behavior" by which persons within a society interact with each other. Murder is illegal in nearly every society on the face of the earth. How that murder is accomplished is simply tool identification. The lack of moral upbringing and interference by the government has removed parental power. Today a child in some cities cannot be spanked out of fear that child protective services will take their child away. Yet, the state makes the parents responsible for the child's behavior, and stands between the child and parent when discipline is most needed. If a child grows up thinking there are not harsh consequences to whatever he does, then he will do whatever he wants. The problem with our society is not the availability of guns it is the absence of a moral standard for our society.

What our nation needs are laws that punish criminal behavior and to stop criminalizing honest citizens who wish only to protect themselves and their families. Both the Department of Justice and the Bureau of Alcohol, Tobacco, and Firearms (ATF) statistics have shown that the majority of violent crimes are committed without firearms, and the vast majority of gun crimes are committed with guns that were illegally obtained, bypassing gun laws. So the net effect of gun control laws is to affect the law abiding citizen and has virtually no effect on the criminal element of our society.

The enactment of "firearms laws" is a relatively recent occurrence for the federal government. The Federal Firearms Act in 1938 was the first act by congress to regulate firearms. This act was based upon the perceived need to regulate the firearms industry and license the dealers, manufacturers, and gunsmiths within the firearms trade. It was based upon the Interstate Commerce Clause of the Constitution. Appropriately it was codified under Title 15 of the US Code—"Commerce and Trade". The new "laws" under the Act included the creation of a Federal Firearms License (FFL), for anyone doing business in the firearm trade. One of the primary goals was to prohibit FFL holders from selling firearms to convicted felons. Requiring FFL holders to keep records of all firearms sales, and for the first time it made any alteration of firearm serial numbers a crime. Some felt this was an infringement on state jurisdiction by enacting a law that reached past the state boundary, in violation of the Constitution.

From 1938 to 1968 everything went along fairly well until the government decided to play a little shell game, and they switched the Firearms Act from

Title 15 to Title 18. Title 18 is entitled "Crimes and Criminal Procedures." Why would the government switch the code section from Title 15 to Title 18 after having been codified under Title 15 for thirty years? The only rational reason is jurisdictional obfuscation, or hiding what would otherwise be apparent as to the limits the government could act upon us, the citizens. You see, under Title 15, the government was within it's rightful jurisdiction of "Commerce and Trade". However, if you are bound by "Commerce and Trade", you cannot enact laws on normal citizens who are not acting in the "trade." Therefore, the government changed, with the stroke of a pen, their Constitutional powers from commerce to crime.

Shortly after President Kennedy's assassination, in 1968, the "Gun Control Act" was passed. It was an attempt by the government to justify broad-sweeping firearms control. The finesse with which the government's lawyers crafted and pushed this bill through can be seen right from the opening lines. The bill is entitled:"*An Act to amend title 18, United States Code, to provide for better control of the interstate traffic in firearms*." Doesn't that title sound allot like Chapter 15? In fact, even though there is much overlap between Title 15 and Title 18, Title 15 was never repealed.

This was done to provide better control of "interstate" traffic in firearms. However, the stated purpose of the act is as follows:

Title I—State Firearms Control Assistance

Purpose

> "**Sec. 101.** The Congress hereby declares that **the purpose of this title is to provide support to Federal, State, and local law enforcement officials in their fight against crime and violence**, and it is not the purpose of this title to place any undue or unnecessary Federal restrictions or burdens on law-abiding citizens with respect to the acquisition, possession, or use of firearms appropriate to the purpose of hunting, trapshooting, target shooting, personal protection, or any other lawful activity, and that this title is not intended to discourage or eliminate the private ownership or use of firearms by law-abiding citizens for lawful purposes, or provide for the imposition by Federal regulations of any procedures or requirements other than those reasonably necessary to implement and effectuate the provisions of this title."

Did you catch that? To support State, and local law enforcement! Where does the Constitution say anything about the federal government assisting law enforcement? Remember, the federal government cannot **legally** do anything that is not specifically enumerated by the Constitution. So where is its justification? It has none; any federal law that falls outside the enumerated powers of the Constitution is repugnant and is void. That does not stop the jack-booted thugs from kicking in your door and enforcing unjust and unconstitutional laws, it just makes them wrong with a gun.

Remember how I said that words and terms can have different meanings depending on how the government defines them? This is no different; in fact, Chapter 44 of Title 18 has page after page of definitions that change the meaning of words and phrases so that they are even different from the meanings given in other chapters of Title 15 from which it sprang.

One particular change is the definition for "interstate commerce" and "foreign commerce." Normally these two terms are found with separate and distinct definitions, but within chapter 44, they are combined to read:

> **18 USC §921(2)**
>
> *"The term **"interstate or foreign commerce"** includes commerce between any **place** in a State and any **place** outside of that State, or within any possession of the United States (not including the Canal Zone) or the District of Columbia, **but such term does not include commerce between places within the same State** but through any place outside of that State. The term "State" includes the District of Columbia, the Commonwealth of Puerto Rico, and the possessions of the United States (not including the Canal Zone)."* [Bold emphasis added]

So far we are within the interstate commerce limitations set by the Constitution. An interesting side note is that Section 5 of Title 18 defines the United States as such: *"**The term "United States"**, as used in this title in a territorial sense, **includes all places and waters**, continental or insular, **subject to the jurisdiction of the United States**, except the Canal Zone."* When they use the term *United States* under Title 18 they mean only the federal jurisdictional definition of "places," where the federal government has jurisdiction as identified in the Constitution. Here they are talking about waterways used in commerce; these are the only areas of federal jurisdiction dealing with waterways.

In the chapter dealing with jurisdiction, we talked about how state and federal jurisdictions were separate, except for certain places within the state, such as forts, magazines, etc., and the District of Columbia and the territories of the United States. In these places, the federal government has full jurisdiction and has police powers that affect the people living in those places. This is also expressed in the Constitution at Article I, Section 8, Clause 17 where it reads:

> *"To exercise exclusive Legislation in all Cases whatsoever, over such District (not exceeding ten Miles square) as may, by Cession of particular States, and the Acceptance of Congress, become the Seat of the Government of the United States, and to exercise like* ***Authority over all Places purchased by the Consent of the Legislature of the State in which the Same shall be, for the Erection of Forts, Magazines, Arsenals, dock-Yards, and other needful Buildings****... "* (Bold emphasis added.)

Here we see the same language from where federal statutes get their Constitutional limitations on the word "places." Within the states of the union it is limited to only those areas of federal lands and waterways which are not within the jurisdiction of the State! It can only be "legally" enforced on federally controlled property.

The English language is very precise and descriptive. English is considered one of the hardest languages to learn and has been chosen as the language of business and science because of the ability to accurately describe ideas and concepts. Why then does Congress feel the need to change the meaning of words? Because it suits their goals! An example, lets say I was to tell you, "All land owners must comply with National Wetlands Act statutes, regardless of state where property is located." In this scenario, you happen to own a couple of acres in the middle of the desert. What would you think? Are you liable to follow these laws? What I did not tell you is that, in a different chapter I changed the definition of "land owner" to mean only persons with land comprised predominately of water or marsh. Do you think you would have had a different view of the law, knowing the definition up front? The government lawyers who write our laws understand how to write laws that give the appearance, or color, of law; even when none exists.

In changing from Title 15 to Title 18, it was meant for you to believe the government had nation-wide jurisdiction under the definition of interstate commerce, when in fact they only have limited federal jurisdiction to the areas enumerated above.

This is quite logical, and it keeps in step with the separation of powers doctrine between state and federal. Can the federal government make state law, or can the state make federal law? Of course not! The federal government cannot define a crime that takes place within the jurisdiction of a state. Also, the federal government does not have police powers within a state of the union, except for the places of federal property or actions against federal agents.

As a summation to this chapter on the Second Amendment and for your edification, the following text comes from the conclusion of the "Right to Keep and Bear Arms" senate report. This report may be found in it's entirety on the GAO web site.

(Authors Note: Bold text comments contained within the text are used to highlight certain concepts. Items at the end of the paragraph and contained within parenthesis are the author's narrative and is not contained in the original text.)

ENFORCEMENT OF FEDERAL FIREARMS LAWS FROM THE PERSPECTIVE OF THE SECOND AMENDMENT

"Federal involvement in firearms possession and transfer was not significant prior to 1934, when the National Firearms Act was adopted. The National Firearms Act as adopted covered only fully automatic weapons (machine guns and submachine guns) and rifles and shotguns whose barrel length or overall length fell below certain limits. Since the Act was adopted under the revenue power, sale of these firearms was not made subject to a ban or permit system. Instead, each transfer was made subject to a $200 excise tax, which must be paid prior to transfer; the identification of the parties to the transfer indirectly accomplished a registration purpose." **(Much of this was in reaction to the revenuers and liquor smugglers during the prohibition era who used machine guns to ply their trade.)**

"The 1934 Act was followed by the Federal Firearms Act of 1938, which placed some ***limitations upon sale of ordinary firearms****. Persons engaged in the business of selling those firearms in interstate commerce were required to obtain a Federal Firearms License, at an annual cost of $1, and to maintain records of the name and address of persons to whom they sold firearms. Sales to persons convicted of violent felonies*

were prohibited, as were interstate shipments to persons who lacked the permits required by the law of their state." **(The cost of FFL's now range in the hundreds of dollars with very tight restrictions that have the effect of eliminating small business.)**

"Thirty years after adoption of the Federal Firearms Act, the Gun Control Act of 1968 worked a major revision of federal law. The Gun Control Act was actually a composite of two statutes. The first of these, adopted as portions of the Omnibus Crime and Safe Streets Act, imposed limitations upon imported firearms, expanded the requirement of dealer licensing to cover anyone "engaged in the business of dealing" in firearms, ***whether in interstate or local commerce****, and expanded the recordkeeping obligations for dealers. It also imposed a variety of* ***direct limitations upon sales of handguns.*** *No transfers were to be permitted between residents of different states (unless the recipient was a federally licensed dealer),* ***even where the transfer was by gift*** *rather than sale and even where the recipient was subject to no state law which could have been evaded. The category of persons to whom dealers could not sell was expanded to cover persons convicted of any felony (other than certain business-related felonies such as antitrust violations), persons subject to a mental commitment order or finding of mental incompetence, persons who were users of marijuana and other drugs, and a number of other categories. Another title of the Act defined persons who were banned from possessing firearms. Paradoxically, these classes were not identical with the list of classes prohibited from purchasing or receiving firearms."* **(Where does the Constitution allow for the federal government to regulate state business? It does not. The Second Amendment states that the rights of the people shall not be infringed. This definitely qualifies as infringement.)**

"The Omnibus Crime and Safe Streets Act was passed on June 5, 1968, and set to take effect in December of that year. Barely two weeks after its passage, Senator Robert F. Kennedy was assassinated while campaigning for the presidency. Less that a week after his death, the second bill which would form part of the Gun Control Act of 1968 was introduced in the House. It

was reported out of Judiciary ten days later, out of Rules Committee two weeks after that, and was on the floor barely a month after its introduction. The second bill worked a variety of changes upon the original Gun Control Act. Most significantly, **it extended to rifles and shotguns the controls which had been imposed solely on handguns,***" (Even though it was a small caliber handgun used to kill Robert Kennedy), "extended the class of persons prohibited from possessing firearms to include those who were users of marijuana and certain other drugs, expanded judicial review of dealer license revocations by mandating a de novo hearing once an appeal was taken, and permitted interstate sales of rifles and shotguns only where the parties resided in contiguous states, both of which had enacted legislation permitting such sales. Similar legislation was passed by the Senate and a conference of the Houses produced a bill which was essentially a modification of the House statute. This became law before the Omnibus Crime Control and Safe Streets Act, and was therefore set for the same effective date."*

"Enforcement of the 1968 Act was delegated to the Department of the Treasury, which had been responsible for enforcing the earlier gun legislation. This responsibility was in turn given to the Alcohol and Tobacco Tax Division of the Internal Revenue Service. This division had traditionally devoted itself to the pursuit of illegal producers of alcohol; at the time of enactment of the Gun Control Act, only 8.3 percent of its arrests were for firearms violations. Following enactment of the Gun Control Act the Alcohol and Tobacco Tax Division was retitled the Alcohol, Tobacco and Firearms Division of the IRS. By July, 1972 it had nearly doubled in size and became a complete Treasury bureau under the name of Bureau of Alcohol, Tobacco and Firearms."

"The mid-1970's saw rapid increases in sugar prices, and these in turn drove the bulk of the "moonshiners" out of business. Over 15,000 illegal distilleries had been raided in 1956; but by 1976 this had fallen to a mere 609. The BATF thus began to devote the bulk of its efforts to the area of firearms law enforcement."

"Complaint regarding the techniques used by the Bureau in an effort to generate firearms cases led to hearings before the Subcommittee on Treasury, Post Office, and General Appropriations of the Senate Appropriations Committee in July 1979 and April 1980, and before the Subcommittee on the Constitution of the Senate Judiciary Committee in October 1980. At these hearings evidence was received from various citizens who had been charged by BATF, from experts who had studied the BATF, and from officials of the Bureau itself."

"Based upon these hearings, ***it is apparent that enforcement tactics made possible by current federal firearms laws are constitutionally, legally, and practically reprehensible.*** *Although Congress adopted the Gun Control Act with the* ***primary object of limiting access of felons and high-risk groups to firearms, the over breadth of the law has led to neglect of precisely this area of enforcement.*** *For example the Subcommittee on the Constitution received correspondence from two members of the Illinois Judiciary, dated in 1980, indicating that they had been totally unable to persuade BATF to accept cases against felons who were in possession of firearms including sawed-off shotguns. The Bureau's own figures demonstrate that in recent years the percentage of its arrests devoted to felons in possession and persons knowingly selling to them have dropped from 14 percent down to 10 percent of their firearms cases. To be sure, genuine criminals are sometimes prosecuted under other sections of the law. Yet, subsequent to these hearings,* ***BATF stated that 55 percent of its gun law prosecutions overall involve persons with no record of a felony conviction, and a third involve citizens with no prior police contact at all.****"*

"The Subcommittee received evidence that the ***BATF has primarily devoted its firearms enforcement efforts to the apprehension, upon technical malum prohibitum charges, of individuals who lack all criminal intent and knowledge.*** *Agents anxious to generate an impressive arrest and gun confiscation quota have repeatedly enticed gun collectors into making a small number of sales — often as few as four — from their personal collections. Although each of the sales was completely legal*

under state and federal law, the agents then charged the collector with having "engaged in the business" of dealing in guns without the required license. Since existing law permits a felony conviction upon these charges ***even where the individual has no criminal knowledge or intent numerous collectors have been ruined by a felony record carrying a potential sentence of five years in federal prison****. Even in cases where the collectors secured acquittal, or grand juries failed to indict, or prosecutors refused to file criminal charges, agents of the* ***Bureau have generally confiscated the entire collection of the potential defendant upon the ground that he intended to use it in that violation of the law. In several cases, the agents have refused to return the collection even after acquittal by jury."***

"The defendant, under existing law is not entitled to an award of attorney's fees, therefore, should he secure return of his collection, an individual who has already spent thousands of dollars establishing his innocence of the criminal charges is required to spend thousands more to civilly prove his innocence of the same acts, without hope of securing any redress. This of course, has given the enforcing agency enormous bargaining power in refusing to return confiscated firearms. Evidence received by the Subcommittee related the confiscation of a shotgun valued at $7,000. Even the Bureau's own valuations indicate that the value of firearms confiscated by their agents is over twice the value which the Bureau has claimed is typical of "street guns" used in crime. ***In recent months, the average value has increased rather than decreased, indicating that the reforms announced by the Bureau have not in fact redirected their agents away from collector's items and toward guns used in crime."***

"The Subcommittee on the Constitution has also obtained evidence of a variety of other misdirected conduct by agents and supervisors of the Bureau. In several cases, ***the Bureau has sought conviction for supposed technical violations based upon policies and interpretations of law which the Bureau had not published in the Federal Register,*** *as required by 5 U.S.C. Sec 552. For instance, beginning in 1975, Bureau officials apparently reached a judgment that a dealer who sells*

to a legitimate purchaser may nonetheless be subject to prosecution or license revocation if he knows that that individual intends to transfer the firearm to a nonresident or other unqualified purchaser.

This position was never published in the Federal Register and is indeed contrary to indications which Bureau officials had given Congress that such sales were not in violation of existing law. Moreover, BATF had informed dealers that an adult purchaser could legally buy for a minor, barred by his age from purchasing a gun on his own. BATF made no effort to suggest that this was applicable only where the barrier was one of age. Rather than informing the dealers of this distinction, Bureau agents set out to produce mass arrests upon these "straw man" sale charges, sending out undercover agents to entice dealers into transfers of this type. The first major use of these charges, in South Carolina in 1975, led to 37 dealers being driven from business, many convicted on felony charges. When one of the judges informed Bureau officials that he felt dealers had not been fairly treated and given information of the policies they were expected to follow, and refused to permit further prosecutions until they were informed, Bureau officials were careful to inform only the dealers in that one state and even then complained in internal memoranda that this was interfering with the creation of the cases. When BATF was later requested to place a warning to dealers on the front of the Form 4473, which each dealer executes when a sale is made, it instead chose to place the warning in fine print upon the back of the form, thus further concealing it from the dealer's sight."

"The Constitution Subcommittee also received evidence that the Bureau has formulated a requirement, of which dealers were not informed that requires a dealer to keep official records of sales even from his private collection. BATF has gone farther than merely failing to publish this requirement. At one point, even as it was prosecuting a dealer on the charge (admitting that he had no criminal intent), the Director of the Bureau wrote Senator S. I. Hayakawa to indicate that there was no such legal requirement and it was completely lawful for a dealer to sell from his collection without recording it. Since that date, the

Director of the Bureau has stated that that is not the Bureau's position and that such sales are completely illegal; after making that statement, however, he was quoted in an interview for a magazine read primarily by licensed firearms dealers as stating that such sales were in fact legal and permitted by the Bureau. ***In these and similar areas, the Bureau has violated not only the dictates of common sense, but of 5 U.S.C. Sec 552, which was intended to prevent "secret lawmaking" by administrative bodies.***

These practices, amply documented in hearings before this Subcommittee, leave little doubt that the ***Bureau has disregarded rights guaranteed by the constitution and laws of the United States.****"*

"It has trampled upon the second amendment by chilling exercise of the right to keep and bear arms by law-abiding citizens."

"It has offended the fourth amendment by unreasonably searching and seizing private property."

"It has ignored the Fifth Amendment by taking private property without just compensation and by entrapping honest citizens without regard for their right to due process of law."

"The rebuttal presented to the Subcommittee by the Bureau was utterly unconvincing. Richard Davis, speaking on behalf of the Treasury Department, asserted vaguely that the Bureau's priorities were aimed at prosecuting willful violators, particularly felons illegally in possession, and at confiscating only guns actually likely to be used in crime. He also asserted that the Bureau has recently made great strides toward achieving these priorities. No documentation was offered for either of these assertions. In hearings before BATF's Appropriations Subcommittee, however, expert evidence was submitted establishing that approximately ***75 percent of BATF gun prosecutions were aimed at ordinary citizens who had neither criminal intent nor knowledge, but were enticed by agents into unknowing technical violations****. (In one case, in fact, the individual was being prosecuted for an act which the Bureau's acting director had stated was perfectly lawful.) In those hearings, moreover, BATF conceded that in fact (1) only 9.8*

percent of their firearm arrests were brought on felons in illicit possession charges; (2) the average value of guns seized was $116, whereas BATF had claimed that "crime guns" were priced at less than half that figure; (3) in the months following the announcement of their new "priorities", the percentage of gun prosecutions aimed at felons had in fact fallen by a third, and the value of confiscated guns had risen. All this indicates that the ***Bureau's vague claims, both of focus upon gun-using criminals and of recent reforms, are empty words. "***

"In light of this evidence, reform of federal firearm laws is necessary to protect the most vital rights of American citizens. *Such legislation is embodied in S. 1030. That legislation would require proof of a willful violation as an element of a federal gun prosecution, forcing enforcing agencies to ignore the easier technical cases and aim solely at the intentional breaches. It would restrict confiscation of firearms to those actually used in an offense, and require their return should the owner be acquitted of the charges. By providing for award of attorney's fees in confiscation cases, or in other cases if the judge finds charges were brought without just basis or from improper motives, this proposal would be largely self-enforcing. S. 1030 would enhance vital protection of constitutional and civil liberties of those Americans who choose to exercise their Second Amendment right to keep and bear arms."*

The revelations into the inner workings of the BATF and its' total disregard for the Constitution and the rights of the citizens of the United States, leaves no doubt that the position of the federal government, in particular the enforcement agency, and its willingness to go to any lengths to defeat the citizens' Second Amendment right. As with any revelation, the full truth is never totally revealed, and it is like viewing an iceberg from afar. You never know how large it is until you get up close. Most importantly, until the American people are willing to stand up to tyranny and oppression, the depths of that oppression will grow deeper. If the BATF, under the Treasury, is willing to lie to Congress, to falsely imprison citizens, to entrap and coerce honest citizens into unknowingly committing infractions and then ravage their lives and make them criminals when there was never any criminal intent, what makes us think the IRS or any other government agency is any different. They are just another branch on the same tree.

I can not say this enough, the birth rights we have as American Citizens are higher than the Constitution. They exist by virtue of our creation and are bestowed at birth and these rights cannot be taken by any government, unless we give them away. The Second Amendment is paramount to all other rights, because without this right, we cannot defend the other rights. I have come to understand that those without a means of defense become victim to those who will force their will upon them. I have personally seen this in Somalia, Pakistan, Kuwait, the Philippines, and Afghanistan. In most cases, the only reason we received respect from the enemy was because we had the means to remove them from the face of the earth. Make no mistake, if it were not for the Second Amendment, this nation would not be here today. Our future still depends on the willingness of "We the People" to stand up and fight to keep this right.

It is a proven axiom that a criminal will not try to commit a crime while a police officer is present. Thus the saying "There is never a policeman around when you need him." There are those who want a society where there are no guns. A society where a woman can walk down a street at night without fear of molestation. Where drugs, gangs, corruption, and evil no longer exists. There is such a place, but it only exists in the stories of Hollywood. The cold reality is that evil does exist and we must protect ourselves and our families against that evil.

So, who is responsible for our protection? Is it the government, the state, the local police? It may surprise you to learn that none of these is the correct answer. Time and time again the courts have ruled, and those rulings have been upheld, that there is no requirement for any level of government to guarantee our *individual* protection. In this nation, the policy of policing is that of "general" peace and order; and no one person or group can have any expectation of individual protection.

There are only two exceptions to this rule, first, when there is a special relationship with the government, such as when an individual is incarcerated. Second, is when the government intentionally places you in danger, such as when they release a criminal who is known to be a danger to himself or others. Other than for these two exceptions, the government is not responsible for your safety and protection. You are!

To illustrate this I would like to present the following cases that illustrate this position:

> In Bowers v. Devito, 686 F.2d 616 (7th Cir. 1982) the courts ruled: *"There is no constitutional right to be protected by the*

state against being murdered by criminals or madmen. It is monstrous if the state fails to protect its residents against such predators but it does not violate the due process clause of the Fourteenth Amendment, or, we suppose, any other provision of the Constitution. ***The Constitution is a charter of negative liberties; it tells the state to let the people alone; it does not require the federal government or the state to provide services, even so elementary a service as maintaining law and order.*** *"*
(Emphasis added)

Warren v. District of Columbia (444 A.2d 1, 1981) state: *"Official police personnel and the government employing them are not generally liable to victims of criminal acts for failure to provide adequate police protection ... this uniformly accepted rule rests upon the fundamental principle that a* ***government and its agents are under no general duty to provide public services, such as police protection, to any particular citizen ... a publicly maintained police force constitutes a basic governmental service provided to benefit the community at large by promoting public peace, safety and good order.***
(Emphasis added)

In still another case, Hartzler v. City of San Jose, 46 Cal.App.3d 6, 120 Cal.Rptr. 5 (1975) A woman called 911 for assistance, stating that her ex-husband had called and said he was coming over to kill her; and he did. The police and governmental groups were sued for not providing protection of the wife. The courts ruled *"The statutory scheme employed makes it clear that failure to provide adequate police protection will not result in governmental liability... nor will a public entity be liable for failure to arrest a person who is violating the law... The statutory scheme shows legislative intent to immunize the police function from tort liability from the inception of its exercise to the point of arrest, regardless of whether the action be labeled 'discretionary' or 'ministerial... In light of the specific holding of the Court of Appeal on this issue in Antique Arts, supra, and in view of the analogous holding in County of Sacramento, we must conclude that* ***the police department enjoys absolute, not merely discretionary, immunity****."*

(Emphasis added)

There are literally hundreds of cases that say exactly the same thing. In the liberal world, I constantly hear that the police are trained to protect the innocent. Quite often this happens solely because they are out on the streets looking for bad guys. Odds are, eventually they will run into a crime and take action. The police are there to bring criminals to justice, which is what they get paid for. However, in order for one to be deemed a criminal they must **first** perpetrate a crime. Only then can the police take action. You and you alone have the primary responsibility for your protection and safety. By law, someone who pays another to commit a crime is just as guilty as if he committed the crime himself. In my estimation, someone who pays another for protection, and is unwilling to take responsibility for their own protection, is guilty of cowardice. Willingness does not equate to capability. Many people are willing to protect themselves, but do not have the capability. If you are not willing to fight, or even kill to protect your own life or the lives of your family, then you cannot ask someone else to do it for you.

We hear time and again from the left that having a gun in the home makes it more likely that the gun will be used against the homeowner by the perpetrator. There are by far more killings by stabbings or blunt force trauma than by guns. With the left's argument all knives should be removed from the population and only plastic brightly colored plastic knives can be sold. Of course this is ridiculous, and so is the gun argument. The gun is only a tool. It has no mind of it's own. It cannot force a person to do anything. But there are two things it does do. First, it magnifies the ethical ills of society. Both in the need for defense against evil, and the atrocity of the evil doer. Second, it allows a 100 pound, would be, victim to fend off a 200 pound aggressor. No pepper spray, cell phone, alarm, or scream can say the same thing.

There are those on both the left and the right who cry out in unison to just enforce the laws already on the books. What in the world are they thinking about? Just because a law is on the books does not mean it is a good law, and it does not necessarily mean that it is constitutional. A good number of laws, currently on the books, although well intentioned, are not constitutional. But until they are challenged they remain on the books and people are being damaged who have never had the intent on committing a crime.

The Constitution states that the Second Amendment "shall not be infringed." How many laws does it take before it is considered infringed? 500? 5,000? 20,000? That's about how many laws we have on the books. Not infringed means exactly that; leave it alone.

The United States was built and survived because of private ownership of arms. Many gun haters cannot abide hearing this; and they manage to forget, or they don't understand the history that brought us through the oppression of the English Kings. One of the sparks to the war of independence was the

Kings' mandate to disarm the people. Our forefathers included in the Constitution the guarantee that the people would never be disarmed again.

The rights from the creator are not removable by government, by law, or even by deed. I do not believe **anyone** should be deprived of their Second Amendment right, even felons once they have served their sentence and have paid the price for their crimes. If we release a criminal who we do not trust back into society, then his sentence was too lenient; and that is a problem with the justice system. Knowing how easily one can get illegal firearms, laws restricting ex-cons from possessing them would only restrict those who do not desire to run afoul of the law again. In that case, they are no different than the rest of us. Remember, it was the Firearms Act of 1938 that restricted felony possession. There was a reason why old western films show people getting their guns back when they are released from jail. Because a person has been to prison does not make them immune to the need to personally protect themselves and their property. If anything it puts them at a greater risk. We should be looking to punish behavior, not tools. The Second Amendment does not place qualifications on who is worthy to be protected. Because the government cannot legally overstep the bounds placed on them by the constitution, they cannot legally revoke any right enjoyed by its' citizens.

There are those who believe that guns are bad. That just having them in the home will place a person more at risk of suicide or murder. They make these claims as though to endow this inanimate object with a will of it's own. That somehow by its mere presence can influence a human being to do something they would otherwise not do. This may be true for Hollywood or fairy tails, but it has no basis in fact or reality.

The firearm is a tool, nothing more nothing less. It has no powers but what the person wielding it provides. If that person be evil, then evil may be produced. If that person be good, then the good man has a means by which he may protect himself and his family from the evil man. If a man be prone to commit assault or even murder, what does he care about gun laws? Will this evil doer decide to not use a gun when he robs, rapes, abducts children, or kills because there is a law stating he may not carry a gun? Of course not! The evil person cares not for the law, therefore gun laws ONLY affect the law abiding citizen, not the criminal. But it is my belief the lawmakers know this. The excuse, of fighting crime, is only the "reason" to pass the law not the desired effect. The desired effect is removal of honest gun ownership. Once this is accomplished the country is then helpless against the rulers of our nation. Another means of checks and balances, the final means, will be abolished.

The last seventy years have been a continual neutering of the American patriot. When all is said and done, the wresting of our God-given rights from the "communist-liberal left and the power-hungry government bureaucrats" may come down to one thing; our Second Amendment Right.

Chapter 11
Illegal Immigration

The topic of illegal immigration goes much deeper than just porous borders; it touches on treasonous acts which go as high as the white house.

Nearly every country in the world maintains its borders with their military. In fact, the primary role of the government is the protection of the people; and what could be a more essential than the protection of the border? There are those who say we cannot use the military on the border, as that would create more of a "police state." Instead we have the U.S. Border Patrol, who take an oath to defend the Constitution from all enemies, foreign and domestic. They wear a uniform, they carry guns, and they work for the federal government. The *only difference* is which department of the executive branch they work for. The Armed Forces work for the Department of Defense and the Border Patrol work for the Department of Homeland Security. Both departments are headed by the President.

There are enough Border Patrol agents on the Mexican border to station one agent every 1,000 feet. On the other hand, on the Canadian border, there are only enough agents to put one agent every 16 miles. Yet conservative estimates show 1.3 million illegal immigrants crossing our southern border yearly. This means that over 3,561 people a day, 7 days a week, 365 days a year illegally enter our country. The Mexican Ambassador, Arturo Sarukhan, stated that if Congress doesn't pass immigration reform soon, legalization efforts may not be revived until a new president takes over in 2009. He stated, *"Comprehensive immigration reform in the United States must begin in Mexico,"* also, *"Mexico must be able to create jobs, economic growth, well-paid jobs, to minimize the factors that generate the departure of Mexican migrants who cross the border."* Again, our neighbors to the south have no plans to assist the United States in securing the borders. They are only interested in what we can do for their country.

And why would Mexico want to close the border? Currently the second largest stream of income going into Mexico is from Mexicans who live in the United States and who send American greenbacks to Mexico. This means billions of dollars contributing to the Mexican economy that otherwise would not be there. So where is the incentive for Mexico to try to slow down the flow of immigrants? If anything, they wish to increase the numbers. Every poor farm worker who crosses the border is one less person to burden on the Mexican economy. In fact, the Mexican government prints pamphlets that teach the people how to cross the border. They even provide rudimentary maps to guide them.

On March 13, 2007, President Bush visited Mexico; and during his speech, he said to the Mexican people:

> *"President Calderon, I appreciate your determination to create new opportunities for the people of Mexico. I share your commitment to building an Americas where the poor and the marginalized begin to feel the blessings of liberty in their daily lives.* ***I respect your views on migration. Because we're working together****, I believe we will make good progress on this important issue. Together, we're working to ensure that we have a secure and* ***modern border that speeds the legitimate flow of people and commerce****, and stop those who threaten our common safety and prosperity.*
>
> *The United States respects rule of law. But in the debate on migration, I remind my fellow citizens that* ***family values do not stop at the Rio Grande River****, that there are decent, hardworking honorable citizens of Mexico who want to make a living for their families. And so, Mr. President,* ***my pledge to you and your government—but, more importantly, the people of Mexico—is I will work as hard as I possibly can to pass comprehensive immigration reform."***

Shortly before the 2006 mid-term elections, the President passed a bill to build a stronger border; and he called for miles of extensive fencing to be built along the Mexican border to stem the tide of illegal aliens that come across our borders every day. Two years later the fences have not been built, nor will they be. No money has been appropriated, and no contracts have been awarded to erect them. Why? To answer this question, we need to look at a few governmental programs, the North American Free Trade Agreement (NAFTA), the Security and Prosperity Partnership (SPP), and the North American Union (NAU).

NAFTA was signed in 1994, and it was touted as a means to facilitate trade among separate sovereign countries. However, as time passed and the details were analyzed, it became clear that rather than promote trade, it provided the basis for what was to follow—an integrated North American economy and the ground rules by which it would be operated.

There have been numerous, in depth analyses on the effects of NAFTA. With the exception of government reports, the majority of these reports decry NAFTA as a failure. The successes the government claims, in their reports, have only been for large corporations and investors. The goal of raising job prospects in Mexico to help ease the border situation have all but failed. NAFTA promised an increase in jobs for Mexicans, and it promised to do away with "maquiladora" industries, which preyed on low-cost labor and deplorable work and living conditions. The net effect has been an increase in these industries.

Following NAFTA, was the SPP which was launched in 2005. SPP's stated objective was to *"ensure continued economic prosperity in Canada, the United States and Mexico, and to increase the security of citizens in all three countries,"* If NAFTA was working so well, why did we need to continue economic prosperity, unless it was for the benefit of large corporations and investors. The SPP has no congressional oversight, even though monies are being spent on its' behalf, as required by the Constitution.

One of the stated goals, for security portion of the SPP, is to extend the external borders of the United States north and south to include Canada and Mexico. All three nations would accept universal individual identification standards, to make free and open cross-border travel. The militaries of all three nations as well as police systems, would be open and shared to facilitate information exchange and training.

Commercially the SPP would provide for a massive highway system to link all of Mexico's industrial and shipping complexes throughout the United States, Mexico, and Canada. Plans are currently underway to build the initial artery, which would be built to go from Texas all the way to Canada.

The government has denied that there are plans to build a "super highway" to link Canada, the U.S., and Mexico. However, on September 28 2006, the 109th Congress House of Representatives bill 487 states: *"Expressing the sense of Congress that the United States should not engage in the construction of a North American Free Trade Agreement (NAFTA) Superhighway System or enter into a North American Union with Mexico and Canada."* If there was no planned superhighway system or plans for a North

American Union, why would representatives of our own government need to present a bill to oppose it? If things don't add up, it probably isn't due to your math skills.

Let's take a look at the resolutions of 487: (Bold emphasis added)

CONCURRENT RESOLUTION

Expressing the sense of Congress that the United States should not engage in the construction of a North American Free Trade Agreement (NAFTA) ***Superhighway System*** *or enter into a* ***North American Union*** *with Mexico and Canada.*

Whereas, according to the Department of Commerce, United States trade ***deficits with Mexico and Canada have significantly widened*** *since the implementation of the North American Free Trade Agreement (NAFTA);*

Whereas the ***economic and physical security of the United States is impaired*** *by the potential loss of control of its borders attendant to the full operation of NAFTA;*

Whereas a NAFTA Superhighway System from the west coast of Mexico through the United States and into Canada has been suggested as part of a North American Union;

Whereas it would be particularly difficult for Americans to collect insurance from Mexican companies which employ Mexican drivers involved in accidents in the United States, which would ***increase the insurance rates for American drivers****;*

Whereas future unrestricted foreign trucking into the United States can pose a safety hazard due to inadequate maintenance and inspection, and can act collaterally as a ***conduit for the entry into the United States of illegal drugs, illegal human smuggling, and terrorist activities****; and*

Whereas a NAFTA Superhighway System would be funded by foreign consortiums and controlled by foreign management, which ***threatens the sovereignty of the United States****:*

Now let's review the Congressional concerns:

- Widening trade deficits between the countries.
- Impaired economic and physical security.
- Safety Concerns for our highways.
- Foreign control over portions of our transportation system.
- Threats to the sovereignty of the United States.

I don't feel that this is appealing or in the best interest of the United States. That is, of course, unless you are interested in global expansion. But in order to have that, you would have to remove state borders, combine the economies of all the nations involved, link the police and military under a central command and control network, provide infrastructure to ease the movement of products and people, and provide a means by which disputes could be adjudicated. Hmm, I think we're almost there!

It is interesting that the government's official position is that there was no signed agreement called the SPP, between the countries. Yet there is an entire government web site, www.spp.gov, dedicated to the program.

On March 31st 2006, President Bush published the 2006 SPP progress report. Within the report the following statements were made:

> ***"North American Emergency Management.*** *A disaster—whether natural or man-made—in one of our countries can have consequences across national borders. Our vision for a North American response, relief and recovery strategy would ensure that critical equipment, supplies and personnel can be deployed expeditiously throughout North America.* ***We commit to develop a common approach to critical infrastructure protection, coordinated responses to cross border incidents, and coordinated training and exercises, with the participation of all levels of government in our countries."***

This all sounds good in theory. Heck, even communism sounds good in theory. It's placing theory into action that creates the problem. Pay close attention to the last highlighted sentence.

My training as an intelligence analyst for the government taught me to look at a commander's statement and to be able to derive tasks to help accomplish any specified objective. There are two types of tasks, either specified or implied. An expressed task states an objective (i.e. unit A will move to point B for insertion). The implied tasks are what lawyers call, "the devil is in the details". In order for unit A to move it must create movement orders, vehicles to transport troops to the airfield, have fuel available, and the mission may require engagement with the enemy so there must be ammunition laid on, etc. There are implied tasks of coordination with other friendlies in the area so you don't take friendly fire. You get the picture.

From the statement above, the implied tasks (paying close attention to the scope of "all levels of government"), will require integrated systems of command and control, communication, targeting, training, logistics, and infrastructure control on par with what he have in America today, but adding Canada and Mexico's military, police, and all other government agencies as well. Remember the statement, "all levels of government." In order to do that, all levels of government must be involved and working together.

The next implied requirement is in dealing with dispute resolution. How do three different countries with varying laws, customs and citizens' rights deal with the inevitable disputes? There is already a resolution in place within NAFTA; it is the SPP's parent agreement. All three countries have agreed to abide by arbitration from the UN and world trade organizations. This would be expanded to cover all areas of dispute, and the binding results would override any one individual country's law. In effect, this would render the Supreme Court mute and the Constitution void when charges are raised from another country. This is in direct conflict with the Judiciaries authority as outlined in the Constitution. Can you feel your national identity slipping away?

Currently this arbitration only covers claims by investors who believe their investments have been harmed by another country's actions or laws. Again, we find that big business and investors are the ones who have the power and the most protections.

> ***"North American Smart, Secure Borders.*** *Our vision is to have a border strategy that results in the* ***fast, efficient and secure movement*** *of low-risk trade and travelers to and within North America, while protecting us from threats including terrorism. In implementing this strategy, we will encourage innovative risk-based approaches to improving security and facilitating trade and travel. These include close coordination on infrastructure investments and vulnerability assessments, screening and processing of travelers, baggage and cargo, a single integrated North American trusted traveler program,* ***and swift law enforcement responses to threats posed by criminals or terrorists, including advancing a trilateral network for the protection of judges and officers.****"*

Notice the phrase, "fast, efficient and secure movement". Implied tasks—what needs to be in place in order to facilitate fast, efficient and secure movement? One report likened the cross-border movement solution to be similar to the automated tolls on America's toll roads. You would need an ID that would meet certain minimum requirements, something like the "Real ID Act" that was passed back in 2005. This ID would facilitate tracking people who cross the border, just like the toll readers do highways. Only we would all be required to obtain this ID and the government would then have the means to track everyone's position as they traveled about the country.

The second phrase has me a little worried. "Swift law enforcement responses." Have you dialed 911 lately? There is a joke that goes something like "dial 911, and then order a pizza, and see which one shows up first." We can't get swift response to an emergency (criminal) threat now, and we want to expand this to include countries that are less trained, less equipped, and who have worse infrastructure? Writing the implied tasks for this problem would fill more than just a couple of pages, however, the cost to the American taxpayer to bring everyone up to the same level would be astronomical. An interesting slant is the specified task for the protection of judges and officers. What judges, and which officers? What would change that would place judges and officers at a higher risk than there is today? Something else is going on that we are not being told. Is this because these judges and officers will hold the power over the three unified countries, and it is going to be so oppressive that they will need this special protection? Many times it is what is *not said* that can have the greatest meaning and impact.

Logic would dictate that in order to integrate all levels of government, security, policing, and emergency response they would have to have authority throughout the tri-nation area. You would also have to have a political command structure, parliament/legislature to create policy (law), and enforcement. My question is, how do you maintain individual sovereignty when you have given away the power to make certain decisions? The European Union started out much like this. It was a free trade agreement that grew, adding more partners; and then they expanded to further include infrastructure and governance for commerce. Then came the need to expand the banking and monetary exchanges. Now we have EU delegates with the same representation as other countries. Countries have lost their individual currencies to the Euro. Corporate legislation and uniform laws have superseded the countries' laws. All this was based on a free trade agreement. Can you see where we are going?

Is it any wonder that our government has not secured the southern border? They don't want it secured; in fact, they plan on opening it even more. Do you really think that building a secure fence for a few million dollars, which is a drop in the bucket for their trillion dollar budgets, is beyond the capability of our government? It has been over two years since the border-fence resolution was passed, and we still have no fence; however the timing of airing the tough-on the border plan at the end of 2005, just before the kick off the mid term elections, is suspect.

Another organization, called the Council on Foreign Relations or CFR, will tell you that they are not associated with any government. They say they are an independent think tank on global foreign relations, and they produce reports that are made available to everyone, but mostly to the government.

The CFR is anything but un-associated. It is not associated in a formal way, but by membership. The list of CFR members looks like a Who's Who in politics. It includes people at all levels of government, including presidents, cabinet members, federal and state officials, large business owners, bankers, and heads of foreign governments. Below is a partial list of CFR and tri-lateral commission members who you might recognize.

David Rockefeller, Chairman Emeritus
Paul Volker, North American Chairman of the Trilateral Commission
William Clinton—President of the United States
George H.W. Bush—President of the United States
Dick Thornburgh—UN
Anthony Lake—National Security Advisor
Albert Gore, Jr.—Vice President of the United States of America
Warren Christopher—Secretary Of State
Colin L. Powell—Chairman Joint Chiefs Of Staff
James Woolsey—Director Central Intelligence Agency
Lloyd Bentsen—Treasury Secretary
Bruce Babbitt—Secretary of Interior
Henry Cisneros—Secretary of Housing and Urban Development
Donna Shalala—Secretary of Health & Human Services
Sandra Day O'Connor—Assoc. Justice, U.S. Supreme Court
Ruth B. Ginsburg—U.S. Court Of Appeals, Wash., DC Circuit
Roger Altman—Deputy Sec. Treasury Department
John M. Niehuss—Dep. Asst. Sec., Intl. Monetary Affairs
George Stephanopoulos—Director, Communications
Willian J. Crowe—Chief Foreign Intelligence Advisory Bd.
Nancy Soderberg—Staff Director, National Secuity Council
Samuel R. Berger—Deputy Advisor, National Security
W. Bowman Cutter—Deputy Assistant, National Economic Council
Alice Rivlin—Deputy Director Office of Management & Budget
Thomas Graham, Jr.—General Council U.S. Arms Control & Disarmament Agency

William Schneier—Chmn., General Advisory Council
Richard Burt—Negotiator On Strategic Defense Arms
David Smith—Negotiator, Defense & Space
William W. Schwarzer—Director Federal Judicial Center
Madeleine Albright—UN Amabassador
Lynn Davis—Under Sec. for International Security Affairs
H. Allen Holms—Asst. Sec., Bureau Of Politico-Military Affairs
John H. Kelly—Asst. Sec., Near East-South Asian Affairs
Alexander F. Watson—Deputy Rep., United Nations
Thomas R. Pickering—Ambassador (Russia)
Morton I. Abramowitz—Ambassador (Turkey)
Michael H. Armacost—Ambassador (Japan)
Shirly Temple Black—Ambassador (Czechoslovakia)
Julia Chang Bloch—Ambassador (Nepal)
Henry E. Catto, Jr.—Ambassador (Great Britain)
Frances Cook—Ambassador (Camaroon)
Edward P. Djerejian—Ambassador (Syria)
Geoge E. Moose—Ambassador (Senegal)
John D. Negroponte—Ambassador (Mexico)
Edward N. Ney—Ambassador (Canada)
Robert B. Oakley—Ambassador (Pakistan)
Robert H. Pelletreau, Jr.—Ambassador (Tunisia)
Christopher H. Phillips—Ambassador (Brunei)
Nicholas Platt—Ambassador (Phillipines)
James W. Spain—Ambassador (Maldives & Sri Lanka)
Terence A. Todman—Ambassador (Argentina)
Frank G. Wisner II—Ambassador (Egypt)
Warren Zimmerman—Ambassador (Yugoslavia)
Senator David L. Boren (D-OK)
Senator William Bradley (D-NJ)
Senator John H. Chafee (R-RI)
Senator William S. Cohen (R-ME)
Senator Christopher J. Dodd (D-CT)
Senator Dianne Feinstein (D-CA)
Senator Bob Graham (D-FL)
Senator Joseph I. Lieberman (D-CT)
Senator George J. MiTChell (D-ME)
Senator Claiborne Pell (D-RI)

Senator Larry Pressler (R-SD
Senator Charles S. Robb (D-VA)
Senator John D. Rockefeller, IV (D-WV)
Senator William Roth, Jr. (R-DE)
Representative Howard L. Berman (D-CA)
Representative Thomas S. Foley (D-WA)
Representative Sam Gejdenson (D-CT)
Representative Richard A. Gephardt (D-MO)
Representative Newton L. Gingrich (R-GA)
Representative Lee H. Hamilton (D-IN)
Representative Amory Houghton, Jr. (R-NY)
Representative Nancy Lee Johnson (R-CT)
Representative Jim Leach (R-IA)
Representative John Lewis (D-GA) Representative Robert T. Matsui (D-CA)
Representative Dave K. Mccurdy (D-OK)
Representative Eleanor Homes Norton (D-DC)
Representative Thomas El Petri (R-WI)
Representative Charles B. Rangel (D-NY)
Representative Carlos A. Romero-Barcelo (D-PR)
Representative Patricia Schroeder (D-CO)
Representative Peter Smith (R-VT)
Representative Olympia J. Snow (R-ME)
Representative John M. Spratt (D-SC)
Representative Louis Stokes (D-OH)
Alan Greenspan—Former Chairman Federal Reserve
E. Gerald Corrigan—V. Chairman./Pres. NY Fed. Res. Bank
Richard N. Cooper—Chairman. Boston Fed. Res. Bank
Sam Y. Cross—Manager, Foreign Open Market Acct
Robert F. Erburu—Chairman. San Francisco Fed. Res. Bank
Robert P. Forrestal—Pres. Atlanta Fed. Res. Bank
Bobby R. Inman—Chairman., Dallas Fed. Res. Bank
Edwin M. Truman—Federal Reserve Staff Dir. International Finance
Paul Volcker—Federal Reserve
Thomas G. Labrecque.—Chairman & CEO Chase Manhattan Corp
Robert R. Douglass.—Vice Chairman Chase Manhattan Corp
Walter V. Shipley.—Chairman Chemical Bank
Robert J. Callander.—President Chemical Bank
William C. Pierce.—Executive Officer Chemical Bank

John S. Reed.—Chairman Citicorp
William R. Rhodes.—Vice Chairman Citicorp
Richard S. Braddock.—President Citicorp
A. Robert Abboud.—CEO First City Bancorp Lewis T. Preston.—Chairman Morgan Guaranty
Charles S. Stanford, Jr. .—Chairman Bankers Trust New York
Alfred Brittain III.—Dir. Bankers Trust New York
Vernon E. Jordan, Jr. .—Dir Bankers Trust New York
Richard L. Gelb.—Dir. Bankers Trust New York
Patricia Carry Stewart.—Dir. Bankers Trust New York
Barry F. Sullivan—First National Bank of Chicago
Cyrus Vance—Manufacturers Hanover Director
G. Robert Durham.—Manufacturers Hanover Director
George B. Munroe.—Manufacturers Hanover Director
Marina V. N. Whitman.—Manufacturers Hanover Director
Charles J. Pilliod, Jr.—Manufacturers Hanover Director
Andrew F. Brimmer.—Dir. Bank America
Ignazio E. Lozano, Jr.—Dir. Bank America
Ruben F. Mettler, Dir.—Bank America
Michael D. Mann, Dir.—International Affairs Securities & Exchange Commission
Les Aspin—Secretary of Defense
Frank G. Wisnerll—Under Secretary for Policy
Henry S. Rowen—Asst. Sec., International Security Affairs
Judy Ann Miller—Dep. Asst. Sec. Nuclear Forces & Arms Control
Michael P. W. Stone—Secretary of the Army
Donald B. Rice—Secretary of the Air Force
Franklin C. Miller—Dep. Asst. Sec. Nuclear Forces & Arms Control
Gen. Colin L. Powell—Chairman Joint Chiefs of Staff
Gen. Carl E. Vuono—Army Joint Chiefs of Staff
Gen. Merril A. Mcpeak—Co Pac AF
Lt. Gen. Bradley C. Hosmer—AF Inspector General
Laurence A. Tisch—CEO CBS
Roswell Gilpatric—CBS
Dan Rather—CBS
John F. Welch—CEO NBC
Tom Brokaw—NBC
David Brinkley—NBC

Thomas S. Murphy—CEO ABC
Barbara Walters—ABC
John Connor—ABC
Diane Sawyer—ABC
Robert Mcneil—PBS
Jim Lehrer—PBS
C. Hunter-Gault—PBS
Stanley Swinton—Associated Press
Harold Anderson—Associated Press
Katharine Graham—Associated Press
Michael Posner—Reuters
Henry Trewhitt—Baltimore Sun
Arnaud De Borchgrave—Washington Times
Joan Ganz Cooney—Pres. Sesame Street
Richard Gelb—New York Times
William Scranton—New York Times John F. Akers—Dir. New York Times
Louis V. Gerstner, Jr.—Dir. New York Times
George B. Munroe—Dir. New York Times
Donald M. Stewart—Dir. New York Times
Cyrus R. Vance, Dir.—New York Times
A.M. Rosenthal—New York Times
Ralph Davidson—Time, Inc.
Donal M. Wilson—Time, Inc.
Henry Grunwald—Time, Inc.
Katharine Graham—Newsweek/Washington Post
N. Deb. Katzenbach—Newsweek/Washington Post
Robert Christopher—Newsweek/Washington Post
Richard Wood—Wall Street Journal
Robert Bartley—Wall Street Journal
Karen House—Wall Street Journal
Wm. F. Buckley, Jr.—National Review
George V. Grune—CEO Readers Digest
William G. Bowen—Dir. Readers Digest

This comprises only a small part of the entire list of 3,000 members. A complete list of past and current members would encompass far too many pages to include here. As you can see, the depth and reach of the CFR is, to say the least, impressive. It's members hold key positions in government, large corporations, the military, national security agencies, high finance, and even include presidents of the United States.

What is really disturbing is to read some of the documents found in the archives of the CFR. The majority of which, in all fairness, are economic studies from around the world. The CFR produces an enormous amount of research and analyses of nations throughout the world and provides a wealth of knowledge.

But there is another side to the CFR, one that is un-American and bent on the destruction of this country as we know it today. The company was founded in 1921 with a stated goal of "advising" members of governments and coordination through sister organizations to bring about global change. Which begs the question, whose global change?

Dr. Carroll Quigley, CFR member, college mentor of President Clinton, author of "Tragedy and Hope," stated: *"The Council on Foreign Relations is the American branch of a society which originated in England ...* [and] *... believes national boundaries should be obliterated and one-world rule established."*

In his book, "Tragedy and Hope," written in 1966, Dr. Carroll Quigley wrote: *"... the powers of financial capitalism had another far-reaching aim, nothing less than to create a world system of financial control in private hands able to dominate the political system of each country and the economy of the world as a whole. This system was to be controlled in a feudalist fashion by the central banks of the world acting in concert, by secret agreements arrived at in frequent private meetings and conferences."* (Does this sound familiar? You may want to revisit the section on Money and the Federal Reserve System.)

Zbigniew Brzezinski was National Security Advisor to five presidents. What was not widely known is that he was also a CFR member and founding member of the Trilateral Commission. He stated:

> *"In the economic-technological field, some international cooperation has already been achieved, but further progress will require greater American sacrifices. More intensive efforts to shape a new world monetary structure will have to be undertaken, with some consequent risk to the present relatively favorable American position."* He also stated that: *"The technotronic era involves the gradual appearance of a more controlled society.* ***Such a society would be dominated by an***

> ***elite, unrestrained by traditional values. Soon it will be possible to assert almost continuous surveillance over every citizen and maintain up-to-date complete files containing even the most personal information about the citizen. These files will be subject to instantaneous retrieval by the authorities."*** (Emphasis added.)

So what is all this leading up to? Prior to the implementation of the SPP, the CFR produced a report entitled, "Building the North American Community," which was sponsored by the CFR, Canadian Council of Chief Executives and the Consejo Mexicano de Asuntos Internacionales (Mexican Counsel for International Affairs.) This document is a roadmap to the destruction of national sovereignty for all three nations in an attempt to foster regional, and then ultimately, global governance.

The report focuses and recommends the following:

1. That the three nations should cooperate and share responsibility in areas of law enforcement, energy security, regulatory policy, dispute resolution, and *continental* defense vice *national* defense. (**This sounds to me like country mergers**)
2. That the countries should rely more on business and less on bureaucracy. (**Exactly what the bankers would be vying for.**)
3. To build an area where there is free movement of trade, capital and people. (**I guess border security is out the window.**)
4. Security boundaries should be around the continent not around individual nations. (**In order to manage this, see 1 above**)
5. They recommend creating a North America security pass. Not only will we have a national ID, we will have a continental ID, which has smart chip technology so we can be tracked wherever we go. (**Getting scared yet?**)
6. By 2010 they want to establish a free flow of people across the interior borders of all three countries.
7. They recommend development of a tri-national threat intelligence center and joint training for law enforcement officials. (**More merger.**)
8. They recommend the development of tri-national ballistics and explosives registration. (**Second Amendment, we don't need any Second Amendment.**)
9. Military defense structures are to be comprised of all three country's militaries. (**Have I mentioned country merger.**)
10. Combine the intelligence-sharing capabilities at both the military

and law enforcement levels. **(Does it sound like they want to build a whole new nation?)**

11. They also want to spread the benefits of economic development. **(This sounds a little like socialism—entitlement rights for the poor to narrow the income gap between the three countries. Why don't they have to work for a living like everyone else?)**
12. Pour more money, resources, businesses, infrastructure, judicial reform, and governmental oversight into Mexico to allow them to grow faster than the U.S. or Canada so they can catch up to us economically.
13. They want to create investment funds in Canada and the U.S. to funnel more capital into Mexico. **(Let's just throw money at this. The more we give them, the less we have for us, thus reducing the income gap.)**
14. Combine national resources for all three countries to share. **(Hmmm, I always thought the national resources for our future generations.)**
15. They want to create common tariffs for all three nations and allow all ports to be used for all of the nations. **(This will require modification of national tax structures, port authorities, Labor Union practices, and security.)**
16. Establish a permanent tribunal for dispute resolution. **(This is the first step in creating a judicial system. This tribunal will supersede national law and constitutions.)**
17. Establish a continental regulatory approach *vice that old national stuff.*
18. Open skies and open roads. No more borders and check points, we should all trust each other; we're a partnership now.
19. Increase labor mobility. **(Sounds like open borders to me.)**
20. They also want us to implement a Social Security Totalization Agreement between the U.S. and Mexico. **(What? We can't make SS work for our own citizens, and they want to add more? It keeps sounding more like socialism.)**
21. Next, a full North American education system. **(Maybe this will fix our broken educations system, NOT.)**
22. Create organizations and governmental departments to facilitate a vision-to-action framework. **(This, my friends, has already started.)**

I did not go into every detail of what the CFR wants in the way of creating this integration, community, union, or whatever you want to call it; but I think you get the picture. Now looking over the list and comparing it to the NAFTA and SPP goals laid out above, do you notice the striking similarities between the two?

Where does the North American Union come into play? I'm sure most of the citizens of the United States have not even heard of the North American Union, although it did get mentioned on CNN once. The North American Union is the coined phrase that is a natural extension of the NAFTA and SPP plans. It dovetails the CFR recommendations with the plans that are already in place.

In a letter dated 4 May, 2005, Secretary of Commerce, Carlos Gutierrez, stated:

> "*Organizationally, I am jointly responsible for the economic, or prosperity, component of the SPP, with my Canadian counterpart, Minister of Industry David Emerson, and my Mexican counterpart, Secretary of Economy Fernando Canales. Secretary of Homeland Security Michael Chertoff, jointly with his Canadian and Mexican counterparts, is responsible for the security component. Secretary of State Condoleezza Rice, jointly with her Canadian and Mexican counterparts, will ensure that the two components are integrated and that the SPP advances our strong relations with Mexico and Canada. ... I have made the SPP one of my top priorities and will utilize the talents and expertise of the people across the Department of Commerce to ensure the SPP is a success.*

Now remember, the SPP is not a treaty. The authorization for moving forward with this comes solely from the President, illegally, and he does not have congressional approval. When top cabinet level authorities talk about integrating components of government with other governments to create a new entity, as described in the SPP; it is, by definition, a union of the countries involved.

There is a lot of propaganda and disinformation about the North American Union, but one fact is clear, there are those in Washington D.C., within the ranks of Congress, who have expressed concern over the North American Union. I guarantee that if Senators and Representatives are discussing this topic, the people of this country are only seeing the tip of the iceberg.

The government has stated that the Security and Prosperity Partnership is not an agreement or a treaty, and no document was signed. But if you visit **www.spp.gov**, the "official" government web site for SPP, they state:

> *"Looking forward, President Bush, Prime Minister Harper and President Fox have identified emergency management; influenza pandemics, including avian influenza; energy security; and safe and secure gateways (border security and facilitation) as key priorities for the SPP. The Leaders also* ***announced the creation of North American Competitiveness Council to fully incorporate the private sector into the SPP process.***

The government defines this as a **process** in which government departments are free to move ahead, without spending authorizations, without the vote of the people, without congressional mandate or authorization, without Constitutional authorization, and with Constitutional prohibitions against performing such actions. However, in a report written by Former Canadian Prime Minster Paul Martin, who met with Bush and Fox in Waco, TX on March 23, 2005, Martin writes:

> *"Thus, on March 23, President Bush, President Fox and I* ***signed*** *the Security and Prosperity Partnership of North America..."* And what is Canada's motivation to do this? The Prime Minister wrote: *"Make no mistake: We are in the midst of a major rebalancing of global power. New nations are rising as military and economic forces. Many established powers are striving to maintain their influence through regional integration and new alliances. In a world of traditional and emerging giants, independent countries like Canada—countries with small populations—risk being swept aside, their influence diminished, their ability to compete hampered. That may sound dramatic, but the stakes are that high."*

The stakes are high; and in order to survive, in his estimation, they must move forward with this plan. Also notice he stated they "signed" the SPP. Why does our government state that nothing was signed and this is just talk? What are they afraid to tell us about?

He went on to say: *"It is a partnership that respects the past but is devoted to building for the future, to ensuring that we as* ***North Americans*** *are able to continue to thrive in a world in which China and India have emerged as economic giants."*

Throughout his presentation, he spoke often of Canadian needs and the Canadian people; but after talking of the SPP, he now refers to them as North

Americans, a subtle yet telling phrase of his commitment to building a new North America that can compete with Europe, China and the other powers of the world.

The problem as I see it, is not just a government doing what it **should not**, it is the other branches of government, and the people, doing absolutely nothing to stop it. It is time to demand change; and if our government is unresponsive, it is our right and duty to replace them, if not by the ballot, then by what-ever means available.

Chapter 12
Property Rights

Property rights can be a bit confusing. Most people think of "real estate" when they talk about property rights, but it goes much deeper than that. Are your skills or your time considered property? What about your earnings? Are they property? What about your thoughts or ideas, your writings, your car or house, your boat, furniture, and pets?

The further we get from the tangible the more things become a little grey. Now let's throw a curve in here by asking, "Do property "rights" exist without the property?" The simple answer is yes; however, the exercise of those rights cannot happen before ownership. Notice that I did not say before possession. For instance, if you own a home and rent it to someone else, who owns the property and who has possession? You can own property but not have possession of it, and the law will limit what you, as the owner, can do while it is in someone else's possession.

No person shall be deprived of life, liberty, or property without due process of law. No one shall be denied equal protection under the law, and taxes shall be uniform and apportioned. Most of us recognize much of the last sentence from the amendments known as the Bill of Rights. The courts have made it clear that income is property, see *James v. United States*, 970 F.2d 750, 755, 756 n. 11 (10th Cir. 1992).

If no person shall be deprived of property without due process of law; and income is deemed to be property, then how is it that they take so much of it by direct taxation without apportionment? The answer is that we let them. (See the chapter on taxation.) We have all become accustomed to accepting a little less freedom; as long as we can go home at the end of the day, put our feet up, and watch a little TV, or go out to eat or to the movies, life isn't so bad. Put it in a different perspective, let's say the local gangster approaches you on the street and says: "Listen bud, when you get your paycheck each week, I want you to cash it and give me 30% because I want to help out my friends who need the money more than you do. For your payment, I will make sure that if anyone breaks into your home, I'll look for him—if I have time. And if you don't pay, I'm going to send my boys over and take you away from your family for awhile". Now replace Bud's name with yours, and replace the gangster with the Federal Government. What is the difference?

What if you're a cabinet-maker and you get approached by a new homeowner saying he would like some new cabinets put up in his house and work-shop. You go to his house, you get all the specifications; and the two of you agree on a cost. You write up a contract and you agree that he will pay you $5,000 for the entire project. All the agreements are signed, and you get started. Three weeks later, the cabinets are all done, perfectly installed, and you present the finished product to the customer. He is thrilled; everything is great. He then proceeds to write out a check and hands it to you; there it is a nice big check for $3,750.00. You blink, look again and say "ahem, excuse me Mr. Customer; but our agreement was for $5,000 not for $3,750." He replies, "oh no, that's $5,000. If you look at the stub, it shows your amount plus the $1,250 to the Gangster for his cut. Everyone has to pay the Gangster his cut." As you can guess, this scenario is between you, your employer, and the Feds.

One of the primary liberties we are supposed to enjoy in this country is the ability to contract with another. This includes contracting our time and talents, and exchanging one property for another. In this case, the exchange was one type of property (cabinets) for another type of property (money). If the material cost came to $3,000 and the carpenter exchanged his time and skills to produce the cabinets for $2,000, is there income, or profit, from the transaction? No, it was an exchange of property, nothing more. This is the same for 90% of the working people in America.

The next thing I want to discuss is Eminent Domain. This is the process whereby the government takes real property, someone's home or land, for public use. In a recent Supreme Court case KELO **et al. v.** CITY OF **NEW LONDON et al.** (certiorari to the supreme court of Connecticut No. 04-108.Argued February 22, 2005--Decided June 23, 2005,) the court ruled that local governments can take property from private citizens and give it to private developers for whatever development project the government deems as a benefit to the community.

The Fourth Amendment allows: *"The right of the people to be secure in their persons, houses, papers, and effects, against unreasonable searches and seizures, shall not be violated...*" I don't know how secure I feel when the government says they can take my house solely because it thinks it will be better for the community. In the Fifth Amendment it states, "*...nor shall private property be taken for public use, without just compensation.*" First, the first half of this sentence says, "For public use." This has always been meant in the most restrictive sense, such as the need for roads or other public infrastructure. It was never meant to be applied in the socialist sense of "the betterment of others over the individual rights." Second, public use does not, in any stretch of the imagination, equate to private use, even at the benefit of the town. You cannot take from someone their home and give it to a private developer to put up a mall just because you think it will add jobs or more income to the town. This is the kind of draconian tactics used in Russia during the height of the soviet empire. The only difference is the appeasement of conscience because you forced upon someone worthless fiat script, called Federal Reserve Notes; in exchange for his mother's home and the place he raised his family.

When reading the Constitution there is a legal concept to apply the plain meaning to what is written. Then if there is doubt, you can go to the meaning as they were used at the time they were written, and to the written commentary of the day; to derive the "intent" of the writers. In this case, the court decided it knew better than the authors and decided to change the meaning of the Constitution to suit their own agenda. Folks, this is legislation from the bench, making laws not interpreting them and this is wrong. The decision of the court stated this: "Court long ago rejected any literal requirement that condemned **property be put into use for the ... public**. Rather, it has embraced the **broader and more natural interpretation of public use as "public purpose."**

They state they can now take your land as long as it has a "public purpose". A mall, a park, public swimming pool, new factory, or convenience stores, are each used by the public. And if they want your land to build it, they can now just take it. Notice the statement, "of a broader more natural interpretation." This is redefining the meaning of the constitution. Since when did they get the power to change the meaning of the Constitution? They didn't, they just did it!

Let's look at what a few of the founding fathers had to say on the topic of property ownership.

John Adams: "*The moment the idea is admitted into society, that property is not as sacred as the laws of God, and that there is* *not a force of law and public justice to protect it, anarchy and tyranny commence. If "Thou shalt not covet," and "Thou shalt not steal," were not commandments of Heaven, they must be made inviolable precepts in every society, before it can be civilized or made free."* As soon as property rights are made inviolable then the society has become uncivilized, and freedom is lost.

James Madison: *"Government is instituted to protect property of every sort; as well that which lies in the various rights of individuals, as that which the term particularly expresses. This being the end of government, that alone is a just government, which impartially secures to every man, whatever is his own."*

Thomas Jefferson: *"The Constitution of most of our states assert that all power is inherent in the people; that they may exercise it by themselves; that it is their right and duty to be at all times armed and that they are entitled to freedom of person, freedom of religion, freedom of property, and freedom of press."* Do you think Mr. Jefferson would be enamored with the current Supreme Court which thinks it's okay to detain people at will, which disallow public prayer, which allows the taking of property for corporate financial gain of the community, and which allows retribution for what we think (hate crimes), let alone what we say, and the redistribution of personal property through taxation? I think not!

In contrast, later in our history came the age of the progressives, who do not believe that our rights are endowed by a creator but are privileges of government, and thus, they can be changed based on the governments' desires. One such progressive was Louis Brandeis, a Supreme Court Justice (1916-1939), who described the interpretation of *property rights* this way: *"**rights** of property and the liberty of the individual **must be remolded**, from time to time, **to meet the changing needs of society.**"* (Bold added.) According to Brandeis, we should remold the rights of individuals around the changing society. How absurd, and this is the position of our Supreme Court today! They truly believe that if society needs a new shopping mall, or new modern homes that will increase property values, then legislatures should decide and then you should lose **your** property. The point lost is that our "rights" are antecedent to the Constitution and to this nation. Rights cannot be altered, abolished, or "remolded" for any society, they are a inseparable from the individual.

I do not approve of drug usage nor condone the violent black market that provides it. Today, in nearly every community around the nation, the government can seize legal, personal property with only the accusation of wrong doing. The mere possession of what is deemed to be a controlled substance provides for automatic forfeiture of property. Again how absurd! As I stated, I do not condone drug use; and I think it is a blight on our communities. However, we should not allow the rights of citizens to be taken away by unjust laws. Rights are **not** granted by the state, and the state has no authority to violate those rights.

The Fourth Amendment, as mentioned above, stipulates that property can only be taken after due process of law, meaning a trial. Then, and only then, should a fine be assessed and means of payment identified. The state contends that if an accused person used a vehicle in the commission of a crime (the possession of a controlled substance) then the state can seize the accused property. With this logic, if any law is broken while in a vehicle, then your property can be seized. The precedence has already been established. It is only a matter of time until further incursions are realized. It is not because of drugs that I object to this law; it is the unconstitutional application of the laws which are repugnant. With this same logic it is only a small step for lawmakers to rationalize that the public safety is better served by seizing any automobile where the operator show disregard for the public safety by exceeding the speed limit by more than 10 miles per hour. If it is the public safety, and all drug laws are based upon public safety that is of concern the confiscation argument has not bounds.

Folks, there is something terribly wrong in America when we think it's okay to kill unborn babies, it's okay to enslave the nation and rob them of one-third or more of their hard earned income, and when it suits the government, to take your property for some unknown community benefit and to steal your property *before* being convicted of a crime. I am sickened at what we have become as a nation. We have turned our backs on our history, our ideals, and our God and the land of brotherly love has turned into a seething cauldron of apathetic cowards. The only hope I see for this nation is either the second coming or a rise of the patriotic citizen, both would be welcome.

Chapter 13
First Amendment

In the 1943 Supreme Court Case of West Virginia Board of Education Vs. Barnette 319 U.S. 624, Justice Robert H Jackson said the following: *"The very purpose of the Bill of Rights was to withdraw certain subjects from the vicissitudes of political controversy, to place them beyond the reach of majorities and officials and to establish them as legal principles to be applied by the courts. One's right to life, liberty and property, to free speech, a free press, freedom of worship and assembly, and other fundamental rights* ***may not be submitted to vote; they depend on the outcomes of no elections.****"* (Bold added)

The amendments of the Constitution are not to be submitted to a vote. This means leave them alone, you (Congress) do not have the power to pass laws concerning these rights. Having said that, this statement is only partially true. Congress can pass any law on any item concerning the *places* under its jurisdiction (D.C., Federal areas and buildings, etc.). With that in mind, it is the enforcement of laws outside of that jurisdiction that allow the subjugation of the American people to laws which our government leaders know do not apply to citizens within the states. This is cowardly and despicable!

The first Amendment does not *give* us any rights. The amendment is comprised of six limitations put on the government. It merely states what the government cannot do, and thus protects citizens rights from government infringement.

The amendment reads as follows:

> *"Congress shall make no law respecting an establishment of religion, or prohibiting the free exercise thereof; or abridging the freedom of speech, or of the press; or the right of the people peaceably to assemble, and to petition the government for a redress of grievances."*

The six protections against government encroachment are:

1. Congress shall make no law respecting an establishment of religion
2. Congress shall make no law prohibiting the exercise of religion
3. Congress shall make no law abridging the freedom of speech
4. Congress shall make no law abridging the freedom of the press
5. Congress shall make no law abridging the right of the people peacefully to assemble
6. Congress shall make no law abridging the right to petition the government for a redress of grievance.

We will look at each of these to determine if the intent of the Constitution is being followed by our government, to include the courts.

1 & 2: Is in regards to the establishment of religion. Probably the most misquoted amendment in the entire Constitution. The phrase most erroneously used is the "separation of church and state." Do you see those words in that phrase? I don't. This phrase simply means that congress cannot make a law that creates a national religion.

Religious persecution was one of the primary reasons for leaving England and severing our association with the motherland. The king had created the Church of England, and he would not recognize any other religions. People were tortured, imprisoned, and even killed for believing contrary to the Church of England.

The authors of the Constitution did not want the government meddling in the private affairs of the citizens, who wished to be left alone to worship as they chose. The freedom of speech and the freedom to assemble created a strong mandate for the government to stay out of the religious affairs of the citizens.

These positions are well established in our historical writings and in the early law of the courts. It was not until recently that a wave of unrelenting legal challenges has weakened this amendment. The primary culprit has been the ACLU, which is no surprise. The ACLU's founder, Thomas Baldwin, has stated that his goal is to establish communism in America; and a leading tenet of communism is the removal of religion.

In *Everson v. Board of Education* 330 U.S. 1 (1947), Supreme Court Justice Hugo Black held that:

> *"The 'establishment of religion' clause of the First Amendment means at least this:* ***Neither a state nor the Federal Government can set up a church.*** *Neither can pass laws which aid one religion, aid all religions or prefer one religion over another.*

Neither can force nor influence a person to go to or to remain away from church against his will or force him to profess a belief or disbelief in any religion. No person can be punished for entertaining or professing religious beliefs or disbeliefs, for church attendance or non-attendance. No tax in any amount, large or small, can be levied to support any religious activities or institutions, whatever they may be called, or whatever form they may adopt to teach or practice religion. Neither a state nor the Federal Government can, openly or secretly, participate in the affairs of any religious organizations or groups and vice versa. In the words of Jefferson, the clause against establishment of religion by law was intended to erect 'a wall of separation between Church and State.'", (15-16). (Bold added)

Here is where we get the infamous "separation of church and state" phrase which many banter about. If you read the language of Justice Black's ruling, it says quite plainly that the government cannot pass laws that affect the free exercise of religion. The power of congress lies in legislation; they make law. That is all. They do not have the ability to force anyone into, out of, or in any way pass laws on religion. The opening line above (in bold) is stating the decision reached by the Supreme Court. Any law which *expands* (broadens) this interpretation is considered interpretive, and **should not be given any weight** in the courts.

His next sentence supports his first. We already know that Congress can "pass no law" establishing religion. The remaining limitations are geared primarily toward the exercise of religion. Again, the First Amendment emphasizes that Congress does not have the power to pass laws involving religion.

The courts and Congress have violated this Constitutional protection time and time again. The individual right of free speech and the exercise of religion should allow citizens to pray when and where they will. Congress has made allowances for Muslims to pray in airports; but they disallow a valedictorian to offer an invocation at school. We do not allow prayer in the classroom, but we have Presidential prayer breakfasts and a prayer is given to open Congressional sessions. We do not allow the Ten Commandments at a VFW post, but we have them on the halls of Congress.

The hypocrisy of this is, in the least, offensive; and more plainly, it is unconstitutional. Congress cannot "legally" prohibit religious free speech nor *require* it. Congress and the government are duplicitous with the communistic ACLU in bringing about and promoting, not freedom of religion, but a society *free OF religion*. They have become the whore of the communist agenda.

Items 3&4: Congress shall make no law abridging the freedom of speech or the press. We know the courts have placed limitations on this. We have all heard the often quoted: "you can't yell fire in a crowded movie theater." I believe you have the right to ***say*** it, however, you are also responsible for the reaction and panic you "cause". This goes back to the premise of personal responsibility. I am also free to print anything I want regarding someone else, but I'm responsible for those words; however, I am responsible for the legal consequences if what I say is not true.

Freedom of speech does not mean that I have the right to stop someone from speaking because it offends me. There is no such thing as a freedom not to be offended. I don't agree with racist positions on either side of the race issue; but I whole-heartedly agree that people have the right to say what they want. I also have the right to think and express my opinions regarding the stupidity of their positions. *They* may be offended; but I have the right to express my views just like they do.

Does my right to freedom of speech go away based on geography? Of course not! Whether I am on a street corner, in a class room, or auditorium, I have the right to express myself. If someone is a non-Christian giving a speech to a body of Christians; the believers may be offended by the words spoken against their beliefs, but they can still support the atheists' right to say it. Even if an atheist or agnostic becomes offended at having to sit through a commencement prayer, they should still support the right to have it offered.

Part of dealing with others in America is civility. Civility is the ability to act correctly even when you find yourself at odds with the situation. This is something I feel we have lost in America. There used to be a time when a preacher would recite scriptures on the street corner. We may not agree with his words but we supported his right to say it. The first step in defeating opposition is to silence the voice of your enemy; in this case, it is literally a battle between the *communist left of our society and freedom.*

Out of all of the sections of this amendment, item 5 is probably the least molested. So far we still have the right to meet together as we see fit; however, our ability to do so without intrusion or monitoring is slowly ebbing.

Item 6: The last vestige of peaceful control by the people upon their government is the right to petition for redress of grievance. The concept of petition stems back to the days of ruling kings in England, and the only way to right a wrong was to petition the King. One would pray for wisdom, understanding and relief of some grievance.

Prior to the Declaration of Independence, the colonists sent a number of petitions to the King of England to ask for a redress of grievance against what they perceived as injustice. In the Declaration of Independence, our forefathers spoke of the response from the King as:

> *"In every stage of these Oppressions We have Petitioned for Redress in the most humble terms: Our repeated Petitions have been answered only by repeated injury. A Prince, whose character is thus marked by every act which may define a Tyrant, is unfit to be the ruler of a free people."*

The King's response was "repeated injury". In reply to a similar event petition for redress by the citizens of our country, the government replied, "The government is answering the question, through our enforcement actions in the courts." The person making the statement was Terry Lemons, a high ranking IRS official in response to citizens asking for clarity about tax law. Why would a government, when asked about the law, respond with threats, and actual, force. This reminds me of a bully on the playground, when caught in a lie, the only response he had was to beat someone up.

What is our government so afraid of that there only response to petitions by honest citizens is a threat of "repeated injury?" It seems that history is repeating itself, and we know what happened when previous rulers would not respond to the people's petition.

On March 23, 1775, Patrick Henry's said the famous words: "give me liberty, or give me death". Many people do not know much about the history behind this quote. He spoke of long suffering, of petition and supplication to the King, and then he said:

> *"Ask yourselves how this gracious reception of our petition comports with those warlike preparations which cover our waters and darken our land....Let us not deceive ourselves, sir. These are the implements of war and subjugation; the last arguments to which kings resort. I ask gentlemen, sir, what means this martial array, if its purpose be not to force us to submission? Can gentlemen assign any other possible motive for it?*
>
> *"Has Great Britain any enemy, in this quarter of the world, to call for all this accumulation of navies and armies? No, sir, she*

> *has none. They are meant for us: they can be meant for no other. They are sent over to bind and rivet upon us those chains which the British ministry have been so long forging. And what have we to oppose to them? Shall we try argument? Sir, we have been trying that for the last ten years. Have we anything new to offer upon the subject? Nothing."*
>
> *"We have held the subject up in every light of which it is capable; but it has been all in vain. Shall we resort to entreaty and humble supplication? What terms shall we find which have not been already exhausted? Let us not, I beseech you, sir, deceive ourselves. Sir, we have done everything that could be done to avert the storm which is now coming on. We have petitioned; we have remonstrated; we have supplicated; we have prostrated ourselves before the throne, and have implored its interposition to arrest the tyrannical hands of the ministry and Parliament. Our petitions have been slighted; our remonstrances have produced additional violence and insult; our supplications have been disregarded; and we have been spurned, with contempt, from the foot of the throne! In vain, after these things, may we indulge the fond hope of peace and reconciliation."*

It seems inconceivable that our government would respond to a petition, by its citizens, with the force of the gun. I have heard people say that it could not happen in this country; however, in researching this issue, I found case after case of armed government response against its' citizens, to enforce questionable laws that were under petition.

When a people are oppressed by its' government, and that government will not answer their pleas, the government will leave the people with little alternative but to fight force with force. At one time or another, it has happened in every country of the world, and if "we the people" cannot get our government to answer our petitions peacefully, then all that is left are non-peaceful methods.

CHAPTER 14
4TH AMENDMENT

"The right of the people to be secure in their persons, houses, papers, and effects, against unreasonable searches and seizures, shall not be violated, and no warrants shall issue, but upon probable cause, supported by oath or affirmation, and particularly describing the place to be searched, and the persons or things to be seized."

There are two governmental limitations stated in this amendment.

1. The citizens are to be secure in their person, home, papers, and property, from unreasonable searches and seizure. In other words they have the privacy to go about their lives without worrying whether the government will invade them. This amendment was to ensure that the government does not trespass on the people nor take anything from the people without following correct legal procedure.
2. The government is restrained from taking either person or property without first getting a warrant, and only after proving probable cause. This, however, is only as valid as the judge is honest. There have been numerous cases in which judges have signed blank warrants, and the details are not filled in until after serving the warrant.

Again, this amendment is not a grant of right, but solely a limitation on the government to ensure that they do not trespass beyond their enumerated powers.

In United States v. Montoya De Hernandez, 473 U.S. 531 (1985), in dealing with the detention of a person at the border, the Supreme Court ruled: *"The 'reasonable suspicion' standard effects a needed balance between private and public interests when law enforcement officials must make a limited intrusion **on less than probable cause**."* (Bold added) On less than probable cause! It seems to me that someone is trying to rewrite the Fourth Amendment. The court is stating that the end justifies the means. In essence it says it is okay to break the law in order to uphold the law. I just don't get it!

In this case the defendant was taken into a secure area, stripped, searched and made to remain naked while two matrons watched her until she was able to produce a bowel movement. This lasted for 18 hours. The court's ruling on this case was, *"Under the circumstances, respondent's detention, while long, uncomfortable, and humiliating, was not unreasonably long."* Remember, there was no probable cause only suspicion based on profiling; and the respondent was detained for 18 hours, stripped naked and humiliated. But that's okay? I remember a time in Germany's history when people were treated like this, and the citizenry did nothing.

Justice Rehnquist, who gave the majority opinion stated: "*Consistently, therefore, with Congress' power to protect the Nation by stopping and examining persons entering this country, the Fourth Amendment's balance of reasonableness is qualitatively different at the international border than in the interior. Routine searches of the persons and effects of entrants are not subject to any requirement of reasonable suspicion, probable cause, or warrant, and first-class mail may be opened without a warrant on less than probable cause, Ramsey, supra. Automotive travelers may be stopped at fixed checkpoints near the border without individualized suspicion even if the stop is based largely on ethnicity, United States v. Martinez-Fuerte, 428 U.S. 543, 562–563 (1976), and boats on inland waters with ready access to the sea may be hailed and boarded with no suspicion whatever. United States v. Villamonte-Marquez, supra.*"

It appears that your rights slowly decrease until, when you reach the border, you no longer have rights! This is totally insane, since when did constitutional rights vary on geographical location? Notice that the Justice thought it was perfectly fine to detain someone when there was no suspicion of wrong doing solely for driving a car across or near the border, and this can be done solely based on profiling (what you look like). "Papers, papers please."

Much of the opinion given here was based on the need for strong security at the border. The justices willingly break constitutional law for safety reasons, implying that this is acceptable because it's in our best interest. I'm sure the Kremlin has used that line many times.

In this case, the woman was found to have been carrying a number of drug balloons within her digestive tract. I do not condone drug smuggling, but I do not agree with the incursions by the Supreme Court on our Constitutional rights. It has been said that it is better to let one guilty man go free than to incarcerate the innocent. Our courts have taken the opposite position indicating that it is better to trample the rights of all so that one may be brought to "justice." It is from these small encroachments that, little by little, our rights are being removed without our notice, until one day it may be too late.

It seems today that Americans only care about their rights when confronted by the government, and they turn a blind eye to the slow bleeding of our constitutional rights. It seems Americans today know more about American Idol than they do about American history. How can we look at the advancement in technology which allows the government to see through walls into our homes or through our clothing and we still don't see the enormous potential for abuse.

Many people today applaud the government's ability to intercept telephone calls, e-mail, and even to open our regular mail or to review our reading habits in the interest of national security. We see all too often police checkpoints to "verify vehicle documents" as a fishing expedition to find drunk drivers. This is all done in the interest of safety; of course. The pretense here is to save lives, again, by trampling just a little on everyone's rights; we may just catch a "bad guy." However, inch by inch, we keep giving up ground on our most fundamental rights.

Benjamin Franklin said: *"Any people that would give up liberty for a little temporary safety deserve neither liberty nor safety."*

On September 6, 2000, Jeffrey Rosen gave testimony to the Senate Judiciary Committed entitled, *The Fourth Amendment and the FBI's Carnivore Program.* A portion of that testimony is as follows:

> *"There is much uncertainty associated with Carnivore. Unlike a conventional wiretap, pen register or trap and trace device, Carnivore gives the FBI access to all of the traffic over an Internet Service Provider's Network, and asks us to trust the government's filters to identify communications from a specified target. This "trust the government" model has been rejected in real space. Traditional wire tapping laws put the responsibility on a communications provider to supply a specified communication to the government on presentation of a court order, and they require the government to minimize the privacy invasion as much as is feasible.*

Although the FBI is legally forbidden from monitoring the communications of citizens who are not targets under Carnivore, the mere knowledge that government agents have the technical capacity to read e-mail messages will greatly increase the uncertainty of innocent citizens at a time of widespread concern over privacy on the Internet. Moreover, the system has the potential to capture the content (as opposed to simply the identifying information) of targets and non targets alike. Although its filter is set to reveal only identifying information of specified communications, the system can be accessed remotely, increasing fears that rogue agents might change the configuration. And one of the safeguards of the system—the audit trail that records precisely which communications were intercepted—is made available to targets only if a prosecution actually results. Innocent citizens who are not targets have no notice when they are being monitored and therefore no confidence that they are not being monitored."

This testimony was taken one full year before the 911 attack on the World Trade Center. Do you think that the government has stepped up its' surveillance and acts on what it feels is in the best interest for America, regardless of infringement of our rights? I think you can guarantee they have, especially since they have admitted to doing so.

In *Katz* v. *United States*, 389 US 347, 359 (1967), Justice Douglas wrote: *'Neither the President nor the Attorney General is a magistrate ... I cannot agree that where spies and saboteurs are involved adequate protection of Fourth Amendment rights is assured when the President and Attorney General assume both the position of adversary-and-prosecutor and disinterested, neutral magistrate.'*

The Supreme Court, supposedly the protectors of the Constitution, does not agree that the Fourth Amendment can be assured, especially when dealing with spies and saboteurs. There have been spies and saboteurs since the beginning of time. The Fourth Amendment was put in place to keep an overreaching government in line, but according to the courts that cannot be assured.

In a recent case from United States District Court out of Michigan, case number 06-CV-10204, the Hon. Anna Diggs Taylor ruled as follows:

"This is a challenge to the legality of a secret program (hereinafter "TSP") undisputedly inaugurated by the National

Security Agency (hereinafter "NSA") at least by 2002 and continuing today, which intercepts without benefit of warrant or other judicial approval, prior or subsequent, the international telephone and internet communications of numerous persons and organizations within this country. The TSP has been acknowledged by this Administration to have been authorized by the President's secret order during 2002 and reauthorized at least thirty times since."

The opinion goes on further to say:

"... it is important to note that if the court were to deny standing based on the unsubstantiated minor distinctions drawn by Defendants, the President's actions in warrant less wiretapping, in contravention of FISA, Title III, and the First and Fourth Amendments, would be immunized from judicial scrutiny. It was never the intent of the Framers to give the President such unfettered control, particularly where his actions blatantly disregard the parameters clearly enumerated in the Bill of Rights. The three separate branches of government were developed as a check and balance for one another. It is within the court's duty to ensure that power is never "condense[d] ... into a single branch of government." Hamdi v. Rumsfeld, 542 U.S. 507, 536 (2004) (plurality opinion). We must always be mindful that "[w]hen the President takes official action, the Court has the authority to determine whether he has acted within the law." Clinton v. Jones, 520 U.S. 681, 703 (1997). "It remains one of the most vital functions of this Court to police with care the separation of the governing powers .... When structure fails, liberty is always in peril." Public Citizen v. U.S. Dept. of Justice, 491 U.S. 440, 468 (1989) (Kennedy, J., concurring)."

The concept that the government will do the right thing and have the best interest of the people in mind may not be correct. The government will do what is best for the government, and it will do everything in its power to remain in power. The individuals within the government are, for the most part, patriotic nationals (which are not the same as patriotic Americans), who believe they are doing what is best for the nation. However, should any citizen call into question any part of the government, that same government which is sworn to defend us, will unleash every power and place our lives under a microscope of scrutiny, which most of us could not endure. The IRS has been used to rob those who expose corruption and wrong doing. Families have been split up and houses ransacked by armed thugs all because they dared to question the government.

The level of technology and sophistication inherent in the federal intelligence collection machine rivals that in science fiction novels. The government has used this technology to gather large scores of data, so much data that they cannot analyze it all and have had to use computers to sort it all out. In their defense, they are looking for the bad guy, and are trying to stop the next horrific act of violence that will one day come again to our shores, but at what price?

On May 20, 2003 in a Statement before the House Committee on the Judiciary Subcommittee on the Constitution, James X. Dempsey Executive Director for the Center for Democracy & Technology testified:

> *"Under the changes that have been made since 9/11, the FBI is authorized by the Attorney General to go looking for information about individuals* ***with no reason to believe they are engaged in, or planning, or connected to any wrongdoing*** *... under the PATRIOT Act and other laws, the FBI may have the authority to scoop up entire databases of information,* ***including data on persons suspected of no wrongdoing****. Our laws are totally inadequate to deal with the reality of decentralized commercial databases and the new techniques of data mining....One important avenue of oversight for this Committee is how the FBI intends to use the technique known as* ***data mining****, which purports to be able to find evidence of possible terrorist preparations by* ***scanning billions of everyday transactions, potentially including a vast array of information about Americans' personal lives such as medical information, travel records and credit card and financial data****. The FBI's Trilogy project includes plans for data mining. According to an undated FBI presentation obtained by the Electronic Privacy Information Center, the FBI's use of public source information (including proprietary commercial databases) has grown 9,600% since 1992."*

Some think the government is doing what it needs to do to protect Americans from those who wish us harm. If we consider the trespassing on our rights protection, then I don't want to be protected. If we give up on what makes this country unique, freedom, then the terrorists have already won.

The constant retreat of Americans from protecting our inalienable rights has taken massive tolls on our precious freedom. We are told that we can't say things which might offend others, so we retreat. We are told to register our firearms, and we retreat. We are told we must have a license to carry a gun in order to defend ourselves, and we retreat. We are told that mere suspicion, not probable cause, now justifies unreasonable search and seizure, and we retreat. We petition the government, and their answer is to enforce those immoral and illegal laws, and we retreat. We are spied upon by our own government, who read our email, and know the books we read, and who open our mail, and we retreat. They unconstitutionally tax our labor, and we retreat. They license and tax our ability to freely move about, and we retreat. When will we stop retreating? When there is nothing left to retreat from?

Chapter 15
Emergency Powers

In an updated Congressional Research Service (CRS) Report dated November 13, 2006 entitled "National Emergency Powers", written by Harold C. Relyea, the opening paragraph states:

> *"The President of the United States has available certain powers that may be exercised in the event that the nation is threatened by crisis, exigency, or emergency circumstances **(other than natural disasters, war, or near-war situations)**. Such powers may be stated explicitly or implied by the Constitution, **assumed** by the Chief Executive to be permissible constitutionally, or inferred from or **specified by statute**. Through legislation, Congress has made a great many **delegations of authority** in this regard over the past 200 years".*
> (Bold Added)

In the first highlighted statement it says that the President has certain powers to deal with emergency circumstances, OTHER than natural disasters, war, or near-war situations. WHAT? I thought natural disasters, war, and near-war situations constituted a national threat, and at a minimum rose to the level of emergency, didn't you? He goes on to say that the president may just assume he has constitutionally-granted powers; or may be granted power from statute, meaning it is enacted by Congress.

What happened to the Constitution? The Constitution created a government with three distinct branches with separate powers and limitations to ensure no one branch of government gained too much power. As we shall see in the upcoming pages, we no longer have three separate branches of government when it comes to emergency powers. We will look at the impact of these consolidated powers as it affects the American people.

Mr. Relyea continues in his report to tell us:

"Some of these authorities, deriving from the Constitution or statutory law, are ***continuously available*** *to the President with little or no qualification. Others —* ***statutory delegations from Congress*** *— exist on a stand-by basis and remain dormant until the President formally declares a national emergency. These delegations or grants of power authorize the President to meet the problems of governing effectively in times of crisis. Under the powers delegated by such statutes,* ***the President may seize property, organize and control the means of production, seize commodities, assign military forces abroad, institute martial law, seize and control all transportation and communication, regulate the operation of private enterprise, restrict travel, and, in a variety of ways, control the lives of United States citizens."***

That is a lot of power to be placed in the hands of one man. Notice however, there is not one mention of defeating an enemy, repelling an invasion, or assistance in the case of a natural disaster. The emergency powers allow the president to "control the lives of United States citizens." If you look at each and every qualified action by the president, with the exception of assigning forces abroad (which as commander in chief he already has the power to do); he may, in effect, change the United States into a communist country. Notice the similarity between the assigned powers given to the President and powers in communist-controlled countries. He has the power to order martial law, to control all transportation and communication, to seize property, and to regulate the operation of private enterprise. A communist state operates in just this manner.

What does the Constitution have to say about Presidential powers?

Article II defines the office of the president and the exact powers he may have.

Section 1 deals with the qualifications and the election process of the president and vice president.

Section 2 describes the first of the powers granted to the president as:

"The President shall be Commander in Chief of the Army and Navy of the United States, and of the Militia ... and he shall have Power to grant Reprieves and Pardons for Offences against the United States, except in Cases of Impeachment."

He shall have Power, by and with the Advice and Consent of the Senate, to make Treaties,... appoint Ambassadors, other

> *public Ministers and Consuls, Judges of the supreme Court, and all other Officers of the United States, whose appointments are not herein otherwise provided for, and which shall be established by Law: but the Congress may by Law vest the Appointment of such inferior Officers, as they think proper, in the President alone, in the Courts of Law, or in the Heads of Departments.*
>
> *The President shall have Power to fill up all Vacancies that may happen during the Recess of the Senate, by granting Commissions which shall expire at the End of their next Session.*

Section 3 describes the final set of powers which are:

> *"He shall from time to time give to the Congress Information of the State of the Union, and recommend to their Consideration such Measures as he shall judge necessary and expedient; he may, on extraordinary Occasions, convene both Houses, or either of them, and in Case of Disagreement between them, with Respect to the Time of Adjournment, he may adjourn them to such Time as he shall think proper; he shall receive Ambassadors and other public Ministers; he shall take Care that the Laws be faithfully executed, and shall Commission all the Officers of the United States."*

Every governmental power and federal law must be founded in the enumerated powers given by the Constitution to that particular branch of the government. If no power is specified, no power is legally conferred. Also, there is no allowance for any branch of government to lend, or otherwise transfer or delegate their power to any other branch or government organization. Solely on this premise alone the United States today is running contrary to the Constitution and contrary to the principles which were put in place to protect citizens from exactly this sort of usurpation of power.

From the preceding, I can find no power granted by the constitution, to the president, the right to declare martial law. In fact, if you look at the enumerated powers, his primary job is as a manager for the United States dealing with foreign countries, the making of treaties, the overseeing of cabinet positions, and the appointment/recommendation of other governmental positions. The other role of the president, as commander-in-chief of the military was designed to create a separation of the war powers from any one branch of government. Again, his position is that of a manager. Along with his cabinet advisors he decides how to manage troop strength, base locations, etc. However, the president was never meant to have the ability to engage in war without a formal declaration from Congress. There is emplaced within the constitution broad scope for the president to direct the military in war-like engagements, such as to repel invasions and other calamities; and in general to provide for the common defense of the nation only when authorized by Congress to do so. That does not give him the power to declare war or commit the country to war, as this is a power reserved for the Congress.

There is great wisdom in separating the command of the military and the enactment of war (or acts of war). A body of men is much less likely to "react" to stressful situations and allow for calmer heads to prevail. Yet, when crises and evil strikes, the elected officials have the backing of the states to declare war, and thus, to provide the authority for a president to prosecute such a war. Short of this declaration, the president, and therefore the nation, is involved in police actions, at best, and global manipulation, or secret combinations at worst. This is not the checks and balances our forefathers wrote into the Constitution and their writings extolling the virtues of this separation of power as well as warnings of dire consequences should the people allow this power to coalesce into a single branch of government. It has become apparent their fears have become well founded.

There are those, however, who believe that the President has the power to do anything he wants unless it is explicitly forbidden by the Constitution. One proponent of this was Theodore Roosevelt, who claimed the "stewardship" theory when he wrote, *"insistence upon the theory that the* ***executive power was limited only by specific restrictions and prohibitions appearing in the Constitution or imposed by the Congress*** *under its constitutional powers."* (From CRS report, Bold added)

Someone who believes in this position might envision kingly powers belonging to the presidency. This I am sure, was never the intent of the founders. Why else would they have written so much about the separation of powers, as well as the Tenth Amendment, which states that all powers not enumerated are reserved to the states or to the people? Why would the Constitution list the powers of the president if they meant to give him open ended powers? If you agree with Roosevelt, wouldn't it make more sense, for the writers of the Constitution to note what the president could not do rather than what he could? No. The writers of the Constitution, in articles and personal correspondence, have been quite clear that the Constitution provides limitations on the government; and it does not grant broad-reaching powers as we see today.

In contrast William Howard Taft viewed the presidential office in more limited terms, writing: *"that the President can exercise no power which cannot be fairly and reasonably traced to some specific grant of power or justly implied and included within such express grant as proper and necessary to its exercise."* (Included in CRS report)

A majority of Constitutional scholars whom I have researched have agreed that the intent of the Constitution was more in line with Taft's view, and they feel that the warnings by the founders against abuse of power would result from the Roosevelt position.

The first real test of Presidential use of emergency powers came under President Lincoln. Shortly before Lincoln was elected; the south had announced that they would secede from the union if Lincoln *was* elected. He was, and the Confederacy was born.

After his election, while Congress was on break, Lincoln made some very controversial and unconstitutional decisions. By March of 1861, seven states had announced their secession from the union. Rather than recall the Congress and raise the issue in the Constitutional manner, President Lincoln decided to issue proclamations (as a King would do) to order blockades of certain southern shipping ports and a call to raise troops. This was a clear violation of the Constitution.

In July, with the newly assembled Congress, President Lincoln explained his reason for not including Congress. He stated, *"...these measures, whether strictly legal or not, were ventured upon under what appeared to be a popular and a public necessity, trusting then, as now, that Congress would readily ratify them. It is believed, that nothing has been done beyond the constitutional competency of Congress."* Notice Lincoln does not say HE had the power to declare these actions, only that this was something felt was sure that Congress would approve. The Congress, by subsequently authorizing the actions of the President, gave their approval for those actions.

When we hear presidents today speaking about emergency powers, "long-standing traditions," or Congressional delegation, they are speaking of the Supreme Courts and Congress' lack of action in holding the executive branch in check. Without the balance of power there are no longer the checks and balances necessary to ensure abuses of power do not continue.

There are many books and research materials available to anyone who may wishes to take the time to read about the history of war powers. Let it be understood, that many presidents have used them but not always with the best intentions.

Emergency powers were given to President Wilson during the First World War; upon completion of the war, he requested they be terminated. Other presidents who have enacted emergency powers have not terminated these powers. FDR was notorious for enacting emergency powers which allowed him broad latitude to achieve his political goals. His first such proclamation came in his first few weeks of taking office, and it was a method he utilized throughout his presidency.

Since the early 1900's presidents have maintained nearly a constant state of "emergency" in order to allow them greater latitude and power. The initial question is why this has been allowed to go on and as there is no basis in the constitution to allow for such a grievous breach of the separation of powers, why do we tolerate it today? The simplest answer is the ignorance of the American people. Ignorance is simply lacking necessary information in order to make an informed decision. This abuse of power is something that has not been told to the people as those on capital hill like their jobs, their money, and their power; and they will do anything to maintain them.

Title 12 United State Code, CHAPTER 2, SUBCHAPTER IV, Section 95b states: *"The actions, regulations, rules, licenses, orders and proclamations heretofore or hereafter taken, promulgated, made, or issued by the President of the United States or the Secretary of the Treasury since March 4, 1933, pursuant to the authority conferred by section 95a of this title, are approved and confirmed."*

What was that? Any action by the president, or Secretary of the Treasury, that has been or *will be done,* are automatically approved and confirmed. How would you like that kind of power? They don't even know what is going to be done, but it's already approved, and made into law. This is the same language that appears in the Act of March, 9 1933, which was put in place by FDR, and which is still in force. That's right, even without the War on Terrorism; we have been under emergency war powers. This is how the presidents, contrary to Constitutional law, have gotten away with all of their proclamations, executive orders, and enactment of laws against the citizens of the United States. Ladies and gentlemen, welcome to our democratic Constitutional Dictatorship.

Chapter 16
Common Law

Bouviers Law dictionary (1856) defines common law as:

"That which derives its force and authority from the universal consent and immemorial practice of the people. It has never received the sanction of the legislature, by an express act, which is the criterion by which it is distinguished from the statute law. It has never been reduced to writing; by this expression, however, it is not meant that all those laws are at present merely oral, or communicated from former ages to the present solely by word of mouth, but that the evidence of our common law is contained in our books of Reports, and depends on the general practice and judicial adjudications of our courts."

"2. The common law is derived from two sources, the ***common law of England, and the practice and decision of our own courts****. In some states the English common law has been adopted by statute. There is no general rule to ascertain what part of the English common law is valid and binding. To run the line of distinction is a subject of embarrassment to courts, and the want of it a great perplexity to the student. It may, however, be observed generally, that it is binding where it has not been superseded by the constitution of the United States, or of the several states, or by their legislative enactments, or varied by custom, and where it is founded in reason and consonant to the genius and manners of the people."*

"3. The phrase 'common law' occurs in the seventh article of the amendments of the Constitution of the United States. In suits at common law, where the value in controversy shall not exceed

> *twenty dollars says that article, 'the right of trial by jury shall be preserved.' The 'common law' here mentioned is the common law of England, and not of any particular state. The term is used in contradistinction to equity, admiralty, and maritime law."*
>
> *"4. The common law of England is not in all respects to be taken as that of the United States, or of the several states; its general principles are adopted only so far as they are applicable to our situation."*

Very few people alive today have attended a trial at common law. What happened to common law, and why are we not using it today?

Prior to the widespread availability of our current legal system, there was the common law. Common law, or what some may call the natural or scientific law, dealt with the interactions of man with man and mans relationship to property. This concept flourished in the new world with it's concepts of liberty and responsibility. It was also the antithesis of the Equity, Maritime or Admiralty Law that England used to suppress the colonies.

With this natural law and the concept of individual freedom, everyone was free to make their own choices in life unless their choices infringed on the freedom of another or if it caused injury, physically or to ones property. For instance, one could ride their horse through town at break neck speeds; but unless I caused some injury it was not against the law, as there was no injured party.

The second type of law, as we know it today is political or statute law. Here things get murky because law becomes a thing of enactment. Rules were put into place solely for the rules sake, and some emotional need of the people.

One major problem with common law is that the rules, although similar, would vary from community to community. As no two communities were identical in makeup and history, the legal necessities inherent to that system would be different. This was based on how law was administered in prior cases. There were no written laws, per se, but more a way of living, when someone trespassed against another, a mediator would listen to both sides of the story and would render a decision. The decisions, in effect, established "laws of behavior."

As communities grew larger and transportation made travel to other communities more common, disputes between groups with varying legal beliefs became more frequent. In these instances the "judge" would have to establish a common ground between both parties, and then he would decide a binding decision.

As this system was based upon philosophical or religious beliefs about how one man should treat another, there came about two fundamental laws upon which all other laws were predicated. The first was honor; your word was your bond. This harkens back to a time when a deal was struck with a hand shake. The second principle was respect for others and their property. On these two fundamentals hung all the laws.

Laws today which describe offenses such as theft, murder, extortion, or a myriad of other crimes, you can see that these laws have been enacted within the last 150 years or so. Under common law, these behaviors have always been prohibited. Common Law deals with the legal interactions between men and their property rather than theoretical, abstract, legal concepts. In essence, common law is the basis for all laws we currently have today; but the spirit of the law has changed from one of justice to one of enforcement or control.

What we have today is the antithesis of common law; it is political law. Political law is based on force; and in many instances, it has no basis in the concepts of morality or right and wrong. More often than not, its genesis was based in knee-jerk reactions to random events and a need for the politico to appear to be involved. Another term for this is mob rule; we make the laws, and we have the force of the mob to keep you in line.

The basis of equality in a Court of Common law is that of an impartial "judge" who monitors the proceedings and who protects the rights of all parties. The jury is the only decider of the fact and the applicability of the law in the case. This system is in contrast to today's judges who work for the state, and who are therefore a party to any dispute brought by the state. Therefore, today's judges cannot be impartial, as they derive their livelihood from the prosecutorial state. In fact, there have been judges, in today's courts who, have refused to allow "law" to be argued in front of a jury or who have refused to allow arguing of constitutional rights.

Another contrast is in the ability of the common man to understand the law. Common law was easily understood by anyone who could read. Under our current political system, the law has become convoluted, written in legalese which takes a team of lawyers to write and twice as many to make it understood. Common law was based on principle of right, wrong, and justice. Today's laws are transient and change with the political sentiment of the day.

As an example, A man walking down the street is met by another man who begins to impede the progress of the first man. The second man then begins to question the validity of the first mans parentage and let's off a string of verbal abuses that would make a sailor blush. The second man then hauls off and hits the first man knocking him to the ground. There are witnesses to both the first and second man actions and a passing policeman takes both into custody. When brought before the judge, under common law, it was quite likely that the behavior of the second man to the first was justified based on the verbal attack against the honor and decency against the first man. And you may have heard the words, "He got what he deserved." In today's court it matters not the reasoning for the assault by the second man against the first, the statute states if you strike another person you are guilty, regardless, and you will be sentenced.

Our laws today are quite simply policy/law en***force***ment; you do what the political powers say or else. No right or wrong, only compliance. Our own Supreme Court has warned us about the evolution of our laws in the case of Laird v. Tatum, 408 U.S. 1 (1972), in which Chief Justice Burger said the following:

> *"The America once extolled as the voice of liberty heard around the world no longer is cast in the image which Jefferson and Madison designed, but more in the Russian image."*

A good example of a political law is the seat belt law. Everyone knows you are safer wearing a seat belt when driving a car; however, stupidity has never been a crime. The political law makes lack of compliance a crime even when there are no injured parties or wrong doing. The only injury occurs is to the words written on paper; no trespass has been committed, no one has been damaged or been injured, a citizen has been penalized for non-compliance. This is simply enforcement for no other reason than "because I said so".

It used to be required that "intent" be established when dealing with a crime. Black's Law Dictionary, Seventh Edition, defines intent as: *"The state of mind accompanying an act, esp. a forbidden act."* I was important to establish the intent of the actor of a crime to determine the severity of the act. This is akin to what we now use as "motive", but they are not the same thing. Motive goes to the inducement to do an act, and intent is the mental state at the time of the incident.

One of the primary reasons for our break with England was the difference between totalitarian political law and the freedom of common law, which is why it was written into the Constitution. Common law is the closest law to freedom. It is the closest for freedom, because in is founded in individual sovereignty, and the belief that a man does what he wants (as a free man) until, or unless it interferes with the freedom or property of another. Then and only then did the "law" take effect.

The clearest way to describe the difference between the two systems, is explaining the difference between liberty and permission.

Under common law, you could be taxed on the purchase of certain items; but you would never need a license to travel, or even to drive a car. A license denotes a privilege granted not an expression of freedom. Under common law, any man could do as he wished to support his family—make furniture, blacksmith, run a general store, etc. Under our current political system, you must first have a license to perform a trade; this is a means of control. If at any time the controlling political power wishes to revoke your license, or demand costly control measures, you are out of business. Between the old Soviet system and our current political system, the only difference is the degree of control. If you wish to do business in Russia, you must get a license/ permission from the government, just like you do here. In Russia, you must relinquish a high percentage of earnings to the government. In our political system the government takes from both the corporations as well as the workers. Our government is becoming more and more like our comrades across the sea.

As we have seen in the previous chapters, governmental powers have grown; while at the same time the freedoms and rights of the citizen have diminished. Under natural or scientific law we are all the same under the law, whether the president or citizen. Today a citizen cannot sue the government without the government's permission. Does this sound like a government "by and for the people?"

Under the common law the fundamental rights to life, liberty, and property were gifts from the creator which could not be revoked, modified, or otherwise infringed upon. The political system is based upon privilege and license; and life, liberty, and property are meted out and controlled by the government.

Today you can still find remnants of common law in our current legal system; but they are few and far between. Nearly all "common law" has been replaced by statute law. It is operating under the political system; and serves that end, not the people. An example of common law still in practice today is the idea of common law marriage. No license from the state (political system) and there may, or may not be, a religious ceremony. Years ago this was the norm.

A precept of common law; was that there had to be some damage or loss. Today we hear about victimless crimes. Laws; such as the seat belt law, traffic laws, drug laws, firearms laws, etc., are considered "victimless crimes." The term "victimless crime" is an oxymoron. You cannot have a "crime" if there is no victim? A paramount right of a defendant is to face his accuser and to establish "harm". Remember the adage "no harm no foul?" If there is no damage to self or property, where is the crime?

In contrast to common law, statutory law only covers what is written; and therefore, constant additional policy is required to "correct" deficiencies in the code when there is no statute to cover a particular situation. However, justice is not the main issue when dealing with statutory law; the violation of a policy (what is written down in a code book) is the main concern. Statutory law is, by purpose and design, a mechanism of social control created by the power elite. No longer is it necessary to prove damage or offense against another, rather it is a concept of the "state" claiming injury to itself. As the state is a creation of fiction, a non-living, non-sentient entity of corporate creation, how can it be injured? The state has established a collective approach to governance, what they deem is best for the masses, as opposed to the Constitution which endows the individual with the power and freedom thereby enhancing the masses.

What damage is created when someone commits an infraction against the State's rules? If you asked the state, they would reply that it damages the public impression of security and control the state has over the populace in their charge. By punishing and advertising the punishment, the state enforces its domination on the masses. This instills fear into the citizens to ensure compliance with state rules, thereby deterring anyone else from breaking the rules. Merely the mechanism of government "control" over it's citizens.

If this represents the protection of the citizens and control of the lawless, then who is the beneficiary of their action? Is it the general population who feel safer knowing the police state is there to protect them? If so, then why do we get that sinking feeling every time a police car pulls in behind us? No my fellow Americans, the beneficiary is the state who maintains the ability to control the sheeple (people acting like sheep). If the citizens will cringe and do what they are told solely because a law was passed then they will think twice when told to pay one half of their entire earnings to the state, solely because they wrote that down as well. Ah, now it makes sense. They could not do this under common law; that had to be changed.

Once again, this highlights how the *freedoms* we once had have slowly been replaced with *privileges* that grow smaller and smaller each year. The constant eroding of our rights, if done all at once, would cause a great upheaval among the people that could not be contained. But as with the proverbial frog in the pot of water, we are slowly being par boiled, and we are seemingly doing the backstroke thinking life is good.

Chapter 17
9th Amendment

The 9th Amendment is arguably the most misunderstood and least quoted amendment in the Bill of Rights; however, it was one of the most discussed and most argued about before its inclusion in the Constitution.

The amendment simply states:

"The enumeration in the Constitution, of certain rights, shall not be construed to deny or disparage others retained by the people."

Basically this amendment states that the citizens of the United States have more rights than just those enumerated in the Constitution, and the government is forbidden to deny us those rights.

There are those that would argue that you cannot defend this position, because you cannot identify what rights were being stipulated. I disagree; any "freedom" enjoyed by the people and those upheld by the Supreme Court, such as privacy, travel, presumption of innocence, etc., are all rights not enumerated. Remember, the Constitution was created to "define" the government and the "limits" of the government. Any powers not enumerated to the government, remained with the states or to the people. So I would say it is much easier to argue how small the government should be and thereby show the expanse of the citizen's rights.

Still a harder question is; do we have the "right" to be free from federal harassment? When our country was first started, and for nearly a century thereafter, the Federal government had virtually NO dealings with the average citizen. It was not until the civil war that the government started creating statues that affected the population and which directly affected the states' sovereignty. Now there is nearly no aspect in which the government is not involved, from the bedroom, to birth, to the boardroom, and to the grave. This is not how this republic is supposed to operate.

During the early stages of our country, before the Constitution, and the creation of the Bill of Rights, there were ongoing arguments. The first being that there was no need to enumerate the rights as they were obvious to all citizens and the government. The second position was that if you listed their rights it would automatically allow for the government to control any that were left off the list.

In the end, it was decided to enumerate government limitations which ensured certain key rights could not be infringed upon by the government. As we can see, the government did not honor their side of the agreement. The Ninth Amendment was written, therefore, to address concerns regarding the other rights enjoyed by the citizens.

It is no mistake that the Ninth Amendment is then followed by the directive of the Tenth Amendment, which says:

> *"The powers not delegated to the United States by the Constitution, nor prohibited by it to the states, are reserved to the states respectively, or to the people."*

The founders probably thought they had this beast, called federal government, reigned in. There was acknowledgement that the people had un-enumerated rights and that the government could only have the powers that were enumerated in the Constitution. All other power was relegated to the States or to the people. There you have the perfect solution, limited government, strong states, and a free-sovereign people. This sounds good, doesn't it? This did not last; however, as greedy, power hungry, professional politicians took control of the government and started twisting the meanings of words, which completely changed the meaning of the Constitution.

No longer was the government bound by the Constitution, but it was redefined, allowing all power to the federal unless specifically denied by the Constitution. This was a completely different view which no one has been able to defend; yet it has been the mantra in our government for over a century.

What are the rights alluded to in the Ninth Amendment? They are, and must be, the natural rights of each individual citizen. It is the inherent right of each citizen to dispose of his person and property as he sees fit without license, tax, or other infringement by the federal government.

Ultimately, it is up to the courts, especially the Supreme Court, to decide this fact in law.

One such case is **GRISWOLD v. CONNECTICUT**, 381 U.S. 479 (1965). In this case, the court ruled that the Ninth Amendment provides for an inherent, and therefore, Constitutional, right of marital privacy which cannot be infringed by any arm of government. Justice Douglas went on to say: *"Specific guarantees in the Bill of Rights have penumbras, formed by emanations from those guarantees that help give them life and substance. Various guarantees create zones of privacy."* Zones of privacy are areas which the government has no business. These include our homes, our papers, our marriages, and bedrooms all those rights are antecedent to the Constitution.

I wish to reiterate that the Constitution does not "grant" any rights. The purpose of the Constitution was to create a government and provide the bounds by which it would operate. As dictated in the Tenth Amendment, if a power was not granted by the Constitution, to the government, it does not exist, **period**. All other powers and rights reside with the states and the people from which all the authority in the Constitution is derived.

The theory, held by some, that the only rights we have are those that are enumerated in the first eight amendments of the Bill of Rights is ludicrous. If that were so, there would be no need for the Ninth Amendment. There are numerous natural rights which have found there way into law; such as the right of self defense. The Bill of Rights does not enumerate such a right, but it is upheld by the courts.

I would venture to say that any right, any desire of man that does not infringe on the rights of another, is a protected right. If I wish to drive down the road without a seat belt, so be it. The government has no "right" to infringe upon its' citizens by making policy when there is no injury in the act.

Some would argue that wearing seat belts saves lives, and this is true. Wearing a life preserver when in the water also saves lives, so why don't we mandate by law that anyone entering a swimming pool must wear a certified floatation device? There are thousands of people who are poisoned each year from household cleaners. Should we then license anyone wishing to use such cleaners, and make them store such cleaners only in approved locked metal containers outside of the home? Should any violations of these laws mean stiff jail sentences? The absurdity is apparent. It is not the government's responsibility to save us from ourselves.

I was once told that the free citizen's right to swing his fist ended somewhere just short of someone else's nose. This means that until there is injury, whether personal, property, or monetary, they are free to do as they wish. All else is nothing more than control by government.

Constitutional lawyer, Lysander Spooner, in a letter to Grover Cleveland in 1886 stated: *"What then, were these 'other rights', that had not been 'enumerated'; but which were nevertheless 'retained by the people'? Plainly they were men's natural 'rights'; for these are the only 'rights' that 'the people' ever had, or, consequently, that they could 'retain,' And as no attempt is made to enumerate these 'other rights' ... and as no exceptions are made of any of them, the necessary, the legal, the inevitable inference is, that they were 'retained'; and that Congress should have no power to violate any of them. Now, if Congress and the courts had attempted to obey this amendment, as they were constitutionally bound to do, they would soon have found that they had really no lawmaking power whatever left to them; because they would have found that they could make no law at all, of their own invention that would not violate men's natural rights."*

This "free man" concept extends to every aspect of life. The statement, "the power to tax is the power to destroy" describes why the federal could not tax the people directly. The earnings and property, of an individual is constitutionally not something that is under the taxing authority of the government. The right to a make a living is understood, and the power to tax that right converts the right into a privilege. If the government is given the power to tax a citizens income then they are given the ability to destroy that income, and it is therefore repugnant to the Constitution and to every free man in this nation.

What did our founding fathers say concerning our rights?

> Our second President, John Adams stated: *"You have rights antecedent to all earthly governments; rights that cannot be repealed or restrained by human laws; rights derived from the Great Legislator of the Universe"*
>
> In 1819 Thomas Jefferson wrote in a letter to Isaac H. Tiffany: *"... rightful liberty is unobstructed action according to our own will within limits drawn around us by the equal rights of others. **I do not add 'within the limits of the law**,' because law is often but the tyrant's will, **and always so when it violates the right of an individual**"* (Bold added)
>
> On November 20, 1772, Samuel Adams wrote: *"Among the natural rights of the colonists are these: first, a right to life; second, to liberty; third, to property; together with the right to support and defend them in the best manner they can. These are evident branches of ... the duty of self-preservation, commonly called the first law of nature. All men have a right to*

*remain in a state of nature as long as they please; and in case of intolerable oppression, civil or religious, to leave the society they belong to, and enter into another.... **Now what liberty can there be where property is taken away without consent?**"* (Bold added) With this in mind, does the IRS have your consent when they take your property?

John Adams stated: "*You have rights antecedent to all earthly governments; rights that cannot be repealed or restrained by human laws; rights derived from the Great Legislator of the Universe.*"

And another quote by Thomas Jefferson, speaks to our responsibility in retaining those rights, said: *"When once a republic is corrupted, there is no possibility of remedying any of the growing evils but by removing the corruption and restoring its lost principles; every other correction is either useless or a new evil."*

The words of Samuel Adams, John Adams, and Thomas Jefferson portray the true meaning of freedom for the American people, it is the individual. So long as the individual is kept free the collective of our society will be forever prosperous, remove the individual freedom and our great nation will fall to collective anarchy.

Chapter 18
16th Amendment

The Government Printing Office (GPO) is the official keeper of government documents, and it makes available to all citizens it's documents, from budget reports to historical documents. One such document is a treatise on the Constitution and the Bill of Rights along with relevant Supreme Court decisions and the history pertaining to the topic in question.

The following are excerpts from the GPO document concerning the Sixteenth Amendment. These excerpts explain the history and reasons for the amendments enactment (pages 1951-1964). The document may be found at the following web site: http://www.gpoaccess.gov/ constitution/html/ amdt16.html.

The 16th Amendment states:

> *"The Congress shall have power to lay and collect taxes on incomes, from whatever source derived, without apportionment among the several States, and without regard to any census or enumeration."*

It then goes into the history and purpose of the amendment, stating: *"The ratification of this Amendment was the direct consequence of the Court's decision in 1895 in Pollock v. Farmers' Loan & Trust Co.,"* (*Pollock v. Farmers' Loan & Trust Company*, 157 U.S. 429 (1895))

The Pollock case was an important Supreme Court case that ruled that a tax on income derived from real property was a *direct tax* under the Constitution; and thus it had to be apportioned to the individual states.

The GPO continues, stating: *"A tax on incomes derived from property, the Court declared, was a "direct tax" which Congress under the terms of Article I, Sec. 2, and Sec. 9, could impose only by the rule of apportionment according to population"*

If things are working as they should; direct taxes must be apportioned to the states as outlined in the Constitution.

Continuing further, the government report gets to the meat of the topic, stating: *"Because of such endeavors the Court thus found it possible to sustain a corporate income tax as an excise "measured by income"* ***on the privilege of doing business in corporate form.*** *"* (Flint v. Stone Tracy Co., 220 U.S. 107 (1911)). *"The adoption of the Sixteenth Amendment, however, put an end to speculation whether the Court, unaided by constitutional amendment, would persist along these lines of construction until it had reversed its holding in the Pollock case. Indeed, in its initial appraisal* (Brushaber v. Union Pac. R.R., 240 U.S. 1 (1916)) *of the Amendment it classified income taxes as being inherently "indirect." "The command of the amendment that all income taxes shall not be subject to apportionment by a consideration of the sources from which the taxed income may be derived, forbids the application to such taxes of the rule applied in the Pollock case by which alone such* ***taxes were removed from the great class of excises, duties, and imports subject to the rule of uniformity and were placed under the other or direct class.***"(Ibid) *"The Sixteenth Amendment conferred* ***no new power of taxation*** *but simply prohibited the previous complete and plenary power of income taxation possessed by Congress from the beginning from being taken out of the category of indirect taxation to which it inherently belonged."* (Stanton v. Baltic Mining Co., 240 U.S. 103, 112 (1916).)

Again, notice the theme running throughout this discourse. Even upon the enactment of the 16th Amendment, this amendment deals solely with business as corporate income on the privilege of doing business in **corporate form**. Notice it does not stop at "doing business." It is the right of all people to "do business," but only when in *corporate form.* Only then do you have government protection and privilege upon which you may be taxed. An excise is synonymous with privilege.

The government goes on to admit that the 16th Amendment merely took the business (excise) duties and imports and placed them under the direct class. We are still dealing with gains from corporate activity, with which the individual has no involvement and was not taxable before the 16th Amendment. The next sentence states the amendment conferred no new power of taxation. If this power did not exist before the amendment then it did not have it after. Again I reiterate, Pollack, Brushaber, and all the other cases during this time were ALL **corporate income cases not personal income tax cases**.

The government goes on to define income: *"Building upon definitions formulated in cases construing the* ***Corporation Tax Act of 1909,"*** (Stratton's Independence v. Howbert, 231 U.S. 399 (1913)) *"the Court initially* ***described income*** *as the "gain derived from capital, from labor, or from both combined," inclusive of the* ***"profit gained through a sale or conversion of capital assets"***; (Eisner v. Macomber, 252 U.S. 189 (1920)) *"in the following array of factual situations it subsequently applied this definition to achieve results that have been productive of extended controversy."*

The government has reiterated that income, as described by Congress and the courts, is and has always been, profit from corporate activity. When you go to work and exchange your time and talents for compensation, is that profit or an exchange of property? It is an agreed upon exchange of property. Money is property, and skill and time are properties. An individual does not earn "profit", which is what is taxed, when he works for another person or company. It is merely an "exchange" of properties you and your employer have agreed upon.

The entire treatise does not break from the aforementioned business explanation. The 16th Amendment was deemed the means by which to enforce taxation of (the privilege of) doing business (in the corporate sense); it was not meant to impact the individual. It has only been the misapplication of tax law that started the taxing of individuals.

When the IRS was asked where it got its' authority to tax the citizens of the United States, it replied from that it was from 16th Amendment. As we have just seen, from the governments own historical accounts, the 16th Amendment was meant for corporate business. In the chapter on taxation, I said that Congress may define the meaning of words or phrases, which they quite often do. They have defined a person to include corporations, partnerships, etc. This, in my opinion, is a direct attempt by the Congress to subvert the Constitution and expand the taxing powers of Congress from the corporate to the individual. However, unless the government decides to put forth another amendment to allow for individual taxation, the majority of citizens are being robbed of their property and Constitutional rights of due process.

There are those in the patriot movement who contend that the 16th Amendment was never ratified and is therefore null and void. In Bill Benson's book, "The Law That Never Was," he makes a convincing argument that the 16th amendment was never legally ratified and evidences further that Secretary of State, Philander Knox, committed fraud when he declared it ratified in February 1913.

All of this may be true however, we find ourselves in the quandary as for what can be done about it. The Treasury Department, with its entire enforcement mechanism, can in no way agree to this finding. If it does, then the entire gravy train stops, and the government would have to admit to wrong-doing. Do you really think they would do such a thing?

In the case of Murphy v. IRS, 362 F. Supp. 2d 206, 211-. 12, 218 (2005), when trying to determine "incomes", the Supreme Court, stated:

> *"**The Sixteenth Amendment simply does not authorize the Congress to tax as "incomes" every sort of revenue a taxpayer may receive**. As the Supreme Court noted long ago, the "**Congress cannot make a thing income which is not so in fact.**" Burk-Waggoner Oil Ass'n v. Hopkins, 269 U.S. 110, 114 (1925). Indeed, because the "the power to tax involves the power to destroy," McCulloch v. Maryland, 17 U.S. (4 Wheat.) 316, 431 (1819), **it would not be consistent with our constitutional government**, and the sanctity of property in our system, **merely to rely upon the legislature to decide what constitutes income.**"*
> (Bold added)

Here the courts have admitted that not all "incomes" are taxable, and congress cannot make a thing income when it is not income. We can then infer the meaning of the term "income," as it was used at the time of the so called ratification of the 16th Amendment, it was corporate gains. Money that comes in from the trade of skill and time is not income in the 16th Amendment sense; and therefore a direct tax on the individual is unconstitutional if not apportioned. And, as the court dictated, the legislature can not be consistent with the Constitution if it tries to change the original meaning of the term income. Either way, direct taxation of the people without apportionment to the states is unconstitutional, and therefore illegal.

Again, I do not disagree with the governments power of taxation, only it's enforcement of taxation, by force, upon that which it does not have the authority to tax.

CHAPTER 19
CONCLUSION

Reading any one of the previous chapters, by it self, might lead a person to conclude that no government is perfect, and things are not so bad. They may decide that mankind, being fallible, may err from time to time; ant that America is still the best country in the world. And it is! The problem is not that America is not a great place to live. The problem is that, on the topic of individual freedom, America is not as great as it was, or as great as it could be, and much more importantly, individual rights are dwindling. For generation's the nations of the world have looked on as America prospered. They envied our strength, our resolve, but most of all they envied our steadfast belief in something greater than the individual, and yet bound to the individual. They envied our belief that the society, as a whole, is better when the individual is free. In no other country in the world has this amount of freedom ever existed before; where the right of the individual was above that of the governing body. And regrettably, the freedom that set us apart also provided the apathy that has allowed it to slowly, and systematically, be taken from us.

Each and every preceding chapter has illuminated a loss of freedom for the Citizen's of the United States. Each and every preceding chapter has a coherent theme that most all of us will have missed, and yet has been a factor in the demise of every single individual freedom. That coherent theme has been collectivism. Whether we couch collectivism in "the needs of the many", "what is best for all", or even "what is best for our country", the end result is still the same; the many over the value of the individual. What most on the collective left do not seem to understand is that by strengthening the individual, the whole is made stronger. By demanding responsibility of the individual, the collective is made responsible. By making the individual free the whole is made free.

There are plans by powerful men in both government and business to control the masses. Some are done with feelings of parental guidance in a desire to do what is best for the country they love. Others, and I fear the majority, are doing so out of greed for power and money. We have discussed the corruption within the government, the slow encroachment, generation after generation, until the government is in every aspect of our lives. Sucking the very life from each and every Citizen of this nation, if you don't think so, ask yourself on April 15th of each year if paying more taxes will make your life better.

Our leaders have given away/delegated their responsibilities, or usurped powers they were never supposed to have. We have instituted a professional political structure where the servant of the people can serve two terms in office and be paid for the rest of his life out of the pockets of those he serves. The politicians make more money as servants of the people than the above average citizen makes, does not pay into Social Security, and has the best health care the Citizens can provide. Yet, the average Citizen, which pays his salary, has none of that.

Each year the price tag of taxation for each Citizen increases. It is projected that with the combined taxation of Federal and state, including fees, the average Citizen will be paying as high as 50% of his entire earnings by the year 2020. 50%! So would say this is the price of freedom, I say this is the price of tyranny.

There is the powerful axiom that states: "The power to tax a thing is the power to destroy a thing." If you believe the government has the "legal" power to tax your personal income then the government has the "legal" power to set the level of taxation. That level can be 1% or it can be 100%, each percentage, and every percentage between, would be legal. It is only a matter of degree. So if you are taxed at 100%; do you become a slave to the government? You do not have a choice so the response must be, YES. Therefore, if you are taxed at 50%, you are a slave to the government 50% of the time. It is only the degree of slavery that is in question, not the fact of whether or not you are a slave. The Constitution has given our representatives the narrow guidelines by which they were to operate taxation, or any other area of government, they have grown far beyond those levels.

I have come to believe that our leaders, at all levels of government, practice selective support for the Constitution. What I mean by this is that they will use the Constitution when it is advantageous to their position, and use some other "compelling need" when it does not. With each new "gun law", "hate crime", expansion of unconstitutional state departments (such as the "departments of"—Education, Welfare, DEA, ATF, etc.) where there is no constitutional right to exist, taxation, denials or limitations on freedom of speech, etc., puts us further from freedom. Each time the government sticks another needle into the voodoo doll called citizens rights; the more the people will start to resist. At some inevitable point the people will rise up in opposition to this repression to retake what is rightfully theirs. The question is what will it take for Americans to say enough is enough?

The choices are narrowing. We legally have four choices left for us:

1. The ballot box—Although we have been doing this for centuries, we have not got this one right. The remedy is to get elected as many, hopefully the majority, within Congress and the Presidency who are strict constitutionalists. We must then devolve government to it's proper and just roles, returning to the states and the people what is rightfully theirs.
2. Petition for redress of grievance—As we have discussed, the First Amendment allows us to petition the government for correction where we believe they have gone astray. As already outlined, the government is not playing well in this regard and has yet to respond to ANY petition. Quite the contrary, to date they have stated they have no requirement to answer and petition but that they will respond with force. The Supreme Court has yet to make a determination and we are awaiting their decision. I don't hold much hope for a positive outcome in this regard.
3. Constitutional Convention—It is within the power of the people, from each of the states, to declare a Constitutional Convention and reign in the government to it's Constitutional position. This would require establishing referendums in every state of the Union and get a two-thirds majority. Once convened each issue would then be raised and require a three-fourths majority to pass. This would require years of preparation, instruction, campaigning, and large financial backing for a very uncertain outcome. Again I don't hold much hope for a positive outcome in this regard either.
4. Start over—The Declaration of Independence establishes the right of "The People", when oppressions become too great, to throw off the oppressive government and reestablish that government to best support the freedom of the people.

As you look over the available options one thing becomes glaringly clear, it is not the government that is going to correct itself. It is not the corporate business world that will come to aid the American people. The recapturing of our freedoms can only come from one source, the American people. Each and every option above requires the will of the people. As the option increases, so does the severity of what it will take to accomplish it.

To date we have risen to number two and thus far have been unsuccessful. We are left with options three and four, neither of which will be easily accomplished. However, if we arrive at three and fail, four will be inevitable. If we never attempt number three, four may be all we have left. I pray that this will never happen and providence provides a peaceful resolution. But make no mistake, those in power, both governmental and private who depend on the tyrannical structure, will fight tooth and nail to hold on to what they have.

In the end it will come down to the strength of the American patriot, whether in the halls of Washington or on the grounds of the battlefield, America must prevail to return the Unalienable rights back to the people or the United States will be relegated to the footnotes of history as the greatest nation that ever was.

Appendix

The Articles of Confederation

To all to whom these Presents shall come, we the undersigned Delegates of the States affixed to our Names, send greeting

Whereas the Delegates of the United States of America, in Congress assembled, did, on the 15th day of November, in the Year of Our Lord One thousand Seven Hundred and Seventy seven, and in the Second Year of the Independence of America, agree to certain articles of Confederation and perpetual Union between the States of New-hampshire, Massachusetts-bay, Rhode-island and Providence Plantations, Connecticut, New York, New Jersey, Pennsylvania, Delaware, Maryland, Virginia, North-Carolina, South-Carolina, and Georgia in the words following, viz.

"Articles of Confederation and perpetual Union between the states of New-hampshire, Massachusetts-bay, Rhode-island and Providence Plantations, Connecticut, New-York, New-Jersey, Pennsylvania, Delaware, Maryland, Virginia, North-Carolina, South-Carolina and Georgia".

Article I*. The Stile of this confederacy shall be "The United States of America".*

Article II*. Each state retains its sovereignty, freedom, and independence, and every Power, Jurisdiction and right, which is not by this confederation expressly delegated to the United States, in Congress assembled.*

Article III*. The said states hereby severally enter into a firm league of friendship with each other, for their common defence, the security of their Liberties, and their mutual and general welfare, binding themselves to assist each other, against all force offered to, or attacks made upon them, or any of them, on account of religion, sovereignty, trade, or any other pretence whatever.*

Article IV*. The better to secure and perpetuate mutual friendship and intercourse among the people of the different states in this union, the free* *inhabitants of each of these states, paupers, vagabonds and fugitives from justice excepted, shall be entitled to all privileges and immunities of free citizens in the several states; and the people of each state shall have free ingress and regress to and from any other state, and shall enjoy therein all the privileges of trade and commerce, subject to the same duties impositions and restrictions as the inhabitants thereof respectively, provided that such restriction shall not extend so far as to prevent the removal of property imported into any state, to any other state, of which the Owner is an inhabitant; provided also that no imposition, duties or restriction shall be laid by any state, on the property of the united states, or either of them. If any Person guilty of, or charged with treason, felony,—or other high misdemeanor in any state, shall flee from Justice, and be found in any of the united states, he shall, upon demand of the Governor or executive power, of the state from which he fled, be delivered up and removed to the state having jurisdiction of his offence. Full faith and credit shall be given in each of these states to the records, acts and judicial proceedings of the courts and magistrates of every other state.*

Article V*. For the more convenient management of the general interests of the united states, delegates shall be annually appointed in such manner as the legislature of each state shall direct, to meet in Congress on the first Monday in November, in every year, with a power reserved to each state, to recal its delegates, or any of them, at any time within the year, and to send others in their stead, for the remainder of the Year. No state shall be represented in Congress by less than two, nor by more than seven Members; and no person shall be capable of being a delegate for more than three years in any term of six years; nor shall any person, being a delegate, be capable of holding any office under the united states, for which he, or another for his benefit receives any salary, fees or emolument of any kind. Each state shall maintain its own delegates in a meeting of the states, and while they act as members of the committee of the states. In determining questions in the united states in Congress assembled, each state shall have one vote.*

Freedom of speech and debate in Congress shall not be impeached or questioned in any Court, or place out of Congress, and the members of congress shall be protected in their persons from arrests and imprisonments, during the time of their going to and from, and attendance on congress, except for treason, felony, or breach of the peace.

Article VI. *No state, without the Consent of the united states in congress assembled, shall send any embassy to, or receive any embassy from, or enter into any conference agreement, alliance or treaty with any King prince or state; nor shall any person holding any office of profit or trust under the united states, or any of them, accept of any present, emolument, office or title of any kind whatever from any king, prince or foreign state; nor shall the united states in congress assembled, or any of them, grant any title of nobility.*

No two or more states shall enter into any treaty, confederation or alliance whatever between them, without the consent of the united states in congress assembled, specifying accurately the purposes for which the same is to be entered into, and how long it shall continue.

No state shall lay any imposts or duties, which may interfere with any stipulations in treaties, entered into by the united states in congress assembled, with any king, prince or state, in pursuance of any treaties already proposed by congress, to the courts of France and Spain.

No vessels of war shall be kept up in time of peace by any state, except such number only, as shall be deemed necessary by the united states in congress assembled, for the defence of such state, or its trade; nor shall any body of forces be kept up by any state, in time of peace, except such number only, as in the judgment of the united states, in congress assembled, shall be deemed requisite to garrison the forts necessary for the defence of such state; but every state shall always keep up a well regulated and disciplined militia, sufficiently armed and accoutered, and shall provide and constantly have ready for use, in public stores, a due number of field pieces and tents, and a proper quantity of arms, ammunition and camp equipage.

No state shall engage in any war without the consent of the united states in congress assembled, unless such state be actually invaded by enemies, or shall have received certain advice of a resolution being formed by some nation of Indians to invade such state, and the danger is so imminent as not to admit of a delay till the united states in congress assembled can be consulted: nor shall any state grant commissions to any ships or vessels of war, nor letters of marque or reprisal, except it be after a declaration of war by the united states in congress assembled, and then only against the kingdom or state and the subjects thereof, against which war has been so declared, and under such regulations as shall be established by the united states in congress assembled, unless such state be infested by pirates, in which case vessels of war may be fitted out for that occasion, and kept so long as the danger shall continue, or until the united states in congress assembled, shall determine otherwise.

Article VII. *When land-forces are raised by any state for the common defence, all officers of or under the rank of colonel, shall be appointed by the legislature of each state respectively, by whom such forces shall be raised, or in such manner as such state shall direct, and all vacancies shall be filled up by the State which first made the appointment.*

Article VIII. *All charges of war, and all other expences that shall be incurred for the common defence or general welfare, and allowed by the united states in congress assembled, shall be defrayed out of a common treasury, which shall be supplied by the several states in proportion to the value of all land within each state, granted to or surveyed for any Person, as such land and the buildings and improvements thereon shall be estimated according to such mode as the united states in congress assembled, shall from time to time direct and appoint. The taxes for paying that proportion shall be laid and levied by the authority and direction of the legislatures of the several states within the time agreed upon by the united states in congress assembled.*

Article IX. *The united states in congress assembled, shall have the sole and exclusive right and power of determining on peace and war, except in the cases mentioned in the sixth article--of sending and receiving ambassadors--entering into treaties and alliances, provided that no treaty of commerce shall be made whereby the legislative power of the respective states shall be restrained from imposing such imposts and duties on foreigners as their own people are subjected to, or from prohibiting the exportation or importation of any species of goods or commodities, whatsoever--of establishing rules for deciding in all cases, what captures on land or water shall be legal, and in what manner prizes taken by land or naval forces in the service of the united states shall be divided or appropriated--of granting letters of marque and reprisal in times of peace--appointing courts for the trial of piracies and* *felonies committed on the high seas and establishing courts for receiving and determining finally appeals in all cases of captures, provided that no member of congress shall be appointed a judge of any of the said courts.*

The united states in congress assembled shall also be the last resort on appeal in all disputes and differences now subsisting or that hereafter may arise between two or more states concerning boundary, jurisdiction or any other cause whatever; which authority shall always be exercised in the manner following. Whenever the legislative or executive authority or lawful agent of any state in controversy with another shall present a petition to congress stating the matter in question and praying for a hearing, notice thereof shall be given by order of congress to the legislative or executive authority of the other state in controversy, and a day assigned for the appearance of the parties by their lawful agents, who shall then be directed to appoint by joint consent, commissioners or judges to constitute a court for hearing and determining the matter in question: but if they cannot agree, congress shall name three persons out of each of the united states, and from the list of such persons each party shall alternately strike out one, the petitioners beginning, until the number shall be reduced to thirteen; and from that number not less than seven, nor more than nine names as congress shall direct, shall in the presence of congress be drawn out by lot, and the persons whose names shall be so drawn or any five of them, shall be commissioners or judges, to hear and finally determine the controversy, so always as a major part of the judges who shall hear the cause shall agree in the determination: and if either party shall neglect to attend at the day appointed, without showing reasons, which congress shall judge sufficient, or being present shall refuse to strike, the congress shall proceed to nominate three persons out of each state, and the secretary of congress shall strike in behalf of such party absent or refusing; and the judgment and sentence of the court to be appointed, in the manner before prescribed, shall be final and conclusive; and if any of the parties shall refuse to submit to the authority of such court, or to appear or defend their claim or cause, the court shall nevertheless proceed to pronounce sentence, or judgment, which shall in like manner be final and decisive, the judgment or sentence and other proceedings being in either case transmitted to congress, and lodged among the acts of congress for the security of the parties concerned: provided that every commissioner, before he sits in judgment, shall take an oath to be administered by one of the judges of the supreme or superior court of the state, where the cause shall be tried,—well and truly to hear and determine the matter in question, according to the best of his judgment, without favour, affection or hope of reward:—provided also, that no state shall be deprived of territory for the benefit of the united states.

All controversies concerning the private right of soil claimed under different grants of two or more states, whose jurisdictions as they may respect such lands, and the states which passed such grants are adjusted, the said grants or either of them being at the same time claimed to have originated antecedent to such settlement of jurisdiction, shall on the petition of either party to the congress of the united states, be finally determined as near as may be in the same manner as is before prescribed for deciding disputes respecting territorial jurisdiction between different states. The united states in congress assembled shall also have the sole and exclusive right and power of regulating the alloy and value of coin struck by their own authority, or by that of the respective states--fixing the standard of weights and measures throughout the united states--regulating the trade and managing all affairs with the Indians, not members of any of the states, provided that the legislative right of any state within its own limits be not infringed or violated--establishing or regulating post offices from one state to another, throughout all the united states, and exacting such postage on the papers passing thro' the same as may be requisite to defray the expences of the said office--appointing all officers of the land forces, in the service of the united states, excepting regimental officers--appointing all the officers of the naval forces, and commissioning all officers whatever in the service of the united states--making rules for the government and regulation of the said land and naval forces, and directing their operations.

The united states in congress assembled shall have authority to appoint a committee, to sit in the recess of congress, to be denominated "A Committee of the States," and to consist of one delegate from each state; and to appoint such other committees and civil officers as may be necessary for managing the general affairs of the united states under their direction--to appoint one of their number to preside, provided that no person be allowed to serve in the office of president more than one year in any term of three years; to ascertain the necessary sums of money to be raised for the service of the united states, and to appropriate and apply the same for defraying the public expences to borrow money, or emit bills on the credit of the united states, transmitting every half year to the respective states an account of the sums of money so borrowed or emitted,--to build and equip a navy--to agree upon the number of land forces, and to make requisitions from each state for its quota, in proportion to the number of white inhabitants in such state; which requisition shall be binding, and thereupon the legislature of each state shall appoint the regimental officers, raise the men and cloth, arm and equip them in a soldier like manner, at the expence of the united states; and the officers and men so cloathed, armed and quipped shall march to the place appointed, and within the time agreed on by the united states in congress assembled: But if the united states in congress assembled shall, on consideration of circumstances judge proper that any state should not raise men, or should raise a smaller number than its quota, and that any other state should raise a greater number of men than the quota thereof, such extra number shall be raised, officered, cloathed, armed and equipped in the same manner as the quota of such state, unless the legislature of such state shall judge that such extra number cannot be safely spared out of the same, in which case they shall raise officer, cloath, arm and equip as many of such extra number as they judge can be safely spared. And the officers and men so cloathed, armed and equipped, shall march to the place appointed, and within the time agreed on by the united states in congress assembled.

The united states in congress assembled shall never engage in a war, nor grant letters of marque and reprisal in time of peace, nor enter into any treaties or alliances, nor coin money, nor regulate the value thereof, nor ascertain the sums and expences necessary for the defence and welfare of the united states, or any of them, nor emit bills, nor borrow money on the credit of the united states, nor appropriate money, nor agree upon the number of vessels of war, to be built or purchased, or the number of land or sea forces to be raised, nor appoint a commander in chief of the army or navy, unless nine states assent to the same: nor shall a question on any other point, except for adjourning from day to day be determined, unless by the votes of a majority of the united states in congress assembled. The congress of the united states shall have power to adjourn to any time within the year, and to any place within the united states, so that no period of adjournment be for a longer duration than the space of six Months, and shall publish the Journal of their proceedings monthly, except such parts thereof relating to treaties, alliances or military operations, as in their judgment require secrecy; and the yeas and nays of the delegates of each state on any question shall be entered on the Journal, when it is desired by any delegate; and the delegates of a state, or any of them, at his or their request shall be furnished with a transcript of the said Journal, except such parts as are above excepted, to lay before the legislatures of the several states.

Article X*. The committee of the states, or any nine of them, shall be authorized to execute, in the recess of congress, such of the powers of congress as the united states in congress assembled, by the consent of nine states, shall from time to time think expedient to vest them with; provided that no power be delegated to the said committee, for the exercise of which, by the articles of confederation, the voice of nine states in the congress of the united states assembled is requisite.*

Article XI*. Canada acceding to this confederation, and joining in the measures of the united states, shall be admitted into, and entitled to all the advantages of this union: but no other colony shall be admitted into the same, unless such admission be agreed to by nine states.*

Article XII*. All bills of credit emitted, monies borrowed and debts contracted by, or under the authority of congress, before the assembling of the united states, in pursuance of the present confederation, shall be deemed and considered as a charge against the united states, for payment and satisfaction whereof the said united states, and the public faith are hereby solemnly pledged.*

Article XIII*. Every state shall abide by the determinations of the united states in congress assembled, on all questions which by this confederation are submitted to them. And the Articles of this confederation shall be inviolably observed by every state, and the union shall be perpetual; nor shall any alteration at any time hereafter be made in any of them; unless such alteration be agreed to in a congress of the united states, and be afterwards confirmed by the legislatures of every state.*

And Whereas it hath pleased the Great Governor of the World to incline the hearts of the legislatures we respectively represent in congress, to approve of, and to authorize us to ratify the said articles of confederation and perpetual union. Know Ye that we the undersigned delegates, by virtue of the power and authority to us given for that purpose, do by these presents, in the name and in behalf of our respective constituents, fully and entirely ratify and confirm each and every of the said articles of confederation and perpetual union, and all and singular the matters and things therein contained: And we do further solemnly plight and engage the faith of our respective constituents, that they shall abide by the determinations of the united states in congress assembled, on all questions, which by the said confederation are submitted to them. And that the articles thereof shall be inviolably observed by the states we respectively represent, and that the union shall be perpetual. In Witness whereof we have hereunto set our hands in Congress. Done at Philadelphia in the state of Pennsylvania the ninth day of July in the Year of our Lord one Thousand seven Hundred and Seventy-eight, and in the third year of the independence of America.

On the part of & behalf of the State of New Hampshire:
Josiah Bartlett, John Wentworth. June—August 8th, 1778.

On the part and behalf of the State of Rhode-Island and Providence Plantations:
William Ellery, Henry Marchant, John Collins.

On the part and behalf of the State of New York:
Jas Duane, Fra: Lewis, Wm Duer, Gouvr Morris.

On the part and behalf of the State of Pennsylvania:
Robert Morris, Daniel Roberdeau, Jon. Bayard Smith, William Clingar, Joseph Reed—22d July, 1778.
On the part and behalf of the State of Maryland:
John Hanson, Daniel Carroll—March 1, 1781

On the part and behalf of the State of North Carolina:
John Penn, Corns Harnett, Jno Williams.—July 21st, 1778

On the part and behalf of the State of Georgia:
Jno Walton, Edwd Telfair, Edwd Langworthy.—24th July, 1778

On the part of & behalf of the State of Massachusetts Bay:
John Hancock, Samuel Adams, Elbridge Gerry, Francis Dana, James Lovell, Samuel Holten.

On the part and behalf of the State of Connecticut:

Roger Sherman, Samuel Huntington, Oliver Wolcott, Titus Hosmer, Andrew Adams

On the Part and in Behalf of the State of New Jersey:
Jno Witherspoon, Nathl Scudder.—November 26th, 1778

On the part and behalf of the State of Delaware:
Thos McKean, Febr 22d, 1779, John Dickinson, May 5th, 1779, Nicholas Van Dyke.

On the part and behalf of the State of Virginia:
Richard Henry Lee, John Banister, Thomas Adams, Jno Harvie, Francis Lightfoot Lee.

On the part and behalf of the State of South Carolina:
Henry Laurens, William Henry Drayton, Jno Mathews, Richd Hutson, Thos Heyward, junr.

Declaration of Independence

[Adopted in Congress 4 July 1776]

The Unanimous Declaration of the Thirteen United States of America

When, in the course of human events, it becomes necessary for one people to dissolve the political bands which have connected them with another, and to assume among the powers of the earth, the separate and equal station to which the laws of nature and of nature's God entitle them, a decent respect to the opinions of mankind requires that they should declare the causes which impel them to the separation.

We hold these truths to be self-evident, that all men are created equal, that they are endowed by their Creator with certain unalienable rights, that among these are life, liberty and the pursuit of happiness. That to secure these rights, governments are instituted among men, deriving their just powers from the consent of the governed. That whenever any form of government becomes destructive to these ends, it is the right of the people to alter or to abolish it, and to institute new government, laying its foundation on such principles and organizing its powers in such form, as to them shall seem most likely to effect their safety and happiness. Prudence, indeed, will dictate that governments long established should not be changed for light and transient causes; and accordingly all experience hath shown that mankind are more disposed to suffer, while evils are sufferable, than to right themselves by abolishing the forms to which they are accustomed.

But when a long train of abuses and usurpations, pursuing invariably the same object evinces a design to reduce them under absolute despotism, it is their right, it is their duty, to throw off such government, and to provide new guards for their future security.—Such has been the patient sufferance of these colonies; and such is now the necessity which constrains them to alter their former systems of government. The history of the present King of Great Britain is a history of repeated injuries and usurpations, all having in direct object the establishment of an absolute tyranny over these states. To prove this, let facts be submitted to a candid world.

He has refused his assent to laws, the most wholesome and necessary for the public good.

He has forbidden his governors to pass laws of immediate and pressing importance, unless suspended in their operation till his assent should be obtained; and when so suspended, he has utterly neglected to attend to them.

He has refused to pass other laws for the accommodation of large districts of people, unless those people would relinquish the right of representation in the legislature, a right inestimable to them and formidable to tyrants only.

He has called together legislative bodies at places unusual, uncomfortable, and distant from the depository of their public records, for the sole purpose of fatiguing them into compliance with his measures.

He has dissolved representative houses repeatedly, for opposing with manly firmness his invasions on the rights of the people.

He has refused for a long time, after such dissolutions, to cause others to be elected; whereby the legislative powers, incapable of annihilation, have returned to the people at large for their exercise; the state remaining in the meantime exposed to all the dangers of invasion from without, and convulsions within.

He has endeavored to prevent the population of these states; for that purpose obstructing the laws for naturalization of foreigners; refusing to pass others to encourage their migration hither, and raising the conditions of new appropriations of lands.

He has obstructed the administration of justice, by refusing his assent to laws for establishing judiciary powers.

He has made judges dependent on his will alone, for the tenure of their offices, and the amount and payment of their salaries.

He has erected a multitude of new offices, and sent hither swarms of officers to harass our people, and eat out their substance.

He has kept among us, in times of peace, standing armies without the consent of our legislature.

He has affected to render the military independent of and superior to civil power.

He has combined with others to subject us to a jurisdiction foreign to our constitution, and unacknowledged by our laws; giving his assent to their acts of pretended legislation:

For quartering large bodies of armed troops among us:

For protecting them, by mock trial, from punishment for any murders which they should commit on the inhabitants of these states:

For cutting off our trade with all parts of the world:

For imposing taxes on us without our consent:

For depriving us in many cases, of the benefits of trial by jury:

For transporting us beyond seas to be tried for pretended offenses:

For abolishing the free system of English laws in a neighboring province, establishing therein an arbitrary government, and enlarging its boundaries so as to render it at once an example and fit instrument for introducing the same absolute rule in these colonies:

For taking away our charters, abolishing our most valuable laws, and altering fundamentally the forms of our governments:

For suspending our own legislatures, and declaring themselves invested with power to legislate for us in all cases whatsoever.

He has abdicated government here, by declaring us out of his protection and waging war against us.

He has plundered our seas, ravaged our coasts, burned our towns, and destroyed the lives of our people.

He is at this time transporting large armies of foreign mercenaries to complete the works of death, desolation and tyranny, already begun with circumstances of cruelty and perfidy scarcely paralleled in the most barbarous ages, and totally unworthy of the head of a civilized nation.

He has constrained our fellow citizens taken captive on the high seas to bear arms against their country, to become the executioners of their friends and brethren, or to fall themselves by their hands.

He has excited domestic insurrections amongst us, and has endeavored to bring on the inhabitants of our frontiers, the merciless Indian savages, whose known rule of warfare, is undistinguished destruction of all ages, sexes and conditions.

In every stage of these oppressions we have petitioned for redress in the most humble terms: our repeated petitions have been answered only by repeated injury. A prince, whose character is thus marked by every act which may define a tyrant, is unfit to be the ruler of a free people.

Nor have we been wanting in attention to our British brethren. We have warned them from time to time of attempts by their legislature to extend an unwarrantable jurisdiction over us. We have reminded them of the circumstances of our emigration and settlement here. We have appealed to their native justice and magnanimity, and we have conjured them by the ties of our common kindred to disavow these usurpations, which, would inevitably interrupt our connections and correspondence. We must, therefore, acquiesce in the necessity, which denounces our separation, and hold them, as we hold the rest of mankind, enemies in war, in peace friends.

We, therefore, the representatives of the United States of America, in General Congress, assembled, appealing to the Supreme Judge of the world for the rectitude of our intentions, do, in the name, and by the authority of the good people of these colonies, solemnly publish and declare, that these united colonies are, and of right ought to be free and independent states; that they are absolved from all allegiance to the British Crown, and that all political connection between them and the state of Great Britain, is and ought to be totally dissolved; and that as free and independent states, they have full power to levey war, conclude peace, contract alliances, establish commerce, and to do all other acts and things which independent states may of right do. And for the support of this declaration, with a firm reliance on the protection of Divine Providence, we mutually pledge to each other our lives, our fortunes and our sacred honor.

Constitution for the United States of America

We the People of the United States, in Order to form a more perfect Union, establish Justice, insure domestic Tranquility, provide for the common defence, promote the general Welfare, and secure the Blessings of Liberty to ourselves and our Posterity, do ordain and establish this Constitution for the United States of America.

Article I.

Section 1. All legislative Powers herein granted shall be vested in a Congress of the United States, which shall consist of a Senate and House of Representatives.

Section 2. The House of Representatives shall be composed of Members chosen every second Year by the People of the several States, and the Electors in each State shall have the Qualifications requisite for Electors of the most numerous Branch of the State Legislature.

No Person shall be a Representative who shall not have attained to the Age of twenty five Years, and been seven Years a Citizen of the United States, and who shall not, when elected, be an Inhabitant of that State in which he shall be chosen.

Representatives and direct Taxes shall be apportioned among the several States which may be included within this Union, according to their respective Numbers, which shall be determined by adding to the whole Number of free Persons, including those bound to Service for a Term of Years, and excluding Indians not taxed, three fifths of all other Persons. The actual Enumeration shall be made within three Years after the first Meeting of the Congress of the United States, and within every subsequent Term of ten Years, in such Manner as they shall by Law direct. The Number of Representatives shall not exceed one for every thirty Thousand, but each State shall have at Least one Representative; and until such enumeration shall be made, the State of New Hampshire shall be entitled to chuse three, Massachusetts eight, Rhode-Island and Providence Plantations one, Connecticut five, New-York six, New Jersey four, Pennsylvania eight, Delaware one, Maryland six, Virginia ten, North Carolina five, South Carolina five, and Georgia three.

When vacancies happen in the Representation from any State, the Executive Authority thereof shall issue Writs of Election to fill such Vacancies.

The House of Representatives shall chuse their Speaker and other Officers; and shall have the sole Power of Impeachment.

Section 3. The Senate of the United States shall be composed of two Senators from each State, chosen by the Legislature thereof, for six Years; and each Senator shall have one Vote.

Immediately after they shall be assembled in Consequence of the first Election, they shall be divided as equally as may be into three Classes.

The Seats of the Senators of the first Class shall be vacated at the Expiration of the second Year, of the second Class at the Expiration of the fourth Year, and of the third Class at the Expiration of the sixth Year, so that one third may be chosen every second Year; and if Vacancies happen by Resignation, or otherwise, during the Recess of the Legislature of any State, the Executive thereof may make temporary Appointments until the next Meeting of the Legislature, which shall then fill such Vacancies.

No Person shall be a Senator who shall not have attained to the Age of thirty Years, and been nine Years a Citizen of the United States, and who shall not, when elected, be an Inhabitant of that State for which he shall be chosen.

The Vice President of the United States shall be President of the Senate, but shall have no Vote, unless they be equally divided.

The Senate shall chuse their other Officers, and also a President pro tempore, in the Absence of the Vice President, or when he shall exercise the Office of President of the United States.

The Senate shall have the sole Power to try all Impeachments. When sitting for that Purpose, they shall be on Oath or Affirmation. When the President of the United States is tried, the Chief Justice shall preside: And no Person shall be convicted without the Concurrence of two thirds of the Members present.

Judgment in Cases of Impeachment shall not extend further than to removal from Office, and disqualification to hold and enjoy any Office of honor, Trust or Profit under the United States: but the Party convicted shall nevertheless be liable and subject to Indictment, Trial, Judgment and Punishment, according to Law.

Section 4. The Times, Places and Manner of holding Elections for Senators and Representatives, shall be prescribed in each State by the Legislature thereof; but the Congress may at any time by Law make or alter such Regulations, except as to the Places of chusing Senators.

The Congress shall assemble at least once in every Year, and such Meeting shall be on the first Monday in December [Modified by Amendment XX], unless they shall by Law appoint a different Day.

Section 5. Each House shall be the Judge of the Elections, Returns and Qualifications of its own Members, and a Majority of each shall constitute a Quorum to do Business; but a smaller Number may adjourn from day to day, and may be authorized to compel the Attendance of absent Members, in such Manner, and under such Penalties as each House may provide.

Each House may determine the Rules of its Proceedings, punish its Members for disorderly Behaviour, and, with the Concurrence of two thirds, expel a Member.

Each House shall keep a Journal of its Proceedings, and from time to time publish the same, excepting such Parts as may in their Judgment require Secrecy; and the Yeas and Nays of the Members of either House on any question shall, at the Desire of one fifth of those Present, be entered on the Journal.

Neither House, during the Session of Congress, shall, without the Consent of the other, adjourn for more than three days, nor to any other Place than that in which the two Houses shall be sitting.

Section 6. The Senators and Representatives shall receive a Compensation for their Services, to be ascertained by Law, and paid out of the Treasury of the United States. They shall in all Cases, except Treason, Felony and Breach of the Peace, be privileged from Arrest during their

Attendance at the Session of their respective Houses, and in going to and returning from the same; and for any Speech or Debate in either House, they shall not be questioned in any other Place.

No Senator or Representative shall, during the Time for which he was elected, be appointed to any civil Office under the Authority of the United States, which shall have been created, or the Emoluments whereof shall have been encreased during such time; and no Person holding any Office under the United States, shall be a Member of either House during his Continuance in Office.

Section 7. All Bills for raising Revenue shall originate in the House of Representatives; but the Senate may propose or concur with Amendments as on other Bills.

Every Bill which shall have passed the House of Representatives and the Senate, shall, before it become a Law, be presented to the President of the United States; If he approve he shall sign it, but if not he shall return it, with his Objections to that House in which it shall have originated, who shall enter the Objections at large on their Journal, and proceed to reconsider it. If after such Reconsideration two thirds of that House shall agree to pass the Bill, it shall be sent, together with the Objections, to the other House, by which it shall likewise be reconsidered, and if approved by two thirds of that House, it shall become a Law. But in all such Cases the Votes of both Houses shall be determined by yeas and Nays, and the Names of the Persons voting for and against the Bill shall be entered on the Journal of each House respectively. If any Bill shall not be returned by the President within ten Days (Sundays excepted) after it shall have been presented to him, the Same shall be a Law, in like Manner as if he had signed it, unless the Congress by their Adjournment prevent its Return, in which Case it shall not be a Law.

Every Order, Resolution, or Vote to which the Concurrence of the Senate and House of Representatives may be necessary (except on a question of Adjournment) shall be presented to the President of the United States; and before the Same shall take Effect, shall be approved by him, or being disapproved by him, shall be repassed by two thirds of the Senate and House of Representatives, according to the Rules and Limitations prescribed in the Case of a Bill.

Section 8. The Congress shall have Power To lay and collect Taxes, Duties, Imposts and Excises, to pay the Debts and provide for the common Defence and general Welfare of the United States; but all Duties, Imposts and Excises shall be uniform throughout the United States;

To borrow Money on the credit of the United States;

To regulate Commerce with foreign Nations, and among the several States, and with the Indian Tribes;

To establish an uniform Rule of Naturalization, and uniform Laws on the subject of Bankruptcies throughout the United States;

To coin Money, regulate the Value thereof, and of foreign Coin, and fix the Standard of Weights and Measures;

To provide for the Punishment of counterfeiting the Securities and current Coin of the United States;

To establish Post Offices and post Roads;

To promote the Progress of Science and useful Arts, by securing for limited Times to Authors and Inventors the exclusive Right to their respective Writings and Discoveries;

To constitute Tribunals inferior to the supreme Court;

To define and punish Piracies and Felonies committed on the high Seas, and Offences against the Law of Nations;

To declare War, grant Letters of Marque and Reprisal, and make Rules concerning Captures on Land and Water;

To raise and support Armies, but no Appropriation of Money to that Use shall be for a longer Term than two Years;

To provide and maintain a Navy;

To make Rules for the Government and Regulation of the land and naval Forces;

To provide for calling forth the Militia to execute the Laws of the Union, suppress Insurrections and repel Invasions;

To provide for organizing, arming, and disciplining, the Militia, and for governing such Part of them as may be employed in the Service of the United States, reserving to the States respectively, the Appointment of the Officers, and the Authority of training the Militia according to the discipline prescribed by Congress;

To exercise exclusive Legislation in all Cases whatsoever, over such District (not exceeding ten Miles square) as may, by Cession of particular States, and the Acceptance of Congress, become the Seat of the Government of the United States, and to exercise like Authority over all Places purchased by the Consent of the Legislature of the State in which the Same shall be, for the Erection of Forts, Magazines, Arsenals, dock-Yards, and other needful Buildings;—And

To make all Laws which shall be necessary and proper for carrying into Execution the foregoing Powers, and all other Powers vested by this Constitution in the Government of the United States, or in any Department or Officer thereof.

Section 9. The Migration or Importation of such Persons as any of the States now existing shall think proper to admit, shall not be prohibited by the Congress prior to the Year one thousand eight hundred and eight, but a Tax or duty may be imposed on such Importation, not exceeding ten dollars for each Person.

The Privilege of the Writ of Habeas Corpus shall not be suspended, unless when in Cases of Rebellion or Invasion the public Safety may require it.

No Bill of Attainder or ex post facto Law shall be passed.

No Capitation, or other direct, Tax shall be laid, unless in Proportion to the Census or Enumeration herein before directed to be taken.

No Tax or Duty shall be laid on Articles exported from any State.

No Preference shall be given by any Regulation of Commerce or Revenue to the Ports of one State over those of another; nor shall Vessels bound to, or from, one State, be obliged to enter, clear, or pay Duties in another.

No Money shall be drawn from the Treasury, but in Consequence of Appropriations made by Law; and a regular Statement and Account of the Receipts and Expenditures of all public Money shall be published from time to time.

No Title of Nobility shall be granted by the United States: And no Person holding any Office of Profit or Trust under them, shall, without the Consent of the Congress, accept of any present, Emolument, Office, or Title, of any kind whatever, from any King, Prince, or foreign State.

Section 10. No State shall enter into any Treaty, Alliance, or Confederation; grant Letters of Marque and Reprisal; coin Money; emit Bills of Credit; make any Thing but gold and silver Coin a Tender in Payment of Debts; pass any Bill of Attainder, ex post facto Law, or Law impairing the Obligation of Contracts, or grant any Title of Nobility.

No State shall, without the Consent of the Congress, lay any Imposts or Duties on Imports or Exports, except what may be absolutely necessary for executing it's inspection Laws; and the net Produce of all Duties and Imposts, laid by any State on Imports or Exports, shall be for the Use of the Treasury of the United States; and all such Laws shall be subject to the Revision and Controul of the Congress.

No State shall, without the Consent of Congress, lay any Duty of Tonnage, keep Troops, or Ships of War in time of Peace, enter into any Agreement or Compact with another State, or with a foreign Power, or engage in War, unless actually invaded, or in such imminent Danger as will not admit of delay.

Article. II.

Section 1. The executive Power shall be vested in a President of the United States of America. He shall hold his Office during the Term of four Years, and, together with the Vice President, chosen for the same Term, be elected, as follows:

Each State shall appoint, in such Manner as the Legislature thereof may direct, a Number of Electors, equal to the whole Number of Senators and Representatives to which the State may be entitled in the Congress: but no Senator or Representative, or Person holding an Office of Trust or Profit under the United States, shall be appointed an Elector.

The Electors shall meet in their respective States, and vote by Ballot for two Persons, of whom one at least shall not be an Inhabitant of the same State with themselves. And they shall make a List of all the Persons voted for, and of the Number of Votes for each; which List they shall sign and certify, and transmit sealed to the Seat of the Government of the United States, directed to the President of the Senate. The President of the Senate shall, in the Presence of the Senate and House of Representatives, open all the Certificates, and the Votes shall then be counted. The Person having the greatest Number of Votes shall be the President, if such Number be a Majority of the whole Number of Electors appointed; and if there be more than one who have such Majority, and have an equal Number of Votes, then the House of Representatives shall immediately chuse by Ballot one of them for President; and if no Person have a Majority, then from the five highest on the List the said House shall in like Manner chuse the President. But in chusing the President, the Votes shall be taken by States, the Representation from each State having one Vote; a quorum for this Purpose shall consist of a Member or Members from two thirds of the States, and a Majority of all the States shall be necessary to a Choice. In every Case, after the Choice of the President, the Person having the greatest Number of Votes of the Electors shall be the Vice President. But if there should remain two or more who have equal Votes, the Senate shall chuse from them by Ballot the Vice President.

The Congress may determine the Time of chusing the Electors, and the Day on which they shall give their Votes; which Day shall be the same throughout the United States.

No Person except a natural born Citizen, or a Citizen of the United States, at the time of the Adoption of this Constitution, shall be eligible to the Office of President; neither shall any Person be eligible to that Office who shall not have attained to the Age of thirty five Years, and been fourteen Years a Resident within the United States.

In Case of the Removal of the President from Office, or of his Death, Resignation, or Inability to discharge the Powers and Duties of the said Office, the Same shall devolve on the Vice President, and the Congress may by Law provide for the Case of Removal, Death, Resignation or Inability, both of the President and Vice President, declaring what Officer shall then act as President, and such Officer shall act accordingly, until the Disability be removed, or a President shall be elected.

The President shall, at stated Times, receive for his Services, a Compensation, which shall neither be increased nor diminished during the Period for which he shall have been elected, and he shall not receive within that Period any other Emolument from the United States, or any of them.

Before he enter on the Execution of his Office, he shall take the following Oath or Affirmation:—"I do solemnly swear (or affirm) that I will faithfully execute the Office of President of the United States, and will to the best of my Ability, preserve, protect and defend the Constitution of the United States."

Section 2. The President shall be Commander in Chief of the Army and Navy of the United States, and of the Militia of the several States, when called into the actual Service of the United States; he may require the Opinion, in writing, of the principal Officer in each of the executive Departments, upon any Subject relating to the Duties of their respective Offices, and he shall have Power to grant Reprieves and Pardons for Offences against the United States, except in Cases of Impeachment.

He shall have Power, by and with the Advice and Consent of the Senate, to make Treaties, provided two thirds of the Senators present concur; and he shall nominate, and by and with the Advice and Consent of the Senate, shall appoint Ambassadors, other public Ministers and Consuls, Judges of the supreme Court, and all other Officers of the United States, whose

Appointments are not herein otherwise provided for, and which shall be established by Law: but the Congress may by Law vest the Appointment of such inferior Officers, as they think proper, in the President alone, in the Courts of Law, or in the Heads of Departments.

The President shall have Power to fill up all Vacancies that may happen during the Recess of the Senate, by granting Commissions which shall expire at the End of their next Session.

Section 3. He shall from time to time give to the Congress Information of the State of the Union, and recommend to their Consideration such Measures as he shall judge necessary and expedient; he may, on extraordinary Occasions, convene both Houses, or either of them, and in Case of

Disagreement between them, with Respect to the Time of Adjournment, he may adjourn them to such Time as he shall think proper; he shall receive Ambassadors and other public Ministers; he shall take Care that the Laws be faithfully executed, and shall Commission all the Officers of the United States.

Section 4. The President, Vice President and all civil Officers of the United States, shall be removed from Office on Impeachment for, and Conviction of, Treason, Bribery, or other high Crimes and Misdemeanors.

Article III.

Section 1. The judicial Power of the United States shall be vested in one supreme Court, and in such inferior Courts as the Congress may from time to time ordain and establish. The Judges, both of the supreme and inferior Courts, shall hold their Offices during good Behaviour, and shall, at stated Times, receive for their Services a Compensation, which shall not be diminished during their Continuance in Office.

Section 2. The judicial Power shall extend to all Cases, in Law and Equity, arising under this Constitution, the Laws of the United States, and Treaties made, or which shall be made, under their Authority;—to all Cases affecting Ambassadors, other public Ministers and Consuls;—to all Cases of admiralty and maritime Jurisdiction;—to Controversies to which the United States shall be a Party;—to Controversies between two or more States;—between a State and Citizens of another State;—between Citizens of different States;—between Citizens of the same State claiming Lands under Grants of different States, and between a State, or the Citizens thereof, and foreign States, Citizens or Subjects.

In all Cases affecting Ambassadors, other public Ministers and Consuls, and those in which a State shall be Party, the supreme Court shall have original Jurisdiction. In all the other Cases before mentioned, the supreme Court shall have appellate Jurisdiction, both as to Law and Fact, with such Exceptions, and under such Regulations as the Congress shall make.

The Trial of all Crimes, except in Cases of Impeachment, shall be by Jury; and such Trial shall be held in the State where the said Crimes shall have been committed; but when not committed within any State, the Trial shall be at such Place or Places as the Congress may by Law have directed.

Section 3. Treason against the United States shall consist only in levying War against them, or in adhering to their Enemies, giving them Aid and Comfort. No Person shall be convicted of Treason unless on the Testimony of two Witnesses to the same overt Act, or on Confession in open Court.

The Congress shall have Power to declare the Punishment of Treason, but no Attainder of Treason shall work Corruption of Blood, or Forfeiture except during the Life of the Person attainted.

Article IV.

Section 1. Full Faith and Credit shall be given in each State to the public Acts, Records, and judicial Proceedings of every other State. And the Congress may by general Laws prescribe the Manner in which such Acts, Records and Proceedings shall be proved, and the Effect thereof.

Section 2. The Citizens of each State shall be entitled to all Privileges and Immunities of Citizens in the several States.

A Person charged in any State with Treason, Felony, or other Crime, who shall flee from Justice, and be found in another State, shall on Demand of the executive Authority of the State from which he fled, be delivered up, to be removed to the State having Jurisdiction of the Crime.

No Person held to Service or Labour in one State, under the Laws thereof, escaping into another, shall, in Consequence of any Law or Regulation therein, be discharged from such Service or Labour, but shall be delivered up on Claim of the Party to whom such Service or Labour may be due.

Section 3. New States may be admitted by the Congress into this Union; but no new State shall be formed or erected within the Jurisdiction of any other State; nor any State be formed by the Junction of two or more States, or Parts of States, without the Consent of the Legislatures of the States concerned as well as of the Congress.

The Congress shall have Power to dispose of and make all needful Rules and Regulations respecting the Territory or other Property belonging to the United States; and nothing in this Constitution shall be so construed as to Prejudice any Claims of the United States, or of any particular State.

Section 4. The United States shall guarantee to every State in this Union a Republican Form of Government, and shall protect each of them against Invasion; and on Application of the Legislature, or of the Executive (when the Legislature cannot be convened), against domestic Violence.

Article. V.

The Congress, whenever two thirds of both Houses shall deem it necessary, shall propose Amendments to this Constitution, or, on the Application of the Legislatures of two thirds of the several States, shall call a Convention for proposing Amendments, which, in either Case, shall be valid to all Intents and Purposes, as Part of this Constitution, when ratified by the Legislatures of three fourths of the several States, or by Conventions in three fourths thereof, as the one or the other Mode of Ratification may be proposed by the Congress; Provided that no Amendment which may be made prior to the Year One thousand eight hundred and eight shall in any Manner affect the first and fourth Clauses in the Ninth Section of the first Article; and that no State, without its Consent, shall be deprived of its equal Suffrage in the Senate.

Article. VI.

All Debts contracted and Engagements entered into, before the Adoption of this Constitution, shall be as valid against the United States under this Constitution, as under the Confederation.

This Constitution, and the Laws of the United States which shall be made in Pursuance thereof; and all Treaties made, or which shall be made, under the Authority of the United States, shall be the supreme Law of the Land; and the Judges in every State shall be bound thereby, any Thing in the Constitution or Laws of any State to the Contrary notwithstanding.

The Senators and Representatives before mentioned, and the Members of the several State Legislatures, and all executive and judicial Officers, both of the United States and of the several States, shall be bound by Oath or Affirmation, to support this Constitution; but no religious Test shall ever be required as a Qualification to any Office or public Trust under the United States.

Article. VII.

The Ratification of the Conventions of nine States, shall be sufficient for the Establishment of this Constitution between the States so ratifying the Same.

The Word, "the," being interlined between the seventh and eighth Lines of the first Page, The Word "Thirty" being partly written on an Erazure in the fifteenth Line of the first Page, The Words "is tried" being interlined between the thirty second and thirty third Lines of the first Page and the Word "the" being interlined between the forty third and forty fourth Lines of the second Page.

Attest William Jackson
Secretary

Done in Convention by the Unanimous Consent of the States present the Seventeenth Day of September in the Year of our Lord one thousand seven hundred and Eighty seven and of the Independence of the United States of America the Twelfth In witness whereof We have hereunto subscribed our Names,

Go. Washington—Presidt.
and deputy from Virginia

New Hampshire
John Langdon
Nicholas Gilman

Massachusetts
Nathaniel Gorham
Rufus King

Connecticut
Wm. Saml. Johnson
Roger Sherman

New York
Alexander Hamilton

New Jersey {
Wil: Livingston
David Brearley.
Wm. Paterson.
Jona: Dayton

Pennsylvania {
B Franklin
Thomas Mifflin
Robt Morris
Geo. Clymer
Thos. Fitz Simons
Jared Ingersoll
James Wilson
Gouv Morris

Delaware {
Geo: Read
Gunning Bedford jun
John Dickinson
Richard Bassett
Jaco: Broom

Maryland {
James Mchenry
Dan of St Thos. Jenifer
Danl Carroll

Virginia {
John Blair
James Madison

North Carolina {
Wm. Blount
Richd. Dobbs Spaight
Hu Williamson

South Carolina {
J. Rutledge
Charles Cotesworth Pinckney
Charles Pinckney
Pierce Butler

Georgia {
William Few
Abr Baldwin

In Convention Monday, September 17th, 1787.

Present

The States of New Hampshire, Massachusetts, Connecticut, Mr. Hamilton from New York, New

Jersey, Pennsylvania, Delaware, Maryland, Virginia, North Carolina, South Carolina and Georgia.

Resolved,

That the preceeding Constitution be laid before the United States in Congress assembled, and that it is the Opinion of this Convention, that it should afterwards be submitted to a Convention of Delegates, chosen in each State by the People thereof, under the Recommendation of its Legislature, for their Assent and Ratification; and that each Convention assenting to, and ratifying the Same, should give Notice thereof to the United States in Congress assembled. Resolved, That it is the Opinion of this Convention, that as soon as the Conventions of nine States shall have ratified this Constitution, the United States in Congress assembled should fix a Day on which Electors should be appointed by the States which have ratified the same, and a Day on which the Electors should assemble to vote for the President, and the Time and Place for commencing Proceedings under this Constitution. That after such Publication the Electors should be appointed, and the Senators and Representatives elected: That the Electors should meet on the Day fixed for the Election of the President, and should transmit their Votes certified, signed, sealed and directed, as the Constitution requires, to the Secretary of the United States in Congress assembled, that the Senators and Representatives should convene at the Time and Place assigned; that the Senators should appoint a President of the Senate, for the sole purpose of receiving, opening and counting the Votes for President; and, that after he shall be chosen, the Congress, together with the President, should, without Delay, proceed to execute this Constitution.

By the Unanimous Order of the Convention Go. Washington--Presidt. W. Jackson Secretary.

The Bill of Rights

Amendments 1-10 of the Constitution

The Conventions of a number of the States having, at the time of adopting the Constitution, expressed a desire, in order to prevent misconstruction or abuse of its powers, that further declaratory and restrictive clauses should be added, and as extending the ground of public confidence in the Government will best insure the beneficent ends of its institution;

Resolved, by the Senate and House of Representatives of the United States of America, in Congress assembled, two-thirds of both Houses concurring, that the following articles be proposed to the Legislatures of the several States, as amendments to the Constitution of the United States; all or any of which articles, when ratified by three-fourths of the said Legislatures, to be valid to all intents and purposes as part of the said Constitution, namely:

Amendment I

Congress shall make no law respecting an establishment of religion, or prohibiting the free exercise thereof; or abridging the freedom of speech, or of the press; or the right of the people peaceably to assemble, and to petition the government for a redress of grievances.

Amendment II

A well regulated militia, being necessary to the security of a free state, the right of the people to keep and bear arms, shall not be infringed.

Amendment III

No soldier shall, in time of peace be quartered in any house, without the consent of the owner, nor in time of war, but in a manner to be prescribed by law.

Amendment IV

The right of the people to be secure in their persons, houses, papers, and effects, against unreasonable searches and seizures, shall not be violated, and no warrants shall issue, but upon probable cause, supported by oath or affirmation, and particularly describing the place to be searched, and the persons or things to be seized.

Amendment V

No person shall be held to answer for a capital, or otherwise infamous crime, unless on a presentment or indictment of a grand jury, except in cases arising in the land or naval forces, or in the militia, when in actual service in time of war or public danger; nor shall any person be subject for the same offense to be twice put in jeopardy of life or limb; nor shall be compelled in any criminal case to be a witness against himself, nor be deprived of life, liberty, or property, without due process of law; nor shall private property be taken for public use, without just compensation.

Amendment VI

In all criminal prosecutions, the accused shall enjoy the right to a speedy and public trial, by an impartial jury of the state and district wherein the crime shall have been committed, which district shall have been previously ascertained by law, and to be informed of the nature and cause of the accusation; to be confronted with the witnesses against him; to have compulsory process for obtaining witnesses in his favor, and to have the assistance of counsel for his defense.

Amendment VII

In suits at common law, where the value in controversy shall exceed twenty dollars, the right of trial by jury shall be preserved, and no fact tried by a jury, shall be otherwise reexamined in any court of the United States, than according to the rules of the common law.

Amendment VIII

Excessive bail shall not be required, nor excessive fines imposed, nor cruel and unusual punishments inflicted.

Amendment IX

The enumeration in the Constitution, of certain rights, shall not be construed to deny or disparage others retained by the people.

Amendment X

The powers not delegated to the United States by the Constitution, nor prohibited by it to the states, are reserved to the states respectively, or to the people.

Amendments 11—27

Amendment XI
Passed by Congress March 4, 1794. Ratified February 7, 1795.

The Judicial power of the United States shall not be construed to extend to any suit in law or equity, commenced or prosecuted against one of the United States by Citizens of another State, or by Citizens or Subjects of any Foreign State.

Amendment XII
Passed by Congress December 9, 1803. Ratified June 15, 1804.
Note: A portion of Article II, section 1 of the Constitution was superseded by the 12th amendment.

The Electors shall meet in their respective states and vote by ballot for President and Vice-President, one of whom, at least, shall not be an inhabitant of the same state with themselves; they shall name in their ballots the person voted for as President, and in distinct ballots the person voted for as Vice-President, and they shall make distinct lists of all persons voted for as President, and of all persons voted for as Vice-President, and of the number of votes for each, which lists they shall sign and certify, and transmit sealed to the seat of the government of the United States, directed to the President of the Senate;—the President of the Senate shall, in the presence of the Senate and House of Representatives, open all the certificates and the votes shall then be counted;—The person having the greatest number of votes for President, shall be the President, if such number be a majority of the whole number of Electors appointed; and if no person have such majority, then from the persons having the highest numbers not exceeding three on the list of those voted for as President, the House of Representatives shall choose immediately, by ballot, the President. But in choosing the President, the votes shall be taken by states, the representation from each state having one vote; a quorum for this purpose shall consist of a member or members from two-thirds of the states, and a majority of all the states shall be necessary to a choice. [And if the House of Representatives shall not choose a President whenever the right of choice shall devolve upon them, before the fourth day of March next following, then the Vice-President shall act as President, as in case of the death or other constitutional disability of the President.—]* The person having the greatest number of votes as Vice-President, shall be the Vice-President, if such number be a majority of the whole number of Electors appointed, and if no person have a majority, then from the two highest numbers on the list, the Senate shall choose the Vice-President; a quorum for the purpose shall consist of two-thirds of the whole number of Senators, and a majority of the whole number shall be necessary to a choice. But no person constitutionally ineligible to the office of President shall be eligible to that of Vice-President of the United States.

**Superseded by section 3 of the 20th amendment.*

Amendment XIII

Passed by Congress January 31, 1865. Ratified December 6, 1865.

Section 1.

Neither slavery nor involuntary servitude, except as a punishment for crime whereof the party shall have been duly convicted, shall exist within the United States, or any place subject to their jurisdiction.

Section 2.

Congress shall have power to enforce this article by appropriate legislation.

Amendment XIV

Passed by Congress June 13, 1866. Ratified July 9, 1868.

Note: Article I, section 2, of the Constitution was modified by section 2 of the 14th amendment.

Section 1.

All persons born or naturalized in the United States, and subject to the jurisdiction thereof, are citizens of the United States and of the State wherein they reside. No State shall make or enforce any law which shall abridge the privileges or immunities of citizens of the United States; nor shall any State deprive any person of life, liberty, or property, without due process of law; nor deny to any person within its jurisdiction the equal protection of the laws.

Section 2.

Representatives shall be apportioned among the several States according to their respective numbers, counting the whole number of persons in each State, excluding Indians not taxed.

But when the right to vote at any election for the choice of electors for President and Vice-President of the United States, Representatives in Congress, the Executive and Judicial officers of a State, or the members of the Legislature thereof, is denied to any of the male inhabitants of such State, being twenty-one years of age,* and citizens of the United States, or in any way abridged, except for participation in rebellion, or other crime, the basis of representation therein shall be reduced in the proportion which the number of such male citizens shall bear to the whole number of male citizens twenty-one years of age in such State.

Section 3.

No person shall be a Senator or Representative in Congress, or elector of President and Vice-President, or hold any office, civil or military, under the United States, or under any State, who, having previously taken an oath, as a member of Congress, or as an officer of the United States, or as a member of any State legislature, or as an executive or judicial officer of any State, to support the Constitution of the United States, shall have engaged in insurrection or rebellion against the same, or given aid or comfort to the enemies thereof. But Congress may by a vote of two-thirds of each House, remove such disability.

Section 4.

The validity of the public debt of the United States, authorized by law, including debts incurred for payment of pensions and bounties for services in suppressing insurrection or rebellion, shall not be questioned. But neither the

United States nor any State shall assume or pay any debt or obligation incurred in aid of insurrection or rebellion against the United States, or any claim for the loss or emancipation of any slave; but all such debts, obligations and claims shall be held illegal and void.

Section 5.

The Congress shall have the power to enforce, by appropriate legislation, the provisions of this article.

**Changed by section 1 of the 26th amendment.*

Amendment XV

Passed by Congress February 26, 1869. Ratified February 3, 1870.

Section 1.

The right of citizens of the United States to vote shall not be denied or abridged by the United States or by any State on account of race, color, or previous condition of servitude--

Section 2.

The Congress shall have the power to enforce this article by appropriate legislation.

Amendment XVI

Passed by Congress July 2, 1909. Ratified February 3, 1913.

The Congress shall have power to lay and collect taxes on incomes, from whatever source derived, without apportionment among the several States, and without regard to any census or enumeration.

Amendment XVII

Passed by Congress May 13, 1912. Ratified April 8, 1913.

The Senate of the United States shall be composed of two Senators from each State, elected by the people thereof, for six years; and each Senator shall have one vote. The electors in each State shall have the qualifications requisite for electors of the most numerous branch of the State legislatures.

When vacancies happen in the representation of any State in the Senate, the executive authority of such State shall issue writs of election to fill such vacancies: *Provided*, That the legislature of any State may empower the executive thereof to make temporary appointments until the people fill the vacancies by election as the legislature may direct.

This amendment shall not be so construed as to affect the election or term of any Senator chosen before it becomes valid as part of the Constitution.

Amendment XVIII

Passed by Congress December 18, 1917. Ratified January 16, 1919. Repealed by amendment 21.

Section 1.

After one year from the ratification of this article the manufacture, sale, or transportation of intoxicating liquors within, the importation thereof into, or the exportation thereof from the United States and all territory subject to the jurisdiction thereof for beverage purposes is hereby prohibited.

Section 2.

The Congress and the several States shall have concurrent power to enforce this article by appropriate legislation.

Section 3.

This article shall be inoperative unless it shall have been ratified as an amendment to the Constitution by the legislatures of the several States, as provided in the Constitution, within seven years from the date of the submission hereof to the States by the Congress.

Amendment XIX

Passed by Congress June 4, 1919. Ratified August 18, 1920.

The right of citizens of the United States to vote shall not be denied or abridged by the United States or by any State on account of sex.

Congress shall have power to enforce this article by appropriate legislation.

Amendment XX

Passed by Congress March 2, 1932. Ratified January 23, 1933.

Section 1.

The terms of the President and the Vice President shall end at noon on the 20th day of January, and the terms of Senators and Representatives at noon on the 3d day of January, of the years in which such terms would have ended if this article had not been ratified; and the terms of their successors shall then begin.

Section 2.

The Congress shall assemble at least once in every year, and such meeting shall begin at noon on the 3d day of January, unless they shall by law appoint a different day.

Section 3.

If, at the time fixed for the beginning of the term of the President, the President elect shall have died, the Vice President elect shall become President. If a President shall not have been chosen before the time fixed for the beginning of his term, or if the President elect shall have failed to qualify, then the Vice President elect shall act as President until a President shall have qualified; and the Congress may by law provide for the case wherein neither a President elect nor a Vice President shall have qualified, declaring who shall then act as President, or the manner in which one who is to act shall be selected, and such person shall act accordingly until a President or Vice President shall have qualified.

Section 4.

The Congress may by law provide for the case of the death of any of the persons from whom the House of Representatives may choose a President whenever the right of choice shall have devolved upon them, and for the case of the death of any of the persons from whom the Senate may choose a Vice President whenever the right of choice shall have devolved upon them.

Section 5.

Sections 1 and 2 shall take effect on the 15th day of October following the ratification of this article.

Section 6.

This article shall be inoperative unless it shall have been ratified as an amendment to the Constitution by the legislatures of three-fourths of the several States within seven years from the date of its submission.

Amendment XXI
Passed by Congress February 20, 1933. Ratified December 5, 1933.

Section 1.
The eighteenth article of amendment to the Constitution of the United States is hereby repealed.
Section 2.
The transportation or importation into any State, Territory, or Possession of the United States for delivery or use therein of intoxicating liquors, in violation of the laws thereof, is hereby prohibited.

Section 3.
This article shall be inoperative unless it shall have been ratified as an amendment to the Constitution by conventions in the several States, as provided in the Constitution, within seven years from the date of the submission hereof to the States by the Congress.

Amendment XXII
Passed by Congress March 21, 1947. Ratified February 27, 1951.

Section 1.
No person shall be elected to the office of the President more than twice, and no person who has held the office of President, or acted as President, for more than two years of a term to which some other person was elected President shall be elected to the office of President more than once. But this Article shall not apply to any person holding the office of President when this Article was proposed by Congress, and shall not prevent any person who may be holding the office of President, or acting as President, during the term within which this Article becomes operative from holding the office of President or acting as President during the remainder of such term.

Section 2.
This article shall be inoperative unless it shall have been ratified as an amendment to the Constitution by the legislatures of three-fourths of the several States within seven years from the date of its submission to the States by the Congress.

Amendment XXIII
Passed by Congress June 16, 1960. Ratified March 29, 1961.

Section 1.
The District constituting the seat of Government of the United States shall appoint in such manner as Congress may direct:
A number of electors of President and Vice President equal to the whole number of Senators and Representatives in Congress to which the District would be entitled if it were a State, but in no event more than the least populous State; they shall be in addition to those appointed by the States, but they shall be considered, for the purposes of the election of President and Vice President, to be electors appointed by a State; and they shall meet in the District and perform such duties as provided by the twelfth article of amendment.

Section 2.
The Congress shall have power to enforce this article by appropriate legislation.

Amendment XXIV
Passed by Congress August 27, 1962. Ratified January 23, 1964.

Section 1.
The right of citizens of the United States to vote in any primary or other election for President or Vice President, for electors for President or Vice President, or for Senator or Representative in Congress, shall not be denied or abridged by the United States or any State by reason of failure to pay poll tax or other tax.

Section 2.
The Congress shall have power to enforce this article by appropriate legislation.

Amendment XXV
Passed by Congress July 6, 1965. Ratified February 10, 1967.

Section 1.

In case of the removal of the President from office or of his death or resignation, the Vice President shall become President.

Section 2.

Whenever there is a vacancy in the office of the Vice President, the President shall nominate a Vice President who shall take office upon confirmation by a majority vote of both Houses of Congress.

Section 3.

Whenever the President transmits to the President pro tempore of the Senate and the Speaker of the House of Representatives his written declaration that he is unable to discharge the powers and duties of his office, and until he transmits to them a written declaration to the contrary, such powers and duties shall be discharged by the Vice President as Acting President.

Section 4.

Whenever the Vice President and a majority of either the principal officers of the executive departments or of such other body as Congress may by law provide, transmit to the President pro tempore of the Senate and the Speaker of the House of Representatives their written declaration that the President is unable to discharge the powers and duties of his office, the Vice President shall immediately assume the powers and duties of the office as Acting President.

Thereafter, when the President transmits to the President pro tempore of the Senate and the Speaker of the House of Representatives his written declaration that no inability exists, he shall resume the powers and duties of his office unless the Vice President and a majority of either the principal officers of the executive department or of such other body as Congress may by law provide, transmit within four days to the President pro tempore of the Senate and the Speaker of the House of Representatives their written declaration that the President is unable to discharge the powers and duties of his office. Thereupon Congress shall decide the issue, assembling within forty-eight hours for that purpose if not in session. If the Congress, within twenty-one days after receipt of the latter written declaration, or, if Congress is not in session, within twenty-one days after Congress is required to assemble, determines by two-thirds vote of both Houses that the President is unable to discharge the powers and duties of his office, the Vice President shall continue to discharge the same as Acting President; otherwise, the President shall resume the powers and duties of his office.

Amendment XXVI
Passed by Congress March 23, 1971. Ratified July 1, 1971.

Section 1.
The right of citizens of the United States, who are eighteen years of age or older, to vote shall not be denied or abridged by the United States or by any State on account of age.

Section 2.
The Congress shall have power to enforce this article by appropriate legislation.

Amendment XXVII
Originally proposed Sept. 25, 1789. Ratified May 7, 1992.

No law, varying the compensation for the services of the Senators and Representatives, shall take effect, until an election of representatives shall have intervened.